CHORDS *by* KEY

FOR GUITAR . . .

AND A WHOLE LOT MORE

The Book That Teaches You To Play-by-Ear, While Teaching You Chords.

BY TIM WEMPLE

CHORDS BY KEY FOR GUITAR . . . AND A WHOLE LOT MORE

The Book That Teaches You To Play-by-Ear, While Teaching You Chords.

Copyright © 2012 Tim Wemple

ISBN-10: 0989077209

ISBN-13: 978-0-9890772-0-0

Cover Photo by Tim Wemple Copyright © 2012 Tim Wemple

DEDICATION

This book is dedicated to my son Seth who passed away in July of 2011 from a brain tumor. He was a great guitar player and aspiring songwriter. But more importantly a great son who taught me what it means to love, give forgiveness and be thankful no matter what the circumstances. We miss your sweet spirit, smile and wit Seth. You will forever be in our hearts.

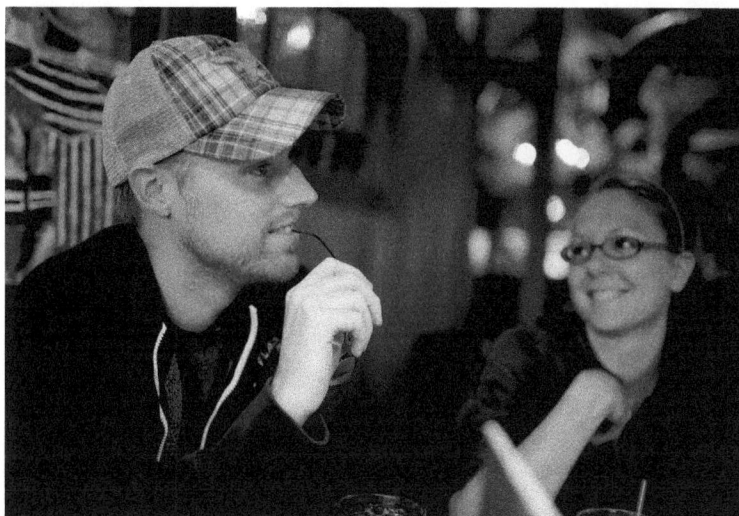

Seth Wemple and his wife Victoria

TABLE OF CONTENTS

CHORD CHARTS

CAPO PLACEMENT CONSIDERATIONS

MAJOR KEY CHORD CHARTS USING A CAPO

CONTEMPORARY WORSHIP CHORDS - KEY OF E AND F — 130

CONTEMPORARY WORSHIP CHORDS - KEY OF G WITH WALKING BASS — 131

MINOR KEY CHORD CHARTS

QUICK REFERENCE GUIDE — 144

CAPO CHARTS — 150

TIPS ON PLAYING-BY-EAR — 151

THE CIRCLE OF FIFTHS — 153

THANK YOU — 154

BLANK WORKSHEETS — 155

INTRODUCTION

THE JOY OF MAKING MUSIC

Okay, let me say right up front, this book is about having fun! It's about the joy of making music. It's about learning to play songs, not just learning to play chords. It's about knoodling—just playing around with different chord combinations and in the process making-up your own songs and learning to play thousands of others. It's like having your own little chord chemistry lab. Just mix things up and see what kind of music you can create.

We live in an age of information. If you want to learn a chord all you have to do is type it into Google. But we also live in an age of information overload. Type "C Major guitar chord" into Google and you get an overwhelming one million websites and two million images to sort through. What we need is a way to manage and organize all this information in a way that's practical and efficient. And that's exactly what this book is all about. It's about organizing chords into useful groups that you can use to start playing songs in the shortest amount of time possible.

If you're a beginner this book will help you prioritize your learning by showing you which chords to start learning first and how to use a capo to maximize what you've learned. If you're a more advanced player then you may be ready for the Roman numeral numbering system. By learning how to number chords you'll be able to speak the language of chord progressions. Understanding this system of numbering chords will give you a fresh perspective on how music is constructed and how to transpose songs with ease. If you're an advanced player then chord formulas may be something you're ready to tackle. Understanding how individual chords are constructed will give you the ability to make any chord, anywhere on the fretboard. You'll also be able to begin studying the more advanced concepts of ascending and descending bass lines and pedal notes in chord progressions.

This book is not limited to just diatonic chords—chords built from the key's scale—but includes all the chords you'll hear in popular music today. You'll learn chords like secondary dominants, quality change chords, flat Majors, dominant 7th

(blues) chords, suspended and add 9 chords, along with their extensions and alterations. On just two pages per key you'll find all the chords you'll need to play just about any song in any key. And the cool thing is you can just play-around with these chords and come up with your own songs and progressions. It's like turning the neck of your guitar into the white keys on a piano—you can't play a bad chord. But that's not all I've included lots of worksheets as well so you can build your own chords and progressions.

I've tried to keep things simple enough not to overwhelm you, yet thorough enough to cover all the bases for both beginners and advanced players. I've taken the 6 most popular guitar keys C, G, D, A, E and F, and divided each keys chords up into small groups. Each group of chords, 67 individual chords in all for each key, have then been prioritized in regards to their commonness in songs. What that means for you is that you'll be playing the most songs possible in the least amount of time possible. For the other keys I've given you chord charts that show you how to use a capo to get the same results.

The underlying premise of the book is to teach you to play by ear. Playing by ear is a skill every musician should develop whether you're a professional playing for other people, or someone who just likes playing for their own enjoyment. Even if you don't have a God given ability to play-by-ear, this book will help you get there. Learning to play-by-ear is a skill that can be achieved with practice and guidance. It can also be a great resource for anyone wanting to use the guitar to write music.

This book is not about learning intervals, or scales, or music theory—though it's all here—it's about playing songs and experiencing the joy of sitting down with just you and your guitar and "making" music. So let's get started having fun!

Fun

HOW TO USE THIS BOOK

Beginners

If you're a complete beginner, the best place to start is with the section on *Fingering*. In this section I'll give you some advice on where to put your fingers and thumb to make chords and how to use the chord charts to find this information. Then in the *Chord Formula* section you may want to read the part about, *So What Good is it Knowing the Chord's Formula?* This will give you some help with knowing what notes you can drop from a chord if you're not ready to play complete barre chords. As you progress in your playing, you'll want to come back to the rest of the sections and build on what you've learned.

Once you've looked at these two sections you can go straight to the key chord charts. My recommendation would be to start with the key of G Major and begin practicing the chords called "Diatonic and Secondary Dominants". (Diatonic is just a fancy word that means all the notes in the chord are in the key's scale.) Start with the top row of chords and work your way down.

With just the top three chords in this group—the I, IV and V chords—you'll be able to play hundreds of songs. Once you've learned these three chords practice transitioning between each of them. Being able to play these top three chords in various combinations is important because you'll be playing them a lot once you begin playing real songs. When you have these chords down and you're comfortable moving from on chord to another, move down to the next three chords.

In the next row you'll see chord boxes with a gray background and an arrow in them. These are the secondary dominant chords. You don't need to know where they came from or why they're named secondary dominants right now, but you do need to know they're special chords, with a special job. The job of a secondary dominant chord is to lead your ear to another chord, the one I've listed just above it. It's important when practicing these chords you practice them in combination with the ones above them. Practice these two chord combos until you know them by heart. These two chord combos or progressions, if you will, are a fundamental part of how music is constructed. Memorizing them will go a long way in helping you learn to play-by-ear and understand one of the most basic concepts in music—building tension and then releasing it.

Now move down to the minor chords vi, ii and iii. I've listed them in this order because they're the relative minors of the Major chords above them, which means you can substitute these minor chords for the Major above and vise versa. (Don't worry about why for now.) When you feel comfortable playing these minor chords practice playing them in combination with the Majors from the first row. Also practice using the secondary dominant chords to lead you to the Majors. For instance if you're playing a ii chord, and want to go to a IV, use the secondary dominant V7/IV (five over four) to make the transition. For the key of G Major that would mean playing an Am, then a G7, followed by the C. Practice the minor and Major chords with and without the secondary dominant chord transitions. (You can also practice transitioning between Major chords with secondary dominants.)

The secondary dominants below the minors are not used as much as the secondary dominants for the Majors. For now you may want to just skip them and move on to the extensions.

All of the extensions keep their same chord family, or basic quality of sound, with the exception of the V chord. The V chord switches from a Major chord to a dominant 7th chord, indicated by the 7 after the Roman numeral—V7. You've already seen this chord above as a secondary dominant, V7/I. In reality this is not a secondary dominant, but the dominant chord of the scale. (Each chord in the scale has a name, dominant being one of them.) As you progress in your studies you'll see that the other secondary dominants come from this same relationship in their own keys. They are the V chord in the scale of the chord they lead to. This is a very important concept in music and one you will want to spend time examining later in your studies. Now for the Flat Majors or borrowed chords as they are sometimes referred to because they're borrowed from the minor key of the same letter name.

The Flat Major chords are found in almost all Rock and Pop music, as well as a lot of contemporary Country. These are chords you'll definitely want to get comfortable playing. However, all keys are not equal when it comes to Flat Majors. For instance don't waste a lot of time learning the Flat Majors for the keys of C and F . The Flat Majors for these two keys can be hard to play in open position and aren't used a lot in these styles of music. If you want to play Rock, Pop or contemporary

Country, you may want to think about going to the keys of D, E or A once you've got the key of G down. If you're only interested in playing old time Country, Folk or Bluegrass then C and F are good keys to learn and you don't need to worry about the Flat Majors. These styles of music rarely use the Flat Major chords. My recommendation would be to start with G, a good key for just about every type of music, and then let the style of music you want to play dictate where to go next.

When you have a good handle on everything on the first page of a key according to the style of music you want to play, you can move on to the second page, or you can move on to another key. The chords on the second page are not used as extensively as those on the first, with the exception of the dominant 7th (blues) chords. These chords should be high on your priority list if you like blues type songs. I say, blues type because these chords can be found in Rock, Pop and Country. A lot of Rock and Blues style songs use just these three chords or the "I" chord in combination with the dominant 7th chords IV7 and V7. These three chords can be a lot of fun just to experiment with and see what you can create. Check-out the *Chord Progression* section on blues progressions to see how these chords are arranged.

Once you have a few keys down you should start thinking about how to use a capo to expand what you know to other keys. Check-out the section on using a capo and the Quick Reference guides to get you started.

INTERMEDIATE

If you're a more experienced player it's time to start learning the Roman numeral numbering system. This will allow you to see how music is put together and how to play songs in different keys. (Something that may not sound all that important, but I'll give you a few reasons later why being able to change keys is a valuable skill.) I call this Roman numeral numbering system the language of chord progressions because it frees up the chords from their key signature and looks at them in relationship to one another. I've included a long list of common chord progressions and songs in the book so you can begin exploring how these progressions and their numbering relate to modern music. I've also included a strategy for creating your own

progressions. You can use the *Chord Substitution* section in each key and the *Chord Substitution Worksheets* to develop your own progressions. As you begin learning the numbers for each chord try playing a single progression in various keys using the Roman numerals as a guide for which chords to play. As you get better at this you'll be able to switch keys and use a capo with ease. For instance a I, IV, V progression in G would be G(I), C(IV), D(V) and that same progression in C would be C(I), F(IV), G(V).

Don't forget the goal of this book is to have fun. As you're learning these chords and how they're numbered, experiment playing them together in different combinations. Hopefully you'll begin to hear different songs as you knoodle around on these pages. When you find something you like, try transposing it to another key using the Roman numerals. What you'll find in this playing-around process is that certain keys lend themselves to certain kinds of progressions better than others. This is especially true when it comes to suspended and add9 chords. Some suspended and add9 chords are just easier to play and sound better than others in certain keys. For instance a Dsus is a lot easier to play than an Esus and has a slightly different sound. A Cadd9 chord is easier to play than a Dadd9 and sounds different. By transposing your progressions to other keys you'll begin to get a feel for which keys are best for certain types of chords and progressions.

Something else to try with the numbering system is to take a chord progression and use a capo to play it with a whole new set of chords—same key with different chord shapes. Even if you're familiar with the chords in a particular key you may want to try using a capo. Different keys have different open strings in their chords and by using a capo you can maximize those open strings for a more open sound. For instance if you're playing a song in the key of A with a lot of minor chords you may want to use a capo to switch the chords you're playing to those of the key of G. With the capo on the second fret, the key of G chords will become the key of A chords. By using a capo you can get a more open sound to the song and if you know the Roman numeral numbering system the switch is easy, just match the Roman numerals up between keys.

For intermediate and advanced players, the real meat of this book is in learning to play-by-ear and understanding the relationships between chords. Playing by ear can be challenging if you're not one of those lucky people with the gift of being able to hear something and just play it. But with this book you'll begin to see the choices for that next chord in a song are not endless, there really are limits. Knowing what those limits are can go a long way in helping you decide what that next chord should be. Learning to play-by-ear for those of us that are not gifted, is about hearing when a chord should change, and then experimenting with a limited number of chords until we find the right one. With practice you can develop your ear so the experimenting part is cut shorter and shorter until eventually you'll just know which chord comes next.

But there is another area that is equally as fun for advanced players and that is chord substitutions and learning to use slash chords to create ascending and descending bass lines, as well as pedal notes in your chord progressions. For me this is one of the most fun areas of playing. By creating walking bass lines and using chord substitutions you have a chance to make a progression your own and have it stand out from all the rest. Adding bass lines to your chord progressions will set your playing apart from just average to truly professional. There is also the area of voice leading which in its most basic form deals with the upper notes of a chord progression. These notes can be made to move chromatically, along with the scale, use common tones in several chords or a melody line can be incorporated into your progression.

For the more advanced player I've included in each chord chart the chord's formula, which can be used as a guide for adding notes or altering notes in a chord. Use the information in the *Chord Formula* section to see what notes can be added or altered. You can also use the *Chord Extension Worksheets* with each key to build your own chords. As I show in the *Worksheet* examples you can literal take one note in a chord and move it up or down and create a chord progression. You can also keep one note the same through several chord changes (a pedal note) and create a chord progression. This is a technique used in hundreds of popular songs. Understanding how a chord is constructed can help you create these advanced chord progressions and help you when your creating your own progressions to name the chords.

There is a lot of material here that can be explored. It's up to you to explore it and exploit it to its full potential. Hopefully the examples given in the next section will get you started in the right direction.

LEVELS

HOW TO USE THE KEY CHORD CHARTS

The chord charts are broken down into groups. Each group can be associated with a certain style of music or function in music.

DIATONIC AND SECONDARY DOMINANT CHORDS

These are the basic chords that form the foundation for most songs regardless of style. I've shown them primarily as open chords, but they can also be played up the neck as barre chords. (Use the Worksheets to see where and how to make them.) When you're trying to learn a song by ear, you'll want to start with these chords. The styles of music that use these chords exclusively are Folk, Country and Western, Hymns, Bluegrass and a lot of Contemporary Country, and Rock, as well.

EXTENSIONS

The extensions are also a staple of almost all styles of music. Pop, Rock, Country and Jazz are just a few examples. When you're trying to learn a song by ear you'll definitely want to consider trying these chords.

FLAT MAJORS

The Flat Major chords or borrowed chords are the chords of Classic Rock. If the song is a Classic Rock song chances are one or more of these chords will be in it. Today a lot of Rock influenced Country songs are using these chords as well.

SUSPENDED CHORDS

The Suspended Chords are also found in Classic Rock and contemporary Country music. They can act as a stand alone chord or they can be used to lead your ear back to a Major chord with the same letter name. For instance an Asus tends to lead your ear to an A Major chord.

ADD9 CHORDS

The Add9 Chords add a little variety to the simple Major chords and are also found in a lot of Classic Rock and some contemporary Country music.

HARMONIC MINOR CHORDS

You can use all the chords in a Major key to play a song in the natural minor key I've shown with the Major key signature, but there are a few other chords that don't fit that you may find with such frequency I decided to include them. They are from the Harmonic minor key.

DOMINANT 7TH (BLUES) CHORDS

The Dominant 7th (Blues) Chords are found in Blues and Rock-n-Roll music. Be aware though many songs have been influenced by Blues so it may be a Country tune or a Classic Rock song and use these chords.

QUALITY CHANGE CHORDS

The Quality Change Chords are chords that give a sense of surprise to a song. Your ear doesn't expect them. They're also used to facilitate key changes. By making a ii chord into a Major for instance which is the V chord in another key you can set-up a key change in a song. You can hear this in Faith Hill's song, *The Way You Love Me* which has several key changes in it.

The IV - iv - I progression adds a sentimental or romantic feeling to a song. Changing the quality of a chord can give the overall song a more sad sound if you switch minors for Majors, or the song may sound more up-beat switching Major for minors.

On the left of the chord box there is an arrow indicating what chord these Quality change chords tend to resolve to. You can use this information to help develop a smoother transition between chords or you can choose to ignore it, it is up to you. Again this information is based on the Dominant idea and you should begin to see how the letter names of each chord tend to pull toward another letter name. It doesn't always need to be a dominant chord it can be any type of chord with the letter name of the dominant V. For instance in the key of G a Em tends to sound good before an Am, and a Am tends to sound good before a D, or the G before a C. The chord that leads to another is based on the 5th tone of the chord it leads to. For example the notes in an Am chord are A(1), C(b3), E(5) so any chord built on the E which is the 5 of Am will lead nicely to the Am. Here is another example. The notes in a D chord are D(1), F#(3), A(5). Any chord then built off of the A will lead nicely to the D. So you can use the notes in the chord to find the chord that leads to it. The dominant 7th tend to have the strongest pull, but the other chord families can be used as well.

ADDITIONAL DIATONIC EXTENSIONS

The Additional Diatonic Extensions are used in Jazz music, but they can also be thought of as "hook" chords. Hook chords are those unusual chords in a song that when you hear them you instantly know what the song is. Some examples would be the E7#9 in Jimi Hendrix's song *Purple Haze*. The Em9/Maj7 from the 007 Theme song. Another example of a chord as a hook would be the G7sus chord in the Beatles' song *A Hard Day's Night*, These chords instantly bring to mind these songs when you hear them. The Additional Diatonic Extensions are to be a starting place for your exploration to find that chord that will set your song apart from all the rest. It's also the place to start looking for that chord in a song you just can't find in the other groups.

Pay particular attention to how a chord sounds when working through these chords. Each has a very distinct sound. The minor 9th chords are very mysterious. The Major 6/9 chords can be good chords to end a song with and the altered dominant 7th chords add a lot of tension to the chord and can be used right before the I chord at the end of a song.

If you're interested in playing Jazz then these will be your meat and potato chords and you will want to explore a lot more than are listed. Use the Chord Extension Worksheets to find more possibilities for how to add notes to your chords and alter the notes in a chord.

Groups

HOW TO USE THE CHORD WORKSHEETS

I've included several Worksheets that you can use to workout your own ideas. Feel free to copy these worksheets and use them as you're going through the book.

CHORD FORMULA WORKSHEET UP THE NECK AND CHORD EXTENSION WORKSHEETS

The *Chord Formula Worksheet* provides you with the basic Major and minor chord shapes up the neck of the guitar, along with the notes that can be added to them and still be within the scale. However, this doesn't mean you can't add notes outside the scale—you can. Just make sure the notes outside the scale don't clash with the melody or lead. On the other hand, you may have a note in the melody that falls outside the scale itself. In that case you would definitely want to explore adding that note into your chord.

One of the fun things to do with this worksheet is to take one note of the basic chord shape and move it up or down to add additional notes to the chord or alter the notes in the chord. You could also take two notes and move them as well. I've given you a few examples of how this would work along with some songs that use this as their chord progression.

Another useful thing you can do with this worksheets is to try and recreate a chord created with one shape, up the neck with another shape. This will allow you to move your progressions around on the fretboard and find fingerings that may be easier to play or inversions that sound better.

(The basic shapes do not include the chords from the first sheet of the Key Charts, so don't forget to add them into the mix as well.)

FOUR NOTE EXTENSIONS UP THE NECK AND CHORD PROGRESSION WORKSHEETS

This worksheet helps you explore playing 4 note chords (Major 7ths, minor 7ths and dominant 7ths) up the neck. If you want to play Jazz this will be your starting point. Use these chords and those from the first page of the Key Charts to put together your chord progressions that move up and down the neck, as well as the open chords. Try creating a progression with open chords and then moving it up the neck with the chords from the *Chord Formula Worksheet* and this worksheet.

This is also where you can begin experimenting with bass lines and voicings in your chord progressions. This to me is one of the most fun things to do on the guitar and will really advance your playing. There are several different ways you can add a bass line to your progressions. You can create a repeating pattern, a chromatic ascending or descending bass movement, a step-wise ascending or descending bass or a common tone bass. Step-wise simply means you work your way up or down the scale notes.

You can also focus your attention on the upper tones in the chord, making the transitions from one chord to another as smooth as possible. This is called voice leading. It functions on the same principles as the bass movement only on the upper strings. You could create a repeating pattern, use a chromatic ascending or descending line or simply follow the scale notes up or down. You can also look for common tones between chords and keep them from one chord to another or use what is called pedal notes that stay the same through the entire chord progression.

As you get better at this you can add the melody notes to the top of the chords and create a chordal melody as well. Even more advanced is to try and create both a bass line and a treble line that work well together. Lots of things to explore.

CHORD SUBSTITUTION WORKSHEET

The *Chord Substitution Worksheet* and the *Chord Progression Worksheet* should be used in combination with each other. Use the *Chord Substitution Worksheets* to develop simple chord progressions into more complex progressions using the principles shown in the *Chord Progression* section: extension and family change substitutions, omission, relative minor and Major substitutions and displacement. You can also use it to reharmonize an already existing progression into something with more interest, color and surprise using: Backcycling, Tritone substitutions and Chromatic and diatonic passing chords.

Power Chord Worksheet

The Power Chord Worksheet provides you with all the power chords for a key along with their inversions. It also includes some Rock-n-Roll type two note chords.

Triad Worksheets

The Triad Worksheets have the triads for the (1st, 2nd and 3rd), (2nd, 3rd and 4th) and (3rd, 4th and 5th) strings. Triads are often used in songs as hooks and many introductions to songs start with triads. Use these sheets to learn the hooks for songs as well as develop your own.

Examples

The examples on the next few pages are to be used as guidelines for what to do with these worksheet. Study them, and then try and apply the same principles to other chords and other keys. These worksheets are important to get you started on developing your playing and understanding how chords work together to form music. This is only the beginning of what can be a lifetime of experimentation and learning.

Worksheets
&
Examples

Chord Extensions Worksheet
Moving Lines in a Chord

D I	DMaj7 I	D7 I7	D6 I
Finger _ _ _ _ _	Finger _ _ _ _ _	Finger _ _ _ _ _	Finger _ _ _ _ _
Scale _ _ _ 1 _	Scale _ _ _ 7 _	Scale _ _ b7 _	Scale _ _ _ 6 _
Note _ _ _ _ _	Note _ _ _ _ _	Note _ _ _ _ _	Note _ _ _ _ _

D with descending line

D I	DMaj7 I	D6 I	DMaj7 I
Finger _ _ _ _ _	Finger _ _ _ _ _	Finger _ _ _ _ _	Finger _ _ _ _ _
Scale _ _ _ 1 _	Scale _ _ _ 7 _	Scale _ _ _ 6 _	Scale _ _ _ 7 _
Note _ _ _ _ _	Note _ _ _ _ _	Note _ _ _ _ _	Note _ _ _ _ _

Gentle On My Mind John Hartford (Key of D) uses D, DMaj7, D6, DMaj7
Glen Campbell

Em ii	EmMaj7 ii	Em7 ii	EMaj7 ii
Finger _ _ _ _ _	Finger _ _ _ _ _	Finger _ _ _ _ _	Finger _ _ _ _ _
Scale _ _ _ 1 _	Scale _ _ 7 _ _	Scale _ b7 _ _	Scale _ _ 7 _ _
Note _ _ _ _ _	Note _ _ _ _ _	Note _ _ _ _ _	Note _ _ _ _ _

Gentle On My Mind also uses a minor chord walk down

Dm vi	DmMaj7 vi	Dm7 vi	Dm6 vi
Finger _ _ _ _ _	Finger _ _ _ _ _	Finger _ _ _ _ _	Finger _ _ _ _ _
Scale _ _ 1 _ _	Scale _ 7 _ _ _	Scale _ b7 _ _	Scale _ 6 _ _
Note _ _ _ _ _	Note _ Dm/C# _	Note _ Dm/C _	Note _ Dm/B _

Uses Bm11 in real song third string open on last chord

Time In A Bottle Jim Croce (Key of Dm)

Dm vi	DmMaj7 vi	Dm7 vi	Dm6 vi
5th	4th	5th	5th
Finger _ 1 3 4 2	Finger _ 1 _ _ _	Finger 4 2 3 1	Finger T _ _ _
Scale _ 1 _ _ _	Scale _ 7 _ _ _	Scale b7 _ _	Scale 6 _ _
Note _ _ _ _ _	Note _ Dm/C# _	Note _ Dm/C _	Note _ Dm/B _

You could also play this same progression up the neck

Chord Extensions Worksheet
Moving Lines in a Chord

C I   Finger / Scale **5** / Note
C+ I+   Finger / Scale **#5** / Note
C6 I   Finger / Scale **6** / Note
C7 I7   Finger / Scale **b7** / Note

Example C Major with ascending line
The Greatest Love of All Whitney Houston key of A uses both the A and D ascending line

C I 5th   Finger / Scale / Note
C+ I+ 5th   Finger / Scale **#5** / Note
C6 I 5th   Finger / Scale **6** / Note
C7 I7 5th   Finger / Scale **b7** / Note

You may find chord shapes using this method you never thought of before like the C6 & C7

Another example of a C Major with an ascending line

A I 5th   Finger / Scale **5** / Note
A+ I+ 5th   Finger / Scale **#5** / Note
A6 I 5th   Finger / Scale **6** / Note
A7 I7 5th   Finger / Scale **b7** / Note

Example Laughing The Guess Who (Key of A)

G7 V7 3rd   Finger / Scale **5** / Note
G7#5 V7 3rd   Finger / Scale **#5** / Note
G13 V7 3rd   Finger / Scale **6=13** / Note
CMaj7 I 3rd   Finger / Scale / Note

Example - G Dominant 7th with an ascending line

G7 V7 3rd   Finger / Scale **5 1** / Note
G7#5b9 V7 3rd   Finger / Scale **#5 b2=b9** / Note
G13add9 V7 3rd   Finger / Scale **6 2=9** / Note
CMaj7 I 3rd   Finger / Scale / Note

Another example of a G7 with two ascending lines

Chord Progression Worksheet
Ascending and Descending Bass lines, and Pedal notes

Combination Progression (Basic I IV Progression & Folk I V7 Progression)
Brown Eyed Girl Van Morrison

Combination Progression (Folk I V Progression & Basic I IV Progression)
When The Saints Go Marching In & Rollin In My Sweet Babies Arms

Relative minor substitutions for G and C
Someone Like You Adele (Key of A)

Standard chord Progression with 7th extensions
(I Love You) For Sentimental Reasons Nat King Cole (key of Db) & Thousands More

Standard Chord Progression with Quality change chord A7
Crazy Patsey Cline (Key of Bb)

Chord Progression Worksheet
Ascending and Descending Bass lines, and Pedal notes

or

Finger _ _ _ _
Scale _ _ _ _
Note _ _ _ _

Folk Progression

Me And Bobby McGee verse Janis Joplin (Key of G)
Hurts So Good chorus John Cougar (Key of A)
Summer Of '69 verse Bryan Adams & Margaritaville verse Jimmy Buffet (Key of D)

Folk Progression Doubled with last G omitted

Have You Ever Seen The Rain verse CCR   Blue Bayou Linda Ronstadt (Key of B) uses V7

Displacement the C and G are switched

I Walk The Line verse Johnny Cash (starts in the Key of F)
Help Me Rhonda chorus Beach Boys (Key of Db) Capo first fret chords from Key of C

Relative minor substitutions

Diamond Girl verse Seals and Crofts & Losing My Religion verse R. E. M.

Minor key Roman numerals shown

Chord Quality change Em - E7

Paint It Black opening verse Rolling Stones (Key of Em)

Chord Progression Worksheet
Ascending and Descending Bass lines, and Pedal notes

C   **I**

Finger _ _ _ _ _
Scale _ _ _ _ _
Note _ _ _ _ _

G/B   **V**

Finger _ _ _ _ _
Scale _ _ _ _ _
Note _ _ _ _ _

Am   **vi**

Finger _ _ _ _ _
Scale _ _ _ _ _
Note _ _ _ _ _

Am/G   **vi**

Finger _ _ _ _ _
Scale _ _ _ _ _
Note _ _ _ _ _

Very Common Step-Wise Descending Bass Line (Key C)

C   **I**

Finger _ _ _ _ _
Scale _1_ _ _5_
Note _ _ _ _ _

G/B   **V**

Finger _ _ _ _ _
Scale _3_ _ _1_
Note _ _ _ _ _

Am7   **vi**

Finger _ _ _ _ _
Scale _1_ _ _♭7_
Note _ _ _ _ _

Am7/G   **vi**

Finger _ _ _ _ _
Scale ♭7_ _ _♭7_
Note _ _ _ _ _

Descending Bass Line with G pedal note (Key C)

C   **I**

5th

Finger _ _ _ _ _
Scale 1_ _ _5_
Note _ _ _ _ _

G/B   **V**

5th

Finger _ _ _ _ _
Scale 3_ _ _1_
Note _ _ _ _ _

Am7   **vi**

5th

Finger _ _ _ _ _
Scale 1_ _ _♭7_
Note _ _ _ _ _

Am7/G   **vi**

3rd

Finger _ _ _ _ _
Scale ♭7_ _ _♭7
Note _ _ _ _ _

To keep the pattern going use the Fadd9/G from above

Descending Bass Line with G pedal note (Key C)

Em   **vi**

Finger _ _ _ _ _
Scale _ _ _ _ _
Note _ _ _ _ _

D/F#   **V**

Finger _T_ _ _ _
Scale _ _ _ _ _
Note _ _ _ _ _

G   **I**

Finger _ _ _ _ _
Scale _ _ _ _ _
Note _ _ _ _ _

Finger _ _ _ _ _
Scale _ _ _ _ _
Note _ _ _ _ _

Ascending Bass Line with (Key G)

G   **I**

Finger _ _ _ _ _
Scale _1_ _ _5_1
Note _ _ _ _ _

Dadd11   **V**

Finger _ _ _ _ _
Scale _3_ _ _1_4
Note _Dsus/F#_

Em7   **vi**

Finger _ _ _ _ _
Scale _1_ _ _♭7♭3
Note _ _ _ _ _

Cadd9   **IV**

Finger _ _ _ _ _
Scale _ _ _2_5
Note _ _ _ _ _

A lot of times the ascending or descending bass will end before the last chord.

Descending Bass Line with two pedal notes (Key G)

Chord Progression Worksheet
Ascending and Descending Bass lines, and Pedal notes

CMaj7 I 3rd
Finger _ _ _ _ _
Scale _ _ _ _ _
Note _ _ _ _ _

C#°7 3rd
Finger _ _ _ _ _
Scale _ _ _ _ _
Note _ _ _ _ _

Dm7 ii 5th
Finger _ _ _ _ _
Scale _ _ _ _ _
Note _ _ _ _ _

G7#5 V7 3rd
Finger _ _ _ _ _
Scale _ _ _ #5 _
Note _ _ _ _ _

Ascending Chromatic Bass Line using Diminished 7th chords

Dm7 ii 5th
Finger _ _ _ _ _
Scale _ _ _ _ _
Note _ _ _ _ _

D#°7 5th
Finger _ _ _ _ _
Scale _ _ _ _ _
Note _ _ _ _ _

Em7 iii 7th
Finger _ _ _ _ _
Scale _ _ _ _ _
Note _ _ _ _ _

FMaj7 IV 8th
Finger _ _ _ _ _
Scale _ _ _ _ _
Note _ _ _ _ _

Ascending Chromatic Bass Line using Diminished 7th chords

Am7 vi 5th
Finger _ _ _ _ _
Scale _ _ _ _ _
Note _ _ _ _ _

Dm7 ii sub Ab7#5 4th
Finger _ _ _ _ _
Scale _ _ _ #5 _
Note _ _ _ _ _

G13 V7 3rd
Finger _ _ _ _ _
Scale _ _ _ 6 _
Note _ _ _ _ _

CMaj7 I 3rd
Finger _ _ _ _ _
Scale _ _ _ _ _
Note _ _ _ _ _

Descending Chromatic Bass Line with Tritone substitution
Also added a pedal note in the first three chords

C I
Finger _ _ _ _ _
Scale _ _ _ _ _
Note _ _ _ _ _

G/B V
Finger _ _ _ _ _
Scale _ _ _ _ _
Note _ _ _ _ _

Bb bVII
Finger _ _ _ _ _
Scale _ _ _ _ _
Note _ _ _ _ _

F/A IV
Finger _ _ _ _ _
Scale _ _ _ _ _
Note _ _ _ _ _

Descending Chromatic Bass Line using Flat Majors (Key C)
Three Times A Lady chorus Commodores (Key Ab) use capo on 8th fret

Am i
Finger _ _ _ _ _
Scale _ _ _ _ _
Note _ _ _ _ _

C/G III
Finger _ _ _ _ _
Scale _ _ _ _ _
Note _ _ _ _ _

F VI
Finger _ _ _ _ _
Scale _ _ _ _ _
Note _ _ _ _ _

E V
Finger _ _ _ _ _
Scale _ _ _ _ _
Note _ _ _ _ _

Descending Bass Line Key of Am The E is from the Harmonic minor key
An Old Fashion Love Song verse Three Dog Night

Chord Progression Worksheet
Ascending and Descending Bass lines, and Pedal notes

CMaj7 I

Finger _ _ _ _ _ _
Scale _ _ _ _ _ _
Note _ _ _ _ _ _

Am7 vi

Finger _ _ _ _ _ _
Scale _ _ _ _ _ _
Note _ _ _ _ _ _

Dm7 ii

Finger _ _ _ _ _ _
Scale _ _ _ _ _ _
Note _ _ _ _ _ _

G7 V7

Finger _ _ _ _ _ _
Scale _ _ _ _ _ _
Note _ _ _ _ _ _

Voice Leading - Common tones
(Just use short segments unless you want a pedal note throughout the progression)

CMaj7 I

Finger _ _ _ _ _ _
Scale _ _ _ _ _ _
Note _ _ _ _ _ _

Am7 vi

Finger _ _ _ _ _ _
Scale _ _ _ _ _ _
Note _ _ _ _ _ _

Dm7 ii

Finger _ _ _ _ _ _
Scale _ _ _ _ _ _
Note _ _ _ _ _ _

G7b9 V7

3rd

Finger _ _ _ _ _ _
Scale _ _ _ _ _ _
Note _ _ _ _ _ _

Voice Leading - Patterns
(The pattern is three frets up or three half steps up)

CMaj7 I

Finger _ _ _ _ _ _
Scale _ _ _ _ _ _
Note _ _ _ _ _ _

Am7 vi

5th

Finger _ _ _ _ _ _
Scale _ _ _ _ _ _
Note _ _ _ _ _ _

Dm7 ii

5th

Finger _ _ _ _ _ _
Scale _ _ _ _ _ _
Note _ _ _ _ _ _

G7 V7

5th

Finger _ _ _ _ _ _
Scale _ _ _ _ _ _
Note _ _ _ _ _ _

Voice Leading - Patterns
(The pattern is two frets up or one whole steps up)

CMaj7 I

Finger _ _ _ _ _ _
Scale _ _ _ _ _ 5
Note _ _ _ _ _ _

Am7 vi

Finger _ _ _ _ _ _
Scale _ _ _ _ _ _
Note _ _ _ _ _ _

DmMaj7 ii

Finger _ _ _ _ _ _
Scale _ _ _ _ 7 _
Note _ _ _ _ _ _

G7 V7

Finger _ _ _ _ _ _
Scale _ _ _ _ 5 _
Note _ _ _ _ _ _

Voice Leading - Chromatic Ascending Line

CMaj7 I

Finger _ _ _ _ _ _
Scale _ _ _ _ _ 5
Note _ _ _ _ _ _

Eb°7

Finger _ _ _ _ _ _
Scale _ _ _ _ _ _
Note _ _ _ _ _ _

Dm7 ii

Finger _ _ _ _ _ _
Scale _ _ _ _ _ _
Note _ _ _ _ _ _

G7add13/F V7

Finger _ _ _ _ _ _
Scale _ _ b7 _ _
Note _ _ _ _ _ _

Voice Leading - Chromatic Descending Line
(The Eb diminished 7th is a tritone substitution)

Chord Progression Worksheet
Ascending and Descending Bass lines, and Pedal notes

CMaj7 I — Finger _ _ _ _ _ / Scale _ _ _ _ _ _ / Note _ _ _ _ _ _

Am7 vi — Finger _ _ _ _ _ / Scale _ _ _ _ _ _ / Note _ _ _ _ _ _

Dm7 ii — 3rd — Finger _ _ _ _ _ / Scale _ _ _ _ _ _ / Note _ _ _ _ _ _

G13 V7 — 3rd — Finger _ _ _ _ _ / Scale _ _ _ _ _ _ / Note _ _ _ _ _ _

Voice Leading - Step-Wise Ascending Line

CMaj7 I — Finger _ _ _ _ _ / Scale _ _ _ _ _ _ / Note _ _ _ _ _ _

Cadd9 I — Finger _ _ _ _ _ / Scale _ _ _ _ _ _ / Note _ _ _ _ _ _

Dm7/F ii — Finger _ _ _ _ _ / Scale _ _ _ _ _ _ / Note _ _ _ _ _ _

G7 V7 — Finger _ _ _ _ _ / Scale _ _ _ _ _ _ / Note _ _ _ _ _ _

Voice Leading - Step-Wise Descending Line
(Relative Major switch with the Am7)

CMaj7 I — Finger _ _ _ _ _ / Scale _ _ _ _ _ _ / Note _ _ _ _ _ _

Am7 vi — Finger _ _ _ _ _ / Scale _ _ _ _ _ _ / Note _ _ _ _ _ _

FMaj7 IV — Finger _ _ _ _ _ / Scale _ _ _ _ _ _ / Note _ _ _ _ _ _

G13 V7 — Finger _ _ _ _ _ / Scale _ _ _ _ _ _ / Note _ _ _ _ _ _

Voice Leading - Pedal Note E
(Relative Major switch with the Dm7)

Finger _ _ _ _ _ / Scale _ _ _ _ _ _ / Note _ _ _ _ _ _

Finger _ _ _ _ _ / Scale _ _ _ _ _ _ / Note _ _ _ _ _ _

Finger _ _ _ _ _ / Scale _ _ _ _ _ _ / Note _ _ _ _ _ _

Finger _ _ _ _ _ / Scale _ _ _ _ _ _ / Note _ _ _ _ _ _

Finger _ _ _ _ _ / Scale _ _ _ _ _ _ / Note _ _ _ _ _ _

Finger _ _ _ _ _ / Scale _ _ _ _ _ _ / Note _ _ _ _ _ _

Finger _ _ _ _ _ / Scale _ _ _ _ _ _ / Note _ _ _ _ _ _

Finger _ _ _ _ _ / Scale _ _ _ _ _ _ / Note _ _ _ _ _ _

Chord Substitution Worksheet

Original Progression (Basic Folk Progression)

ii-V7 substition

Relative minor substitution for C to Am7

This is the basic Standard Chord Progression and there are literally 1000s of songs that use it.

Extension added to C to make it a CMaj7

Quality change of the Am7 to an A7

Chord Substitution Worksheet

C I | **G V** | or | **C I** | **G V7**

Finger _ _ _ _ _   Scale _ _ _ _ _   Note _ _ _ _ _

Folk Progression
Margaritaville verse Jimmy Buffet & Me And Bobby McGee verse Janis Joplin
Hurts So Good chorus John Courgar & Summer Of '69 verse Bryan Adams

C I | **G7 V7** | **C I** |

Finger _ _ _ _ _   Scale _ _ _ _ _   Note _ _ _ _ _

Ommision - The Folk Progression is Doubled with last G ommitted
Blue Bayou verse Lind Ronstadt & Have You Ever Seen The Rain verse CCR

G V | **C I** | |

Finger _ _ _ _ _   Scale _ _ _ _ _   Note _ _ _ _ _

Displacement - the C and G are switched
I Walk The Line verse Johnny Cash & Help Me Rhonda chorus Beach Boys

Am vi | **Em iii** | or | **Am7 vi** | **Em7 iii**

Finger _ _ _ _ _   Scale _ _ _ _ _   Note _ _ _ _ _

Relative minor substitutions
Diamond Girl verse Seals and Crofts
$ Lossing My Religion verse R.E.M.

Aint No Woman (Like The One I've Got) verse Four Tops

Am i | **E7 V7** | Minor key Roman numerals shown |

Finger _ _ _ _ _   Scale _ _ _ _ _   Note _ _ _ _ _

Chord Quality change Em - E7
You've Got A Friend verse James Taylor
Paint It Black opening verse Rolling Stones

25

Chord Substitution Worksheet

Happy Birthday Key of G, Time signature is 3/4

Original   G (I)   D (V)

Substitutes   G   *Eb7   D   D7

Happy   birth - day   to   you.   Happy   birth - day   to

Notes: The Eb7 is the tritone substitution for A7 which could be used by backcycling from D, you can think of it as a kind of double substitution. The D7 is backcycled from G. The D7 and A7 could also be looked at as secondary Dominant chords you should be very familiar with already.

G (I)   C (IV)   C (IV)   G (I)   D (V)

G   Bm7   G7   CMaj7   Am   Em7   Am7   D7

you.   Happy   birth - day   dear   John.   Happy   birth - day   to

Notes: Bm7 Secondary Relative minor of G, G7 Backcycle from C, CMaj7 Extension, Am Relative minor of C, Em7-Am7-D7 backcycle from G, Gadd9 extension.

G (I)

Gadd9

you.

Notes: The add9 and 6/9 chords make good ending chords.
They have a more resolved sound to them.

Twinkle Twinkle Little Star Key of C, Time signature is 2/4 (Chordal Melody)

C (I)   F (IV)   C (I)

C (open)   Em7 (7th fret)   *FMaj7 (8th fret)   Em7 (7th fret)

Twin - kle   twin - kle   lit - tle   Star

*Second time around use a Dm7 5th Fret (melody first string) for the FMaj7

Note: Play the melody on the second string on all these chords.

F (IV)   C (I)   G (V)   C (I)

Dm7 (5th fret)   CMaj7 (3rd fret)   G7 (3rd fret)   C (open)

How   I   won - der   what   you   are

Note: All the substitutions are extensions, relative minor and secondary relative minor substitutions.

Em (iii)   Dm (ii)   C (I)   G (V)

Em7 (7th fret)   Dm7 (5th fret)   CMaj7 (3rd fret)   G7 (3rd fret)

Up   a - bove   the   clouds   so   high

Power Chord Worksheet

E5   I
7th

Finger _ _ _ _ _
Scale _ _ _ _ _
Note _ _ _ _ _

D5   bVII
5th

Finger _ _ _ _ _
Scale _ _ _ _ _
Note _ _ _ _ _

E5   I
7th

Finger _ _ _ _ _
Scale _ _ _ _ _
Note _ _ _ _ _

D5   bVII
5th

Finger _ _ _ _ _
Scale _ _ _ _ _
Note _ _ _ _ _

Intro and Verse

C5   bVI
3rd

Finger _ _ _ _ _
Scale _ _ _ _ _
Note _ _ _ _ _

B5   V

Finger _ _ _ _ _
Scale _ _ _ _ _
Note _ _ _ _ _

Finger _ _ _ _ _
Scale _ _ _ _ _
Note _ _ _ _ _

Finger _ _ _ _ _
Scale _ _ _ _ _
Note _ _ _ _ _

end of chorus
Cocaine Eric Clapton (Key E)

E5   I
7th

Finger _ _ _ _ _
Scale _ _ _ _ _
Note _ _ _ _ _

D5   bVII
5th

Finger _ _ _ _ _
Scale _ _ _ _ _
Note _ _ _ _ _

A5   IV
x o

Finger _ _ _ _ _
Scale _ _ _ _ _
Note _ _ _ _ _

B5   V

Finger _ _ _ _ _
Scale _ _ _ _ _
Note _ _ _ _ _

Living After Midnight Judas Priest   (Key E)

E5   vi
7th

Finger _ _ _ _ _
Scale _ _ _ _ _
Note _ _ _ _ _

G5   I
3rd

Finger _ _ _ _ _
Scale _ _ _ _ _
Note _ _ _ _ _

A5   ii
5th

Finger _ _ _ _ _
Scale _ _ _ _ _
Note _ _ _ _ _

C5   IV
3rd

Finger _ _ _ _ _
Scale _ _ _ _ _
Note _ _ _ _ _

(Key Em) Use chord letter names to determine the key

D5   V
5th

Finger _ _ _ _ _
Scale _ _ _ _ _
Note _ _ _ _ _

Finger _ _ _ _ _
Scale _ _ _ _ _
Note _ _ _ _ _

Finger _ _ _ _ _
Scale _ _ _ _ _
Note _ _ _ _ _

Finger _ _ _ _ _
Scale _ _ _ _ _
Note _ _ _ _ _

Rock You Like A Hurricane Scorpions

Power Chord Worksheet

G5 °° vi	Bb5 I	Db5 bIII	C5 ii
Finger _ _ _ _ _	Finger _ _ _ _ _	3rd / Finger _ _ _ _ _	3rd / Finger _ _ _ _ _
Scale _ 5 1 _ _	Scale _ 5 1 _ _	Scale _ 5 1 _ _	Scale _ 5 1 _ _
Note _ _ _ _ _	Note _ _ _ _ _	Note _ _ _ _ _	Note _ _ _ _ _

(Key Gm) used quick reference guide

Smoke On The Water Deep Purple (Second Inversion Power Chords)

G5 vi	Bb5 I	Db5 bIII	C5 ii
8th	8th	8th	8th
Finger _ _ _ _ _	Finger _ _ _ _ _	Finger _ _ _ _ _	Finger _ _ _ _ _
Scale _ 5 1 _ _	Scale _ 5 1 _ _	Scale _ 5 1 _ _	Scale _ 5 1 _ _
Note _ _ _ _ _	Note _ _ _ _ _	Note _ _ _ _ _	Note _ _ _ _ _

Second Inversion Chords up the neck

Smoke On The Water Deep Purple (Second Inversion Power Chords)

B5 V	A5 IV	E5 I	
7th	7th	7th	
Finger _ _ _ _ _	Finger _ _ _ _ _	Finger _ _ _ _ _	Finger _ _ _ _ _
Scale _ 5 1 _ _	Scale _ 5 1 _ _	Scale _ 1 5 _ _	Scale _ _ _ _ _
Note _ _ _ _ _	Note _ _ _ _ _	Note _ _ _ _ _	Note _ _ _ _ _

E5 I	E5/Eb I	D5 bVII	D5/Db bVII
7th	6th	5th	4th
Finger _ _ _ _ _	Finger _ _ _ _ _	Finger _ _ _ _ _	Finger _ _ _ _ _
Scale _ _ _ _ _	Scale _ _ _ _ _	Scale _ _ _ _ _	Scale _ _ _ _ _
Note _ _ _ _ _	Note _ _ _ _ _	Note _ _ _ _ _	Note _ _ _ _ _

Chromatic Bass line

C5 bVI			
3rd			
Finger _ _ _ _ _	Finger _ _ _ _ _	Finger _ _ _ _ _	Finger _ _ _ _ _
Scale _ _ _ _ _	Scale _ _ _ _ _	Scale _ _ _ _ _	Scale _ _ _ _ _
Note _ _ _ _ _	Note _ _ _ _ _	Note _ _ _ _ _	Note _ _ _ _ _

Hold On Loosely 38 Special (Key E)

Triad Worksheet

D ⋁	C IV	G I	D ⋁
10th	8th	7th	
Finger _ _ _ _ _	Finger _ _ _ _ _	Finger _ _ _ _ _	Finger _ _ _ _ _
Scale _ _ _ _ _	Scale _ _ _ _ _	Scale _ _ _ _ _	Scale _ _ _ _ _
Note _ _ _ _ _	Note _ _ _ _ _	Note _ _ _ _ _	Note _ _ _ _ _

(Key G) Intro
Feel Like Makin' Love Bad Company

F IV	Em iii	Dm ii	C I
13th	12th	10th	8th
Finger _ _ _ _ _	Finger _ _ _ _ _	Finger _ _ _ _ _	Finger _ _ _ _ _
Scale _ _ 3 _ I	Scale _ _ _ b3 I	Scale _ _ b3 _ I	Scale _ _ _ 3 I
Note _ _ _ _ _	Note _ _ _ _ _	Note _ _ _ _ _	Note _ _ _ _ _

Am vi	G ⋁	F IV	
5th	3rd		
Finger _ _ _ _ _	Finger _ _ _ _ _	Finger _ _ _ _ _	Finger _ _ _ _ _
Scale _ _ b3 _ I	Scale _ _ _ 3 I	Scale _ _ _ 3 I	Scale _ _ _ _ _
Note _ _ _ _ _	Note _ _ _ _ _	Note _ _ _ _ _	Note _ _ _ _ _

(Key C) Intro D pedal note
Wanted Dead or Alive Bon Jovi

A I	D IV	A I	Bm ii
9th	10th	9th	7th
Finger _ _ h-o _	Finger _ _ _ _ _	Finger _ _ h-o _	Finger _ _ _ _ _
Scale _ _ p-o _	Scale _ _ _ _ _	Scale _ _ p-o _	Scale _ _ _ _ _
Note _ _ _ _ _	Note _ _ _ _ _	Note _ _ _ _ _	Note _ _ _ _ _

(key of A) Intro
Domino Van Morisson

Finger _ _ _ _ _	Finger _ _ _ _ _	Finger _ _ _ _ _	Finger _ _ _ _ _
Scale _ _ _ _ _	Scale _ _ _ _ _	Scale _ _ _ _ _	Scale _ _ _ _ _
Note _ _ _ _ _	Note _ _ _ _ _	Note _ _ _ _ _	Note _ _ _ _ _

Triad Worksheet

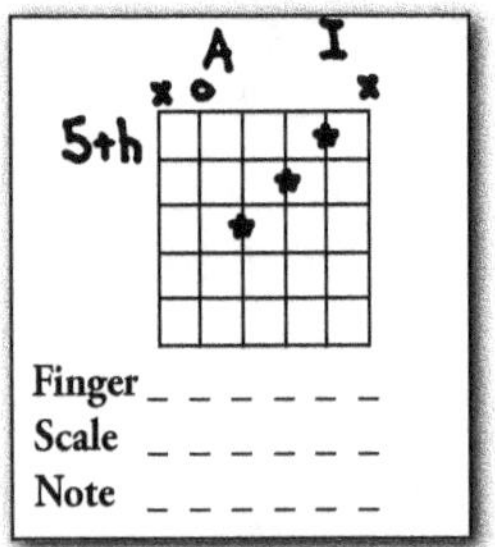

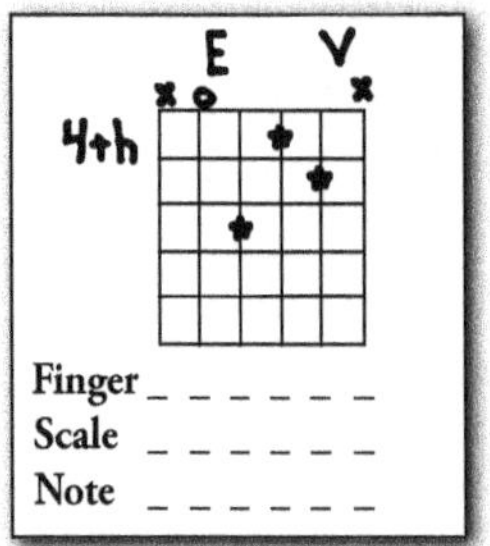

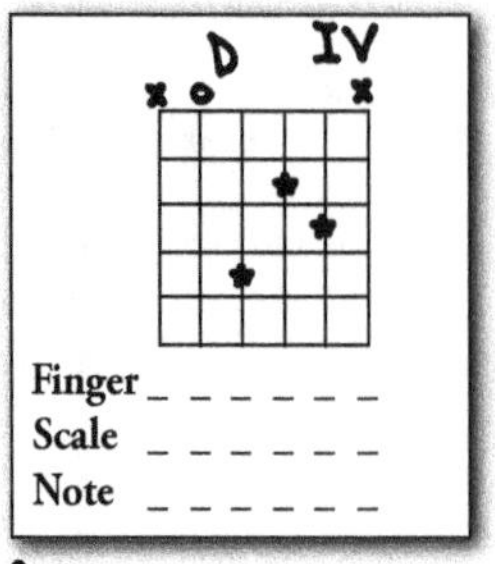

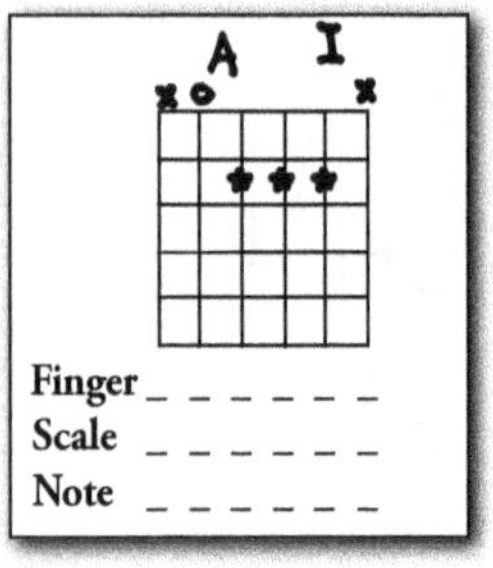

Row 1 (chord diagrams): A I (5th), E V (4th), D IV, A I — each with Finger / Scale / Note blanks

(Key A) Intro (uses A Pedal note)
Crazy Train Ozzy Osbourne

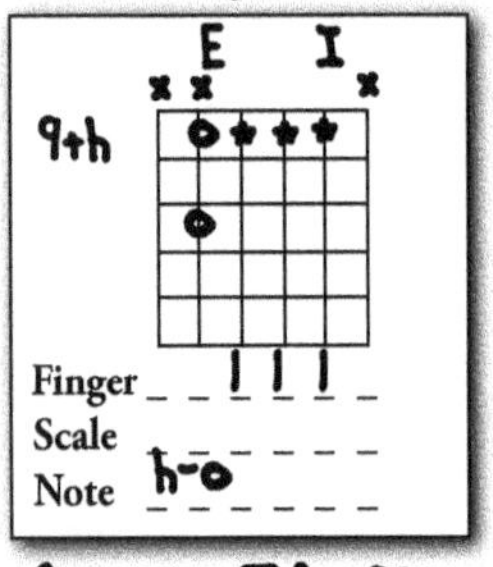

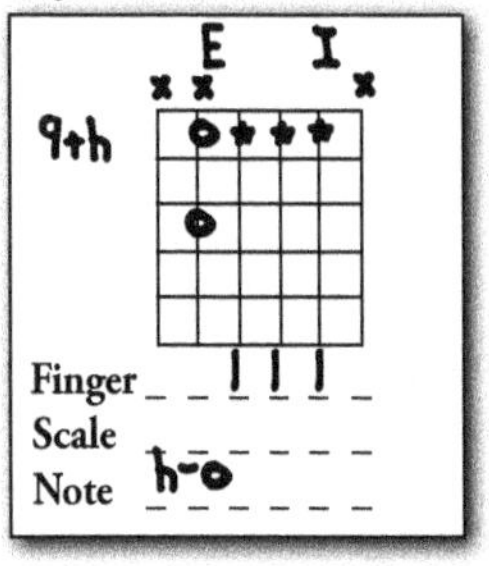

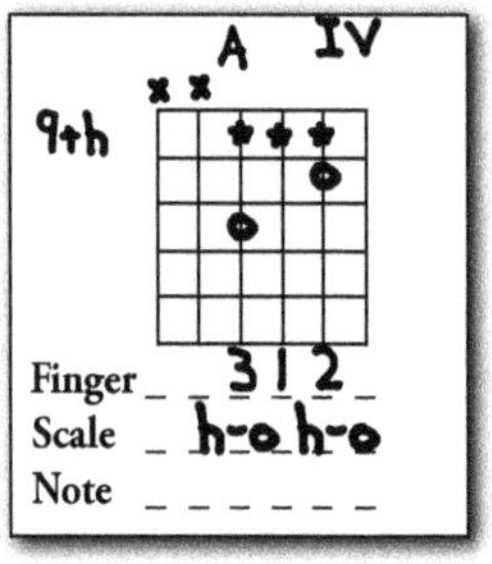

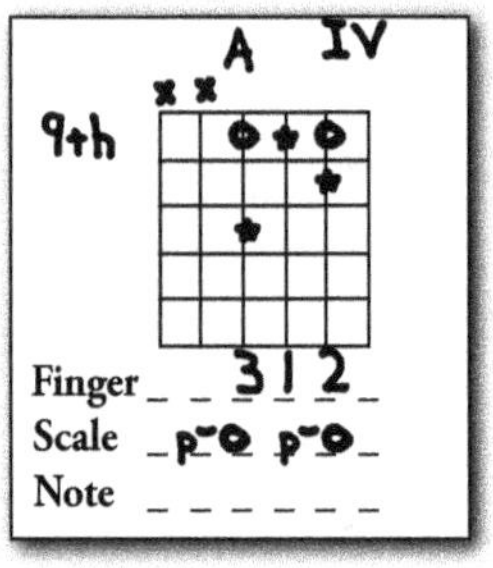

Row 2: E I (9th) Finger | | | Note h-o, E I (9th) Finger | | | Note h-o, A IV (9th) Finger 3 1 2 Scale h-o h-o, A IV (9th) Finger 3 1 2 Scale p-o p-o

(Key E) Intro
Listen To The Music Doobie Brothers

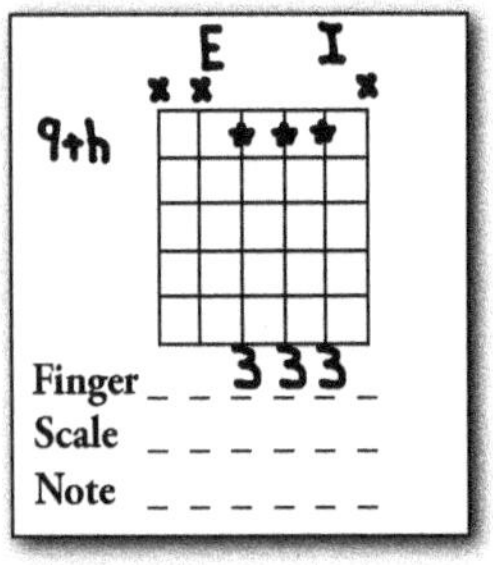

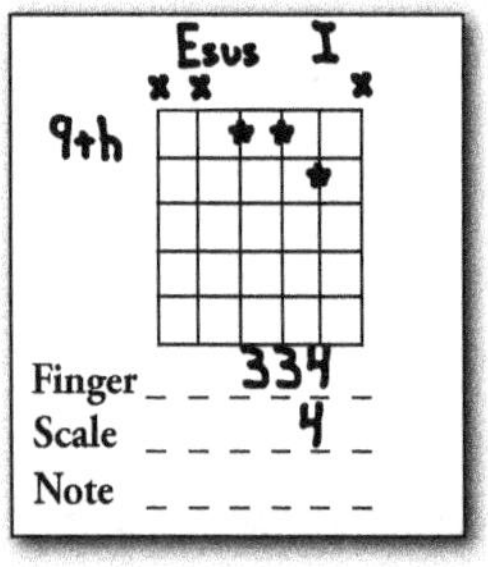

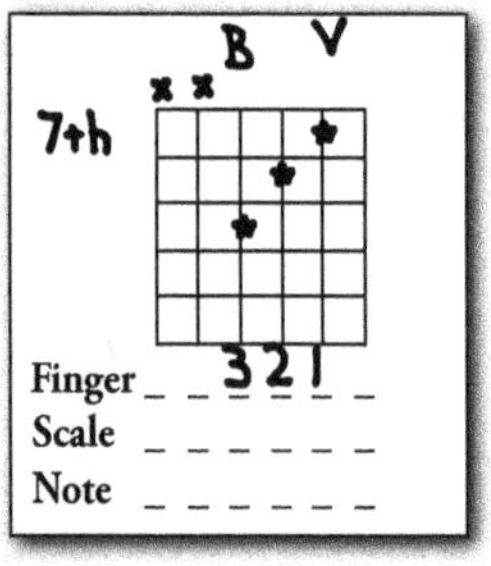

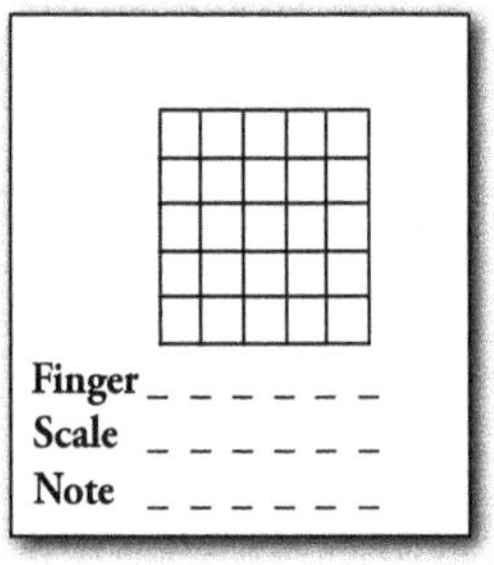

Row 3: E I (9th) Finger 3 3 3, Esus I (9th) Finger 3 3 4 Scale 4, B V (7th) Finger 3 2 1, (blank)

Pedal note in the bass is E (5th string 7th fret) repeat twice

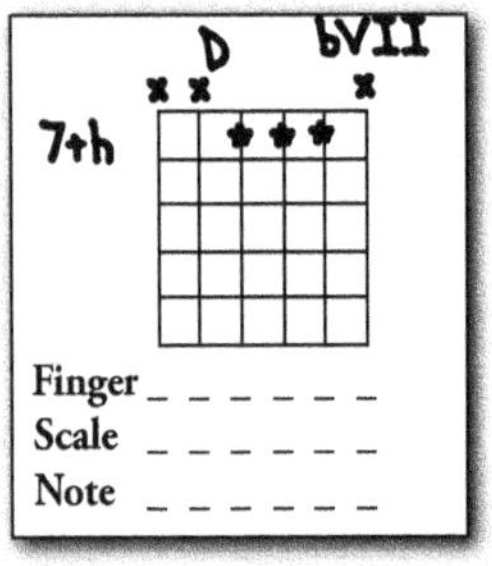

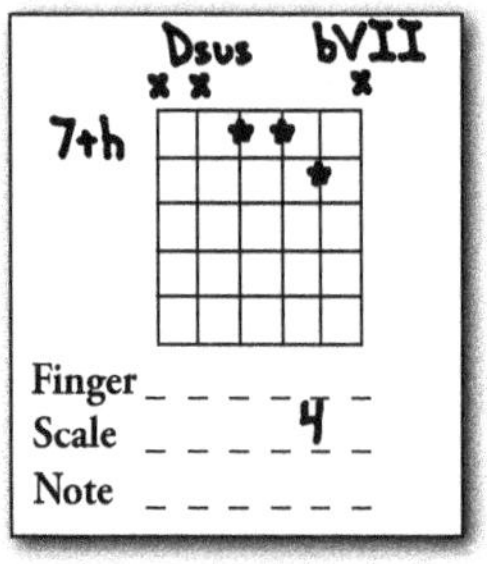

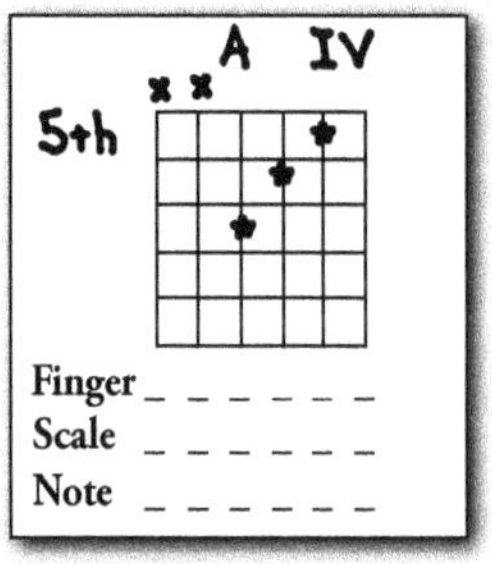

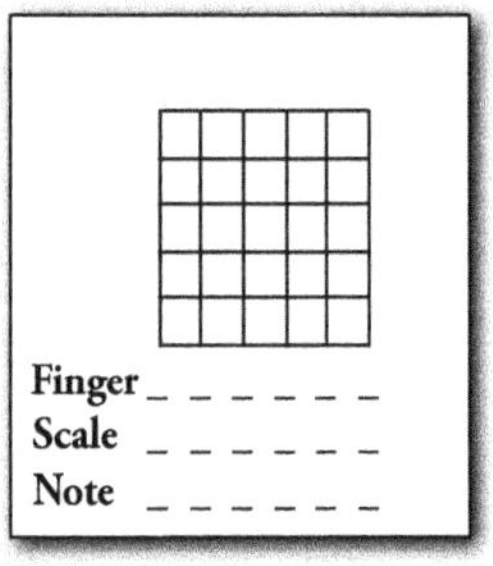

Row 4: D bVII (7th) Finger, Dsus bVII (7th) Finger Scale 4, A IV (5th) Finger, (blank)

(Key E) Intro   Pedal note in the bass is D (5th string 5th fret)
Panama Eddy Van Hallen (Key E)

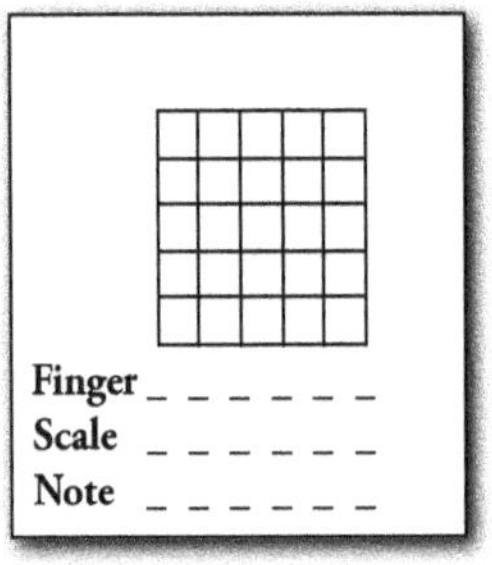

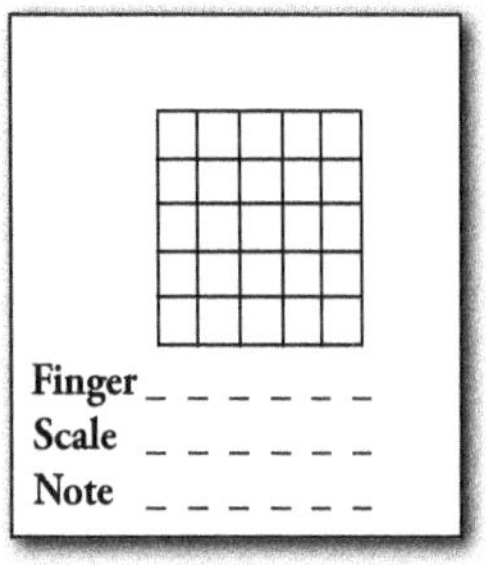

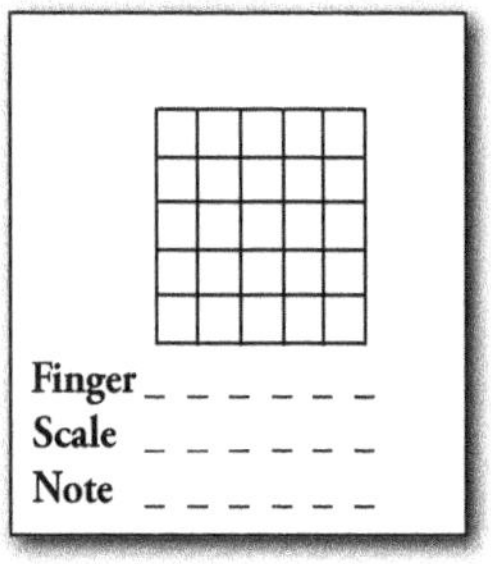

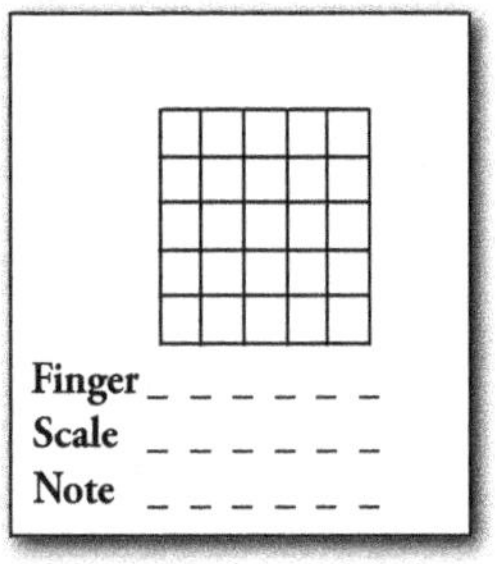

Row 5: four blank chord diagrams, each with Finger / Scale / Note blanks

THE CHORD CHARTS

Chord Name

At the top of the chord box is the chord's name. There are three basic families of chords with very distinct sound qualities; Majors, minors and dominants. The chord symbol for a Major chord consists of the letter name of the chord and nothing else, with two exceptions. If the letter name of the chord is followed by a 6, it means the chord is a Major sixth chord. If the letter name of a chord is followed by "Maj" it also means the chord is Major type chord. The "Maj" after the chord's letter name will be followed by a number indicating what additional note is added to the basic Major chord. For instance the chord symbol, CMaj7, would be called a C Major seventh chord, and a CMaj9 chord would be called C Major Ninth. In general Major chords have a happy up-beat sound to them. If the letter name of the chord is followed by a lower-case "m", it means the chord is a minor chord. Cm for instance is the chord symbol for the C minor chord. (There are other ways of notating Major and minor chords which are less common and can be found in the *Chord Formula* section of this book.) Minor chords can also have numbers after the lower-case "m". For instance Cm7, Cm9 or Cm6, which would be called a C minor seven, C minor nine and a C minor six chord. Minor chords have a sad or melancholy sound to them. If a chord is from the dominant chord family it will have a number after the letter name of the chord—C7, C9 or C11 for instance, which would be a C seven, C nine and a C eleven chord. (The only exception to this is the C6, which is a Major chord as discussed above.) Dominant chords have a tension or dissonance in their sound that wants to be resolved by another chord. Dominant chords are also very popular blues chords that give the music an edginess to the sound.

Major and minor chords in their most basic form consist of only three different notes. You may play more than three notes in a chord, but those additional notes will be one of the three basic notes in the chord doubled or played an octave higher or lower. When you add additional notes to a chord the additional notes are called embellishments or extensions of the basic chord. CMaj7 and Cm7 are extensions of the basic C Major chord and C minor chord. Dominant chords in their most basic form are notated with a 7 after the letter name of the chord and consist of four different notes. Dominant chords can also have additional notes added to their four basic notes and those additional notes are notated as 9, 11 or 13. You can learn more about this in the *Chord Formula* section of the book, along with what are called altered chords where one of the notes from the chord's Major scale has been raised or lowered a half step.

There are also two lesser used chord families, called diminished and augmented chords. These two chords have additional tension in their sound above and beyond the dominant chords. Diminished chords are notated with a degree symbol after them and augmented chords a plus sign, Co (C diminished) and C+ (C augmented). These chords are primarily used as passing chords—chords that get you from one chord to another—because of the instability and tension in the chord.

There are a couple of other types of chords you should be familiar with as well—the suspended and "add" chords. It's not important you understand why these chords are called suspended and "add" chords right now, but you should be able to name them. Suspended chords are notated with a "sus" after the letter name of the chord, for instance Csus, which would be called a C suspended chord. This chord is sometimes notated Csus4, which is the same as a C suspended chord, sometimes called a C suspended four chord. Sometimes people shorten the name to just a C sus as well. The other type of suspended chord is the suspended two chord notated "sus2".

For those chords with the "add" after the letter name you would simply say the "add" followed by whatever number was after it. For instance a Cadd9 chord would be called C add nine. Another common way of writing these chord is with a slash between the letter name and number. For instance, the C add nine chord may also be written C/9. (Don't confuse this with slash chords that have a letter after the slash, these are a completely different kind of chord.)

This section has just been to help you with naming chords. For a more thorough explanation of the different chord families and how chords are made refer to the *Chord Formula* section.

ROMAN NUMERAL NUMBERING SYSTEM

If you already have some experience playing, you're probably ready to start thinking about how chords are numbered. At the top of every chord chart box you'll see the name of the chord followed by a Roman numeral in parentheses. These Roman numerals are the language of chord progressions. They allow us to talk about chord progressions independent of key, which means independent of the letter name of the chord.

Here are a few things you'll need to know about the Roman numeral numbering system. When a Roman numeral is in upper-case it means the chord is Major and when the Roman numeral is in lower-case it means the chord is minor. Another way of thinking of it is, if the Roman numeral is in lower-case it means the 3rd of the chord is flatted. (If you don't know your chord formulas, don't worry, just remember upper-case means Major and lower-case minor.)

If the Roman Numeral has a "7" after it, it means the chord is some kind of dominant chord, either just a 7th chord or any of the many alterations and extensions; C9, C13, C7#5, C7b9 etc.. Another way of thinking about this in terms of chord's formula. If the Roman numeral is followed by a 7 it means the chord has a flat 7 in it.

Diminished chords are written in lower-case with a degree symbol after the Roman numeral and augmented chords are written in upper-case with a plus sign. In the case of the diminished chords the lower-case means the 3rd is flatted and the degree symbol means the 5th is flatted as well. For the Augmented chords the plus means the fifth is sharp.

Just one left to go called a half diminished. Half diminished chords look like diminished chord symbols except they have a slash through the degree symbol. Half diminished chords can also be written as Cm7b5.

Now let's talk about where these numbers come from and how to use them. The Roman numerals tell you the location of the letter name of the chord in the key's Major or minor scale. (For the most part we'll be talking only about the Major keys, but it's the same for the minor keys as well.) So for instance, if someone were to say play the one chord in the key of C, you would play a C Major chord, because C is the first note in a C Major scale. If they were to say play a I, IV, V progression in the key of C, you would play C, F and G, because the C is the first note in the C Major scale, the F is the fourth note and the G is the fifth. (C Major scale: C, D, E, F, G, A, B)

Let's look at another example to make sure you've got it. This time let's say someone were to say play a I, IV, V progression in the key of G. What would you play? (G Major scale is G, A, B, C, D, E, F#) If you said G, C and D you'd be right because in the G Major scale, G is the first note in the scale, C is the forth note and D is the fifth. By learning the Roman numerals for each chord in each key you can move from one key to another with ease. It may sound like a lot of extra work but there are some big payoffs for understanding how this works.

When you build three note chords off of a Major scale, using Major third intervals, there is a pattern of Major, minor and diminished chords that occurs. That pattern is I, ii, iii, IV, V, vi, vii°. The first, fourth and fifth chords are always Major and the second, third and sixth chords are always minor. The seventh chord is a diminished chord. (Each one of these chords has a name as well: I=Tonic, ii=Supertonic, iii=Mediant, IV=Subdominant, V=Dominant, vi=Submediant, vii=Leading Note)

A (I)		Bm (ii)		E7 (V7)		G#dim7 (vii°7)		Aaug (I+)
Finger X 0 1 2 3 0		Finger X 1 3 4 2 1		Finger 0 2 0 1 0 0		Finger 2 X 1 3 1 X		Finger X 0 1 2 3 X
Scale X 1 5 1 3 5		Scale X 1 5 1 b3 5		Scale 1 5 b7 3 5 1		Scale 1 X bb7 b3 b5 X		Scale X 3 #5 1 3 X
Note X A E A C# E		Note X B F# B D F#		Note E B D G# B E		Note G# X F B D X		Note X C# F A C# X

Here are a few examples of how the Roman numerals can tell you which chord family they represent.

If you add another note to each of these chords, making them four note chords, you get the extensions IMaj7, iim7, iiim7, IVMaj7, vim7. You also get a chord that changes from a Major chord to a dominant, the V chord becomes a V7 chord. For the key of C Major you would have the following chords; CMaj7, Dm7, Em7, FMaj7, G7, Am7 and Bdim7. The important thing to notice here is that the family or quality of the chords stay the same with the exception of the V chord. The V chord instead of being a Major chord becomes a dominant chord. (To learn more about the different families of chords refer to the section on *Chord Formulas*.)

Chords built off of a Major scale are referred to as diatonic chords, and as you would imagine, sound good together because none of the notes in the chords fall outside of the scale. Its kind of like sitting at a piano and only playing the white keys. But there are several other chords that are not diatonic that sound good with these chords and are used extensively in modern music. They're the bIII, bVI and bVII chords which I refer to as the Flat Majors. (These Flat Major chords come from the minor scale with the same letter name as the Major scale.) These chords are very popular in Rock, Pop and a lot of contemporary Country music. In the key of C these chords would be Eb, Ab and Bb. There are also what I call family or quality change chords like the II, III, iv and v. These chords in the key of C would be D, E, Fm and Gm. And then you have what are called secondary dominant chords that I've shown in the chord charts with gray backgrounds. These chords come from the fact that the V7 to I combination is so strong that you can take a chord outside the key and add it to a key it doesn't belong in as long as it resolves to one of the chords in the key. These "secondary" dominants, as they're called, are the V7 chords from the chords scale they lead to. (The V7/I is really not a secondary dominant, but rather the dominant chord for that key. I've listed it this way, just a memory help, but since it is part of the key it really would not be considered a "secondary" dominant.) The secondary dominant chords do not always have to be dominant family chords. You can use Major or minor chords. I've listed them as dominant family chords because the dominant chord family has the strongest pull to the one chord.

By using Roman numerals instead of chord names, progressions can be written once and applied to any key. But they also tell us important things about how music is constructed. As you gain experience you'll begin to see relationships between chords you may not have noticed before, like the V7 to I progression, for instance. One of the goals of studying this book should be to learn the Roman numerals for each chord as well as the chord's name. With this knowledge, you'll be well on your way to understanding music and being able to transpose music to any key.

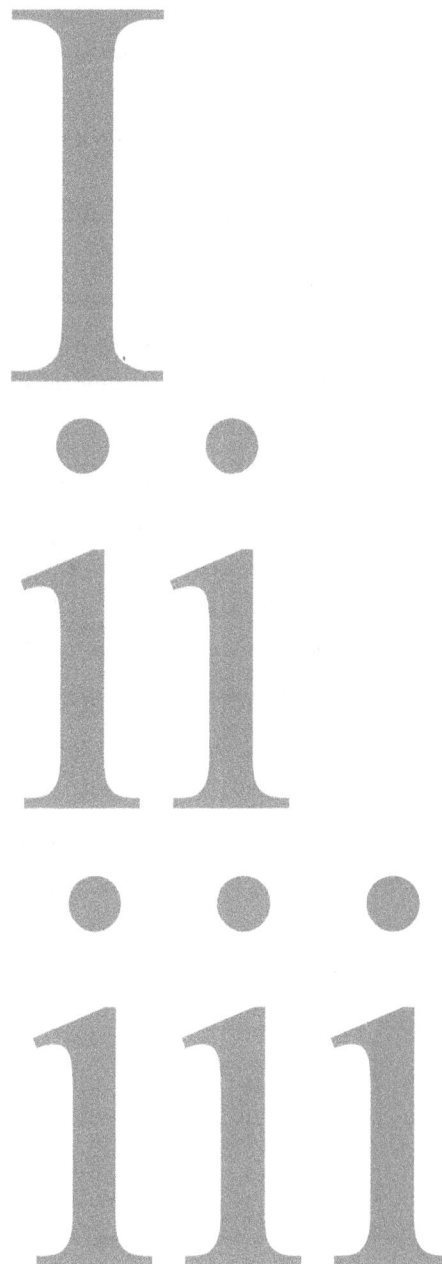

I

ii

iii

FINGERING

Below the chord chart itself you'll find the word "Finger" followed by a set of numbers or an X or T. These numbers and the T represent which fingers to use to make the chord: 1=index, 2=middle, 3=ring, 4=pinky and the T is used for the thumb. The X indicates the string is not played or muted.

There's usually more than one way you can place your fingers to make a chord, so these are really just suggestions. When you're first learning to play it's hard to get your fingers to do anything, so these are really just suggestions to get you started. But just because I say this finger goes here, and this one goes here, etc. Doesn't mean you have to do it that way.

A couple of chords that you'll see people make different ways are the G and F chords. The G chord for instance can be played using the middle and ring finger on the lower strings or the index and middle finger. The F chord can be played as a barre chord or you can use your thumb over the top of the neck to get the lower F on the sixth string.

there are a couple of different choices and you should experiment to see which works best for the chord changes you're making.

1st
2nd

G	**G**	**G**	**F**	**F**	**F**
Finger 3 2 0 0 0 4	Finger 2 1 0 0 0 3	Finger 2 1 0 0 0 4	Finger 1 3 4 2 1 1	Finger T 3 4 2 1 1	Finger T X 3 2 1 1
Scale 1 3 5 1 3 1	Scale 1 3 5 1 3 1	Scale 1 3 5 1 3 1	Scale 1 5 1 3 5 1	Scale 1 5 1 3 5 1	Scale 1 X 1 3 5 1
Note G B D G B G	Note G B D G B G	Note G B D G B G	Note F C F A C F	Note F C F A C F	Note F X F A C F

Here are a few different ways the G and F chord can be made.

Another chord with a few different ways to make it is the B chord and all the versions of this barre chord moved up the neck. You can use individual fingers or you can use a single finger to barre across the 2nd, 3rd and 4th strings.

B	**B**	**B**
Finger X 1 2 3 4 1	Finger X 1 3 3 3 1	Finger X 1 4 4 4 1
Scale X 1 5 1 3 5	Scale X 1 5 1 3 5	Scale X 1 5 1 3 5
Note X B F# B D# F#	Note X B F# B D# F#	Note X B F# B D# F#

3rd
4th

As you progress in your playing the chord progression itself should really be your guide for what fingers to use. So my recommendation is experiment and don't let yourself get tied into thinking there is only one way to make a chord. Often

ECONOMY OF MOTION

There are a couple of different thoughts on how to move your fingers when it comes to beginners. Some people will advise when learning new chords to take your fingers completely off the fingerboard in between each chord. The thought is by doing it this way you build up what is called muscle memory in your fingers and are able to find the chords quicker with practice.

The other approach is to try and find pivot points, fingers in a chord that don't need to be raised, but can be left down between two chords. So in this approach you wouldn't remove all your fingers from the fretboard, only the ones that change position.

C (I)		
Finger	X 3 2 0 1 0	
Scale	X 1 3 5 1 3	
Note	X C E G C E	

F (IV)		
Finger	X X 3 2 1 1	
Scale	X X 1 3 5 1	
Note	X X F A C F	

G (V)		
Finger	3 2 0 0 0 4	
Scale	1 3 5 1 3 1	
Note	G B D G B G	

Am (vi)		
Finger	X 0 2 3 1 0	
Scale	X 1 5 1 ♭3 5	
Note	X A E A C E	

Dm (ii)		
Finger	X X 0 2 3 1	
Scale	X X 1 5 1 ♭3	
Note	X X D A D F	

Em (iii)		
Finger	0 2 3 0 0 0	
Scale	1 5 1 ♭3 5 1	
Note	E B E G B E	

Here are a few examples going from a Major chord to its relative minor below you can leave fingers down between chords.

When transitioning from the C to the Am all you have to do is move one finger and you can keep the rest down. The same is true for the F to Dm. For the G to Em you lift off the fourth finger and move the third.

You can also form the relative minor 7th chords by simply raising a finger. Here are the C, F and G chords with their relative minor 7th chords.

In my humble opinion you should use the pivot idea when at all possible. The reason being is it takes muscle control to lift a finger off the fretboard, as well as reposition your fingers, and you need both skills. Using the pivot method will increase your speed in transitioning from one chord to the next. For an extreme example of this idea check-out the *Contemporary*

Worship Chord section. Here you'll find it's possible to play almost every chord in a key without moving any fingers except up and down the fretboard.

WHERE DO YOU PUT YOUR THUMB?

One more thing about fingering, and that is where do you put your thumb? There are great players on both sides of this issue as well. Some put their thumb on the very back of the neck of the guitar, and some hang their thumb over the top of the neck.

There are advantages and disadvantages to both ways of playing. I can tell you that putting your thumb on the back of the neck will give you greater leverage when you need strength to make a barre chord. But I will also tell you having your thumb over the top of the neck can be a great advantage for playing a note on the sixth string in certain situations.

My suggestion is try both. You'll probably find yourself favoring one over the other, but don't rule anything out. Try to use both methods when they make sense.

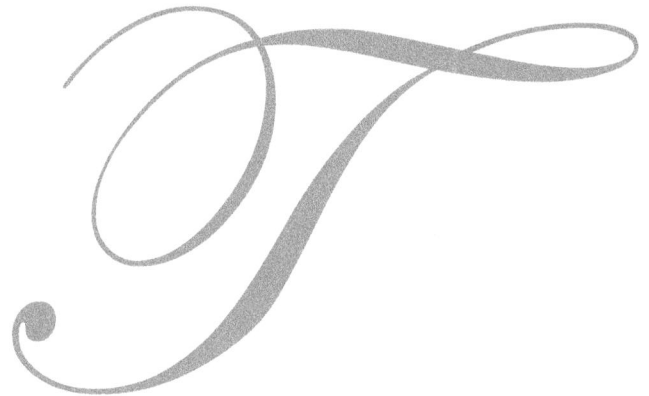

C (I)		
Finger	X 3 2 0 1 0	
Scale	X 1 3 5 1 3	
Note	X C E G C E	

F (IV)		
Finger	X X 3 2 1 1	
Scale	X X 1 3 5 1	
Note	X X F A C F	

G (V)		
Finger	3 2 0 0 0 4	
Scale	1 3 5 1 3 1	
Note	G B D G B G	

Am7 (vi)		
Finger	X 0 2 0 1 0	
Scale	X 1 5 ♭7 3 5	
Note	X A E G C E	

Dm7 (ii)		
Finger	X X 0 2 1 1	
Scale	X X 1 5 ♭7 ♭3	
Note	X X D A C F	

Em7 (iii)		
Finger	0 2 0 0 0 0	
Scale	1 5 ♭7 3 5 1	
Note	E B D G B E	

Here are some chord transitions made by simply raising fingers.

CHORD FORMULAS

WHAT DO THE NUMBERS MEAN?

Under each chord chart you'll see the word "Scale" followed by a group of numbers. This group of numbers represent the chord's formula. Each number corresponds to where that note is located in the Major scale of the chord's letter name. For instance if the chord were an "F" then the numbers would correspond to where each note was located in an F Major scale. Major chords consist of the first, third and fifth notes of the Major scale, while minor chords consist of the first, flatted 3rd and fifth notes. (Flatted simply means you lower the note's pitch one half step or one fret on the guitar. Some people call this a semitone as well.) A dominant 7th chord has the formula one, three, five, flat seven.

Here are some of the basic chord formulas and how you may see them written using a "C chord" for the examples:

Major chords = 1, 3, 5   (C)

Major 7th chords: = 1, 3, 5, 7   (CMaj7, CΔ7)

Minor chords = 1, b3, 5   (Cm, C-)

Minor 7th chords = 1, b3, 5, b7   (Cm7, C-7)

Dominant 7th chords = 1, 3, 5, b7   (C7)

Diminished chords = 1, b3, b5   (Cdim, C^{o})

Diminished 7th chords = 1, b3, b5, bb7(6)   (Cdim7, C^{o}7, C^{o})*

Half diminished = 1, b3, b5, b7   (C$^{\o}$7, Cm7b5)

Augmented chords = 1, 3, #5   (C^{+})

*Diminished chords are usually played as diminished 7th chords and may not have the 7 in the chord's name. Also the double flatted 7 would be the same as playing the 6th note of the scale.

Suspended chords replace the 3 with either a 4 or a 2. If the 3 is still in the chord though the word "add" is used to indicate that these other notes have been added to the chord and don't actually "replace" the 3. The additional notes would be shown as an 11 for the 4 and a 9 for the 2. More on why that is below.

Suspended 4 chords = 1, 4, 5   (Csus, Csus4)

add 11 chords = 1, 3, 5, 4   (Cadd11)

Suspended 2 chords = 1, 2, 5   (Csus2)

add 9 Chords = 1, 3, 5, 2   (Cadd9)

The basic formulas covers the odd numbers 1, 3, 5 and 7 with the exception of the suspended chords. To add an even number to a chord you use the odds 9 for 2, 11 for 4 and 6 for 13.

1	2	3	4	5	6	7	1	2	3	4	5	6	7
							8	9	10	11	12	13	

The exception to this rule is the Major 6th and minor 6th chords.

Major 6th chord = 1, 3, 5, 6   (C6)

minor 6th = 1, b3, 5, 6   (Cm6)

C — Finger X 3 2 0 1 0 / Scale X 1 3 5 1 3 / Note X C E G C E

CMaj7 — Finger X 3 2 0 0 0 / Scale X 1 3 5 7 3 / Note X C E G B E

C6 — Finger X 4 2 3 1 0 / Scale X 1 3 6 1 3 / Note X C E A C E

Cm — Finger X 4 1 0 2 X / Scale X 1 ♭3 5 1 X / Note X C D♯ G C X

Cm7 — Finger X 3 1 4 1 X / Scale X 1 ♭3 ♭7 1 X / Note X C D♯ A♯ C X

Cm6 — Finger X 3 1 2 1 X / Scale X 1 ♭3 6 1 X / Note X C D♯ A C X

C7 — Finger X 3 2 0 1 0 / Scale X 1 3 ♭7 1 3 / Note X C E A♯ C E

Csus — Finger X 3 4 0 1 1 / Scale X 1 4 5 1 4 / Note X C F G C F

Csus2 — Finger X 2 0 0 3 4 / Scale X 1 2 5 2 5 / Note X C D G D G

Cadd9 — Finger X 3 2 0 4 0 / Scale X 1 3 5 2 3 / Note X C E G D E

C° — Finger X X 1 3 2 4 / Scale X X ♭3 ♭♭7 1 ♭5 / Note X X D♯ A C F♯

C+ — Finger X 3 2 1 1 X / Scale X 1 3 ♯5 1 X / Note X C E G♯ C X

Here are a few examples of what the basic chord formulas would look for a C chord.

SO WHAT GOOD IS IT KNOWING THE CHORD'S FORMULA?

The most important thing for beginners is it gives you an idea of which notes you can drop and which you need to keep and still be playing the same chord. Not all the notes in a chord need to be played. Knowing which notes can be dropped because they're doubles or not essential to the chord's quality of sound offers a lot of possibilities for playing one chord. Some of the notes you can drop without harming the chords quality of sound are any doubles, the fifth and even the root can be dropped in some cases. You'd also want to keep the sevenths or a note indicated in the chord's symbol like a sharp 5 or flatted 9th etc.. Here are a few examples of how this would work with a simple B Major barre chord you'll find in the key of F. If you're a beginner it may be a lot easier to start playing the second example rather than the first until you've built up some strength in your fretting hand.

B — Finger X 1 2 3 4 1 / Scale X 1 5 1 3 5 / Note X B F♯ B D♯ F♯

B — Finger X X 2 3 4 1 / Scale X X 5 1 3 5 / Note X X F♯ B D♯ F♯

B — Finger X X X 3 4 1 / Scale X X X 1 3 5 / Note X X X B D♯ F♯

B — Finger X 1 2 3 4 X / Scale X 1 5 1 3 X / Note X B F♯ B D♯ X

B — Finger X X 1 1 1 X / Scale X X 5 1 3 X / Note X X F♯ B D♯ X

B — Finger X 1 X 3 4 1 / Scale X 1 X 1 3 5 / Note X B X B D♯ F♯

The other way knowing the chord's formula can help is if you want to make the same quality of chord with a different letter name. Let's say you really like the sound of a particular C6/9 chord and want to use it to make an F6/9. All you need to do is look for the note in the chord that gives the chord its letter name, the 1, and move it so that it is playing an F. Here are a couple of examples. You can use this technique to help decide what chord you're playing when you have a capo on the guitar as well.

C6/9 — Finger X 2 1 1 3 4 / Scale X 1 3 6 2 5 / Note X C E A D G

F6/9 — 7th — Finger X 2 1 1 3 3 / Scale X 1 3 6 2 5 / Note X F A D G C

CMaj7 — 3rd — Finger X 1 3 2 4 1 / Scale X 1 5 7 3 5 / Note X C G B E G

FMaj7 — 8th — Finger X 1 3 2 4 1 / Scale X 1 5 7 3 5 / Note X F C E A C

This does require learning the notes on the fretboard, but if you just concentrate on the 4th, 5th and 6th strings you'll have most of the notes you'll need. Just count up from E for the sixth string skipping a note between each letter name except (B and C) and (E and F) and you can fill in the skipped frets with either sharps if you raise the note or flats if you lower it. So the note between F and G could be an F♯ or a G♭. For the fifth string you would start on A and work your way up using the same principles as the E string. For the fourth string you would start on D. This will at least get you started. Remember the notes repeat themselves after G, so once you get to G you go to A. (There is a chart at the end of the book in the *Tips for Playing-by-ear* section showing the notes on the fretboard.)

You can also use the formulas as you advance in your knowledge of chord construction to alter a chord. For instance 7th chords can have the 5th sharped or flatted and they can have a sharp or flat 9 added. Remember 9=2, 11=4 and 13=6.

G7		G7#5		G7#5♭9	
3rd		x x	3rd	x	3rd
Finger	1 3 1 2 1 1	**Finger**	1 X 2 3 3 X	**Finger**	1 X 2 3 3 3
Scale	1 5 ♭7 3 5 1	**Scale**	1 X ♭7 3 #5 X	**Scale**	1 X ♭7 3 #5 ♭2
Note	G D F B D G	**Note**	G X F B D#X	**Note**	G X F B D#G#

To cover everything that could be learned from chord formulas would take another book. But hopefully this will get you started and peak your interest because this is just the tip of the iceberg. The main thing you need to remember when moving notes up or down in a chord is that there are frets between all the numbers except (3 and 4) and (7 and 1). So for instance if you want to move up to a 2 from a 1 you need to move up two frets. Or lets say you want to play a 6 in your chord you would need to move up two frets from the 5 or two frets down from the 7. If you're moving from the 1 to the 6 it would be 3 frets down because there isn't a fret between 7 and 1. If you want to replace the 3 with a 4 and make a chord a suspended you would only move up one fret because you don't skip a fret between 3 and 4.

If you keep these two things in mind, where the root notes are in the chord and where the skips are in the scale, the sky is the limit for what chords you can make. Practice looking at the formulas below the chords and seeing how each chord was constructed and why it's called what it's called.

CHORD FORMULAS

MAJOR CHORD FAMILY (1, 3, 5)

Major = 1, 3, 5   (C)

Major 7th = 1, 3, 5, 7   (CMaj7)

Major 6th = 1, 3, 5, 6   (C6)

Major 9th = 1, 3, 5, 7, 2   (CMaj9)

Major add 9 = 1, 3, 5, 2   (Cadd9 , C/9)

Major 6/9th = 1, 3, [5], 6, 2   (C6add9, C6/9)

Major 7/6th = 1, 3, 5, 6, 7   (CMaj7/6)

Major 11th = 1, [3], 5, 7, [2], 4 (CMaj11, CMaj7add11)

Major 13th = 1, 3, [5], 7, [2], [4], 6   (CMaj13, CMaj7add13)

A "/" can also be used to indicate an "add" chord which means a note has been added to the basic chord formula.

Notes with a bracket around them are commonly left out of the chord.

MINOR CHORD FAMILY (1, b3, 5)

minor = 1, b3, 5   (Cm, C-)

minor 7th = 1, b3, 5, b7   (Cm7, C-7)

minor 6 = 1, b3, 5, 6   (Cm6, C-6)

minor 9 = 1, b3, [5], b7, 2   (Cm9, C-9)

minor 11 = 1, b3, [5], b7, [2], 4   (Cm11, C-11)

minor 13 = **1, b3, [5], b7, [2], [4], 6** (Cm13, C-13)

minor 7/11th = **1, b3, [5], b7, 4** (Cm7/11)

minor add 9 = **1, b3, [5], 2** (Cmadd9)

minor 6/9th = **1, b3, [5], 6, 2** (Cm6/9, Cm6add9, C-6add9)

minor Maj7 = **1, b3, 5, 7** (CmMaj7)

minor Major 9 = **1, b3, [5], 7, 2** (CmMaj7/9, CmMaj9, CmMaj7add9)

DOMINANT CHORD FAMILY (1, 3, 5, b7)

Dominant 7th = **1, 3, 5, b7** (C7)

Dominant 7/6 = **1, 3, [5], b7, 6** (C7/6, C7add6, C7/13)

Dominant 7/11 = **1, 3, [5], b7, 4** (C7/11)

Dominant 7 suspended = **1, 4, 5, b7** (C7sus)

Dominant 7/6 suspended = **1, 4, 5, b7, 6** (C7/6sus)

Dominant 9th = **1, 3, [5], b7, 2** (C9)

Dominant 11th = **1, [3], 5, b7, [2], 4** (C11, C7add11)

Dominant 13th = **1, [3], 5, b7, [2], [4], 6** (C13, Cadd13, C9/6)

Dominant 13 suspended = **1, 4, 5, b7, [2], [4], 6** (C13sus)

Dominant 7/6/11th = **1, [3], 5, b7, 4, 6** (C7/6/11)

Dominant 11/13 = **1, [3], 5, b7, [2], 4, 6** (C11/13)

DIMINISHED (1, b3, b5) AND AUGMENTED (1, 3, #5)

Diminished = **1, b3, b5** (C^{O}, Cdim, Cmb5, Cm-5)

Diminished 7th = **1, b3, b5, bb7(6)** (C^{O}, C^{O}7, Cdim7)

Half Diminished = **1, b3, b5, b7** (C$^{\emptyset}$7, Cm7b5)

Augmented = **1, 3, #5** (C^{+}, Caug, C#5, C+5)

SUSPENDED (Suspended chords replace the 3 of the chord with a 2 or 4)

suspended = **1, 4, 5** (Csus, Csus4)

suspended 7th = **1, 4, 5, b7** (C7sus, C7sus4)

Suspended 2 = **1, 2, 5** (Csus2)

ALTERED CHORDS (Altered chords alter one of the notes of the Major scale by making it sharp or flat)

C7b5 (C7-5) = 1, 3, b5 , b7

C7#5 (C7+5) = 1, 3, #5, b7

C7b9 (C7-9) = 1, [3], b7, b2

C7#9 (C7+9) (Caug9)= 1, 3, [5], b7, #2

C7b5b9 (C7-5-9) = 1, [3], b5, b9

C7#5b9 (C7+5-9) = 1, [3], #5, b9

C7b5#9 (C7-5+9) = 1, [3], b5, #9

$$E = MC^2$$

C7#5#9 (C7+5+9) = 1, [3], #5, #9

C7#11 (C+11) = 1, 3, [5], b7, 2, #4

C7b9#11 (C7-9+11) = 1, [3], [5], b7, b2, b4

C9b5 (C9-5) = 1, [3], b5, b7, 2

C9#5 (C9+5) = 1, [3], #5, b7, 2

C11b9 (C11-9) = 1, [3], [5], b7, b2, 4

C13b9 (C13-9) = 1, [3], [5], b7, b9, [4], 6

C13b5b9 (C13-5-9) = [1], [3], b5 , b7, b2, [4], 6

C13#11 (C13+11) = 1, [3], [5], b7, 2, #4, 6

C13b9#11 (C13-9+11) = [1], [3], [5], b7, b9, #4, 6

Altered chords have a note in them that has been made into a sharp or flat that is not in the chord's Major scale. Altered chords are one of rare times you can drop the 3rd of the chord.

Power Chord

C5 = 1, 5 (C5)

DIATONIC EXTENSIONS

Here is a list of extensions that can be used for the diatonic chords which are within the key's scale.

I - (7) Maj7, (2) sus2, add9, Maj7/9, Maj9, (4) sus, add11, Maj7add11, Maj11, (6) 6, 6/9, Maj7/13, Maj9/13, Maj13

ii - (b7) m7, (2) sus2, m9, madd9, m7/9, (4) sus, m11, madd11, m7/11, (6) m6, m6/9, m13, m7/13

iii - (b7) m7, (4) sus, madd11, m7/11, (#5) m7#5 or m7b13

IV - (7) Maj7, (2) add9, Maj9, (6) 6, 6/9, Maj7/13, Maj9/13, Maj13

V - (2) sus2, add9, (4) sus, (6) 6

V7 - (b7) 7, (2) 7sus2, 9, (4) 7sus, 11, (6) 7/6, 7add13, 13

vi - (b7) m7, (2) sus2, m9, madd9, m7/9, (4) sus, m11, madd11, m7/11, (#5) m7#5 or m7b13

vii⁰ - (b7) m7,b5

The ii and vi chord can be changed into suspended chords as well. *Dust In The Wind* by Kansas is a good example of how the vi chord can be used as both a sus and sus2 chord.

This doesn't mean you can't use extension that fall outside the key's scale, but you will want to be mindful of the melody and make sure it sounds good together. Use extensions that are outside the scale when the melody falls outside the scale or as a passing chord between two diatonic chords You can use this passing chord as a kind of bridge between the two chords for a smoother transition. For example Dm7 to D°7 to CMaj7 or C to C⁺ to F.

Dominant 7th chords are also great candidates for using notes outside the scale. Dominant 7th chords by nature have a lot of tension in them and want to resolve to the I chord. By adding notes outside the scale you add even more tension. Here are a couple of examples of chord substitutions you may want to try with a G7 chord. Instead of playing a G7 - C progression try playing a G7#5 or a G7#5b9 instead of the G7.

BASS NOTES

How to Find Additional Bass Notes

The first and fifth notes of a chord's Major scale make great notes for bass notes in a chord. However to show this for every chord would have required two or more chord charts for every chord. So what I decided to do instead is put the root note or one in the bass of each chord and tell you how to find the fifth, which is quite simple. The fifth is always on the next lower string than the 1 on the same fret. There is only one exception and that's when the 1 is on the second string, then the 5 is on the next lower string a fret lower. For the most part you'll not be looking for a bass note this high, so just remember lower string same fret to find the 5 from a 1. If I've shown a chord with a 5 in the bass you just reverse the process. The 1 will be on the next higher string same fret.

CMaj9	Dm9	C6
X X	X	X O
Finger X 2 1 4 3 X	**Finger** X 3 1 4 4 4	**Finger** X 4 3 2 1 0
Scale X 1 3 7 2 X	**Scale** X 1 ♭3 ♭7 2 5	**Scale** X 1 3 6 1 3
Note X C E B D X	**Note** X D F C E A	**Note** X C E A C E

CMaj9	Dm9	C6
X X	X	X O
Finger 2 X 1 4 3 X	**Finger** 3 X 1 4 4 4	**Finger** 4 X 3 2 1 0
Scale 5 X 3 7 2 X	**Scale** 5 X ♭3 ♭7 2 5	**Scale** 5 X 3 6 1 3
Note G X E B D X	**Note** A X F C E A	**Note** G X E A C E

Here are a few examples showing the 1 and 5 relationship.

The other way to find additional bass notes for a chord is to look at what is played on the high E string and then play it on the low E string. This also works in reverse. Since both strings are tuned to E any fret that can be played on one string can be played on the other.

D	E♭
X X O	X X
Finger X X 0 1 3 2	**Finger** X X 1 2 3 3
Scale X X 1 5 1 3	**Scale** X X 1 5 1 3
Note X X D A D F♯	**Note** X X E♭ B♭ E♭ G

D/F♯	E♭/G
X O	X X
Finger T X 0 1 3 2	**Finger** 2 X 1 3 4 X
Scale 3 X 1 5 1 3	**Scale** 3 X 1 5 1 X
Note F♯ X D A C F♯	**Note** G X E♭ B♭ E♭ X

Here are a couple of examples of the first string, sixth string switch. In the second example, the Eb, actually becomes a much more playable chord. These types of switches are often used for walking bass lines in chord progressions. Sometimes the bass note is written after the chord. When you see a note after a slash that means that note is played in the bass of the chord. This is what is called a slash chord which we will talk about later in the book.

BASS BASS
BASS BASS
BASS BASS

OPTIONAL NOTES

You Can Play a Different Note On the Same String

There are times when you can play a different note on a string that is still in the chord's formula. The basic G chord is a good example. Many people play the D on the second string instead of the B. They both are G chords consisting of the notes G, B and D. The only difference is the order of notes in the chord have been changed. Here are two examples of how you can change a note in a chord to another note on the same string. Use the chord's formula to help you locate additional notes. Again remember that you skip a fret between all the numbers except (3 and 4) and (7 and 1). So for the C chord you move down to the 4 on the first fret and then skip a fret to get to the 5.

	G	G	C	C
Finger	3 2 0 0 0 4	2 1 0 0 3 4	X 3 2 0 1 0	X 3 2 0 1 4
Scale	1 3 5 1 3 1	1 3 5 1 5 1	X 1 3 5 1 3	X 1 3 5 1 5
Note	G B D G B G	G B D G D G	X C E G C E	X C E G C G

This also works with minor 7th chords. Here are a couple of examples were the b7 is played instead of the 5. If you wanted you could just add it and return the other note to the 1 as shown in the Em7 example.

	Em7	Em7	Em7	Bm7	Bm7
Finger	0 2 0 0 0 0	0 2 0 0 0 0	0 2 3 0 0 0	X 1 3 1 2 1	X 1 3 1 2 4
Scale	1 5 b7 3 5 1	1 5 b7 3 b7 1	1 5 1 b3 b7 1	X 1 5 b7 3 5	X 1 5 b7 3 b7
Note	E B D G B E	E B D G D E	E B E G D E	X B F#A D F#	X B F#A D A

Dominant chords can also be played a couple of different ways using this principle.

	E7	E7	E7	A7	A7	A7
Finger	0 2 0 1 0 0	0 2 0 1 4 0	0 2 3 1 4 0	X 0 1 0 2 0	X 0 1 0 2 3	X 0 1 2 3 4
Scale	1 5 b7 3 5 1	1 5 b7 3 b7 1	1 5 1 3 b7 1	X 1 5 b7 3 5	X 1 5 b7 3 b7	X 1 5 1 3 b7
Note	E B DG#B E	E B DG#D E	E B E G#D E	X A E GC#E	X A E GC#G	X A E AC#G

Try this out on all the chords. If you're not familiar with chord formulas or how to move from one number in a formula to another, just look at the notes in the chord and see if there are other places you can play the note. Just make sure you have at least one note present from the original chord. A good example of finding additional notes using the notes themselves would be the F#7 chord. By looking at the notes in the original chord and the open strings it's possible to play this chord without making the more difficult barre chord. This technique is very useful for diminished and augmented chords as well.

	F#7	F#7
Finger	1 3 1 2 1 1	X 3 4 2 1 0
Scale	1 5 b7 3 5 1	X 5 b7 3 5 b7
Note	F#C#E A#C#F#	XC#F#A#C#E

HOW TO USE A CAPO

Multiplying What You Know

Learning to use a capo can make playing songs in a difficult key as easy as strapping on a capo to your guitar. The problem is you need to know where to put it and what chords to play.

Digital keyboard players today have what's called transpose on their synths and pianos. With just the touch of a button they can take a piece of music written in a difficult key with a lot of black keys and make it one with only white keys. The capo does the same thing for guitarists. It allows you to play a song in a difficult key like Gb for instance, which requires a lot of barre chords, and play it like it was written in the key of F, E or D. It also allows you to multiply your knowledge. With a capo you can play in several different keys with chords you already know from a single key. The trick with all this is knowing where to put the capo and how it changes the chords letter name.

I've included the most popular keys for guitar in this book, the keys of C, G, D, A, E and F, along with a condensed set of chords using a capo for Bb, Eb, Ab and Gb. But with a capo you can play in any key you want, even playing the easier keys with chords you know from another easy key. (Will get into why you might want to do that later.) The question is how do you know where to put the capo and what chords to use? So let's dive in and see how this works.

The key to this, no pun intended, is that the chords you're going to be playing will look like one chord, but sound like another. To determine what the chord will sound like take the fret the capo is on and add that to the letter name of the chord you're playing. For instance if you put a capo on the second fret of your guitar and play a C chord, the chord will sound like a D because D is one whole step or two frets higher than a C. Move the capo up to the fourth fret and play a C chord and it will sound like a E because an E is four half steps above C. Here's a chart you can use to determine the new letter name of the chord you're playing. Just move clockwise around the wheel. (Don't confuse this chart with the circle of fifths, this is just a chromatic scale, which means it contains all the notes in an octave moving up in half steps.)

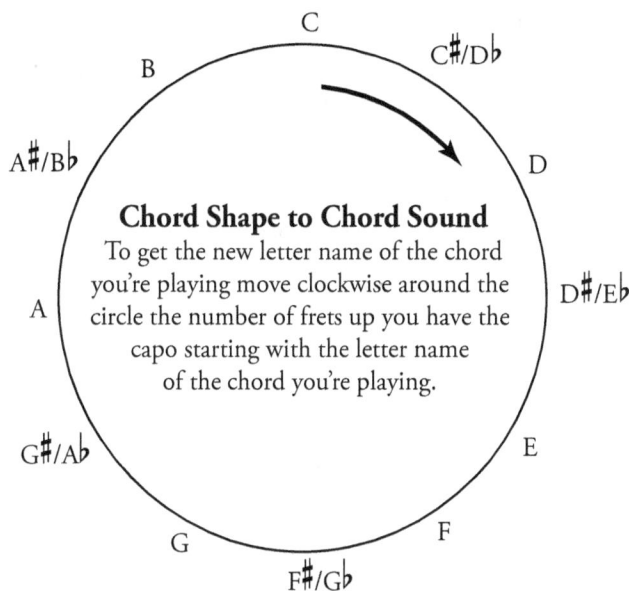

Chord Shape to Chord Sound
To get the new letter name of the chord you're playing move clockwise around the circle the number of frets up you have the capo starting with the letter name of the chord you're playing.

Okay that's the fundamentals of how a capo works, but it's really not all that practical in terms of playing. You don't want to have to sit there and figure out every chord on a chord by chord basis. What you really want to do is transpose the whole key, not individual chords. So how do you do that?

When you're trying to decide where to put your capo based on the music your listening to or the sheet music you're using you'll need to move around the wheel counter-clockwise. For example if the music is in the key of Ab you would want to put the capo on the first fret and play the chords from the key of G. If you look at the chart you'll see that the key of G is the next chord counter-clockwise from Ab. So by putting the capo on the first fret a G chord becomes an Ab. But here's the cool thing. All the chords you learned for the Key of G can now be used for the Key of Ab, not just the G(I), but the Am(ii) becomes a Bbm(ii), and the Bm(iii) becomes a Cm(iii), and the C(IV) becomes Db(IV), and the D(V) becomes an Eb(V), and the Em(vi) becomes Fm(vi). So all the chords from the key of G become the chords for the key of Ab.

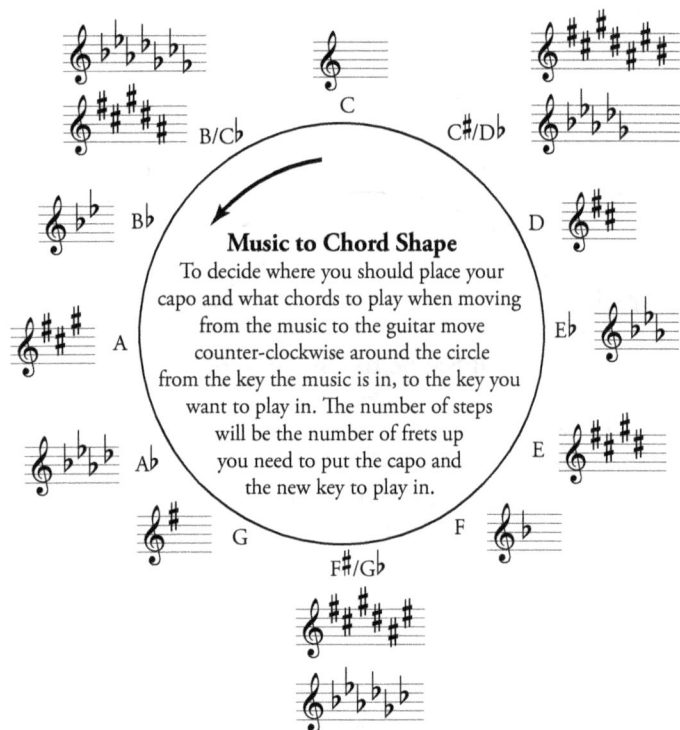

Music to Chord Shape

To decide where you should place your capo and what chords to play when moving from the music to the guitar move counter-clockwise around the circle from the key the music is in, to the key you want to play in. The number of steps will be the number of frets up you need to put the capo and the new key to play in.

This is when memorizing those Roman numerals can really come in handy. All you have to do is just match up the Roman numerals to decide what chord to play to get the new chord. Granted you're not going to be real familiar with what a IV or V chord is in Ab, but you'll be surprised how easy it is with a little practice. It's easy because you know it's going to be one of the chord shapes you already know from the key of G. I've included in the back of the book a list of all the keys along with their chord names and Roman numerals. That way you'll be able to see which chords go with which Roman numerals for the less used keys.

I've also listed at the end of the Quick Reference guide some suggestions on where to place the capo and what the new key would be for your chord shapes. It takes some practice, but once you use it a few times you'll find it comes pretty easy.

Let's try one more example just to make sure you understand it. Lets say that a piece of music is preformed in the key of Gb, it's at the bottom of the circle. Gb is a common key for vocalist so you may very well run into this situation. You have three practical choices for where you might place the capo to play in this difficult key for guitarists. You could put it on the first fret and play the chords from the key of F, or you could put it on the second fret and play the chords from the key of E, or you could put it on the fourth fret and play the chords from the key of D. If you look at the circle you'll see that F is one counter-clockwise step from Gb, E is two and D is four.

WHY USE A CAPO?

Besides the obvious thing we've covered so far—that it makes playing difficult keys easier—there are other reasons to consider using a capo.

Each key has its own unique sound because each key's chords are different. Yes a C chord, is a C chord, is a C chord, but each can have a little different sound depending on the shape that is used to play it. For instance if you play an A chord with a capo on the second fret and play what looks like a G chord it is going to sound different. Why? Because each has a different arrangement of notes in it. Every A Major chord has the notes A, C# and E, but they don't all have the same arrangement of those notes in the chord. Some notes are different because they're in a different octave, sometimes different notes are doubled, and the big one is some notes are played on open strings and some are fretted, which can make a big difference in how a chord sounds. That's why even when the key is an easy one you may see a guitarist using a capo. This is especially true when you consider the suspended and add9 chords. In some keys those particular chords just sound better. Compare an Esus chord with an Esus chord played with a capo on the second fret using the Dsus shape. Big difference.

You may also see someone using a capo for an easy or difficult key if there is more than one guitarist playing rhythm. By using a capo each guitar will have a little different sound and will add a lot more variety and complexity to the sound.

HELPFUL HINTS

Okay having said it's easy with practice it can also be a little confusing at first, so let me give you a few pointers that can help.

When you put a capo on your guitar just think about it as being a permanent barre, like a barre chord that doesn't move and use the 1 or root of the chord to get your new letter name. If you use the root note of a chord to determine the new letter names things get a lot easier to figure-out. Check-out the root notes for each of the chords on the next page to see what I mean.

G (I) ○ ○ ○

Finger	3	2	0	0	0	4
Scale	1	3	5	1	3	1
Note	G	B	D	G	B	G

C (IV) X ○ ○

Finger	X	3	2	0	1	0
Scale	X	1	3	5	1	3
Note	X	C	E	G	C	E

D (V) X X ○

Finger	X	X	0	1	3	2
Scale	X	X	1	5	1	3
Note	X	X	D	A	D	F#

Ab (I) G ○ ○ ○

Finger	3	2	0	0	0	4
Scale	1	3	5	1	3	1
Note	Ab	C	Eb	Ab	C	Ab

Db (IV) C X ○ ○

Finger	X	3	2	0	1	0
Scale	X	1	3	5	1	3
Note	X	Db	F	Ab	Db	F

Eb (V) D X X ○

Finger	X	X	0	1	3	2
Scale	X	X	1	5	1	3
Note	X	X	Eb	Bb	Eb	G

Also don't get confused when using real barre chords with a capo. The letter name for these chords will not change. You can either think of them in terms of their root note or you can think of them in terms of how many frets they're up from the capo, as if the capo were the new nut of the guitar. You just have to decide on one method or the other or you'll get confused fast. Just remember the capo doesn't affect a real barre chord.

The other thing that can help is to just think in terms of steps or semitones. When you have the capo on the first or second fret it's pretty easy to just think this chord is one or two steps above the one I'm playing. Remember just count up however many frets the capo is to get the new name of the chord you're playing. So for example let's say you're playing a G chord with the capo on the first fret. If you count up on half step from G you have Ab, C become Db (one half step up), D become Eb (one half step up), etc.. In the Key section of the book I've given you the basic chords for the keys of Bb, Eb, Ab and Gb using a capo. If you look to the right of the name and Roman numeral you'll also see the name of the chord from the key you will be playing in parentheses. Use these as your training wheels until you get used to this whole concept of using a capo.

TWO MORE REASONS FOR USING A CAPO

Here are a couple of scenarios where knowing how to use a capo can really help as well.

Let's say you have some sheet music or a Fake book and you want to play along with the song off a CD or on YouTube, but when you start playing something is obviously wrong. It just doesn't sound right. Chances are the music is written in a different key than it's normally preformed. It happens all the time. So what do you do?

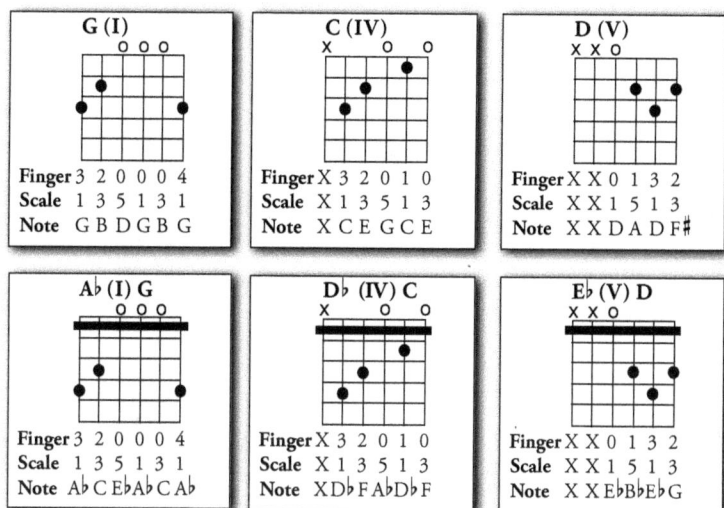

The first thing you do is make sure your guitar is tuned. I know it sounds so obvious but I've done it a million times and slight changes in the weather can make a big difference. Use a digital tuner or tuning fork so you know your guitar is in tune and not just in tune with itself.

The next thing you have to do is determine the performance key. If you have the sheet music to the song the easiest way to determine the performance key is to find a melody note in the song where the singer holds that note and try and match it on the guitar. Once you have it look back at the sheet music and see which note the sheet music says it should be. Then count up or down in frets from the note you found to the one in the sheet music and this will tell you how many steps up or down you need to go with the key as well. (Don't just rely on a single note. I've found sometimes the singer and the music may differ, so you may need to try a couple of different notes.)

So for instance lets say you find a melody note that according to the sheet music should be an E, but when you play along with the singer you find it's being sung as an Eb. If the song is in the key of G that would mean you would need to step down from G one half step to the key of Gb—a common key for vocalist. Once you have that figured out it's just a matter of deciding which chords you want to use to play it and where you need to put the capo. Use the same method we used above to determine where you should put the capo. You may want to try a few different places to see if there are any chords that work better with the song.

Another way of determining the key of a song if you don't have the sheet music is to try and match the first or last chord in the song. The first and last chords are usually the "I" chord in the key of the song. So if the song starts on a C Major chord the song is probably in the key of C Major. Just go through all the "I" chords from the keys I've given you until one sounds right.

If none of them sound right put the capo on the first fret and try again. Keep moving it up until you find one that sounds right. If you don't find anything after the fourth fret it may be the song starts on a different chord than the I. Try playing the IV chord or it could be a song in a minor key that starts on a vi chords. Just keep experimenting with chords and capo until you find that beginning chord.

So from our previous example of the song in Gb you would have needed a capo to find the Gb chord. Since Gb is a popular key for vocalist it might save you some time to just start with an F after you put the capo on the first fret and see if it works. Once you have the chord see if things work. You may need to make adjustments if the song starts on the IV. You'll know when the chords from the key are just not working that you probably need to change keys.

The other time knowing how to use a capo comes in handy is when playing with a vocalist that needs the key changed. Hopefully you can just move the capo up and play the same chords. But if you need to move down you'll need to think about changing the chords you are playing. Just determine how many steps down you need to go and again return to the chart to see where the best place would be to put your capo. If the song originally was in G and the singer needs it lowered a half step you wont be able to use your key of G chords, but will have to change to the chords of the F, E or D keys.

Capo

CHORD PROGRESSIONS
The Essence of Music

I originally started this section of the book with over 150 different chord progressions. But when I was finished it really didn't seem all that practical. Who's going to be able to remember 150 different progressions? That's when I decided to teach you how to make your own from a few basic progressions. With the techniques I'll be showing you, you'll be able to build those 150 original progressions and more, but instead of just memorizing a bunch of Roman numerals, you'll be able to see how they were created.

The foundation on which a lot of Western music is built is the I-IV progression. This progressions can be transformed into a variety of different variations using four different techniques: extensions and chord family changes, chord substitutions, omissions and displacement. Let's look at each of these and see how they can be applied to this basic progression to make real songs.

Let's look at a few songs with just the I-IV progression first so you get a feel for how it sounds.

Angel of Harlem verse (U2 1989) Key of C

Do You Believe In Magic verse (Lovin' Spoonful 1965) Key of C

Downtown Train chorus (Rod Stewart 1989) Key Bb - use capo on third fret and play the key of G chords

Feel Like Makin' Love verse (Bad Company 1975) Key of D (I-quick bVIII-IV)

Forever In Blue Jeans verse (Neil Diamond 1979) Key of A

Forever Young verse (Rod Stewart 1988) Key of E

For What It's Worth (Stop, Hey What's That Sound) verse (Buffalo Springfield 1967) Key of E

Garden Party verse (Rick Nelson 1972) Key of D

Glory Days verse/chorus (Bruce Springsteen 1985) Key of A uses Major and sus chords

In The Midnight Hour verse (Wilson Pickett 1965) Key of E

Lady Madonna verse (Beatles 1968) Key of A

Love Me Do verse (Beatles 1963) Key of G

Once Bitten Twice Shy chorus (Great White 1989) Key of C

One More Night chorus (Phil Collins 1985) Key Bb - use capo on first fret and play the key of A chords

Peaceful Easy Feeling verse (Eagles 1973) Key of E

Rocket Man chorus (Elton John 1972) Key of Gm

Rock Me Gently verse (Andy Kim 1974) Key of C

Some Kind of Wonderful chorus (Grand Funk 1975) Key of D

Sunshine On My Shoulders verse (John Denver 1974) Key of Bb - use capo on third fret play the key of G chords

Take It To The Limit verse (Eagles 1976) Key of B - use capo on fourth fret and play the key of G chords

You Can't Always Get What You Want verse/chorus (Rolling Stones 1969) Key of C

You Sexy Thing verse/chorus (Hot Chocolate 1976) Key of F

Extension And Family Substitutions

This is just a very small list of songs using the basic I and IV chords. When you start adding extensions to these chords the number of songs are just to numerous to list. A few examples would be:

I-IVMaj7

Tonight's The Night (Gonna Be Alright) verse (Rod Stewart 1976) Key of B - use capo on second fret and play the key of A chords

The Living Years verse (Mike & The Mechanics 1989) Key of Ab - use capo on first fret and play the key of G chords

IMaj7-IV

A Rainy Night In Georgia verse (Johnny Mathis 1957) Key of D

Does Anybody Really Know What Time It Is? chorus (Chicago 1971) Key of D

I-IMaj7-IV

Imagine verse (John Lennon 1971) Key of B

IMaj7 - IVMaj7

We've Only Just Begun bridge (Carpenters 1970) Key of E

Song Of The Wind verse (Santana 1972) Key of C

Tin Man verse (America 1974) Key of G

I Can't Tell You Why verse (Eagles 1980) Key of D

Isus2-IV

Hold My Hand verse (Hootie & The Blowfish 1994) Key of B

Iadd9-IVadd9

The End Of The Innocence verse (Don Henley 1989) Key of Ab - use capo on first fret and play the key of G chords

You can also change the chord family from Major to minor or dominant chords.

I-IV7

Last Train To Clarksville verse (Monkees 1966) Key of Ab

I-IV9

Hi-De-Ho verse (Blood, Sweat & Tears 1970) Key of C

I-IMaj7-I7-IV-iv6

I Love The Night Life chorus (Alicia Bridges 1978) Key of C

I-I7-IV-iv6

Desperado verse (Eagles 1973) Key of G

I-I11-IVsus4-IV

Rhythm Of The Night verse (DeBarge 1985) Key of D

I7-IV7

Respect chorus (Aretha Franklin 1967) Key of C

Feeling Alright verse/chorus (Joe Cocker 1972) Key of C

I7-IV7sus4-IV7

Don't Bring Me Down verse (Animals 1966) Key of C

I13-IV11

God Bless The Child verse (Blood, Sweat & Tears 1969) Key of C

OMISSIONS

In this variation we are going to leave out one of the chords when it repeats making a I-IV-I progression.

I-IV-I

Do Wah Diddy Diddy verse (Manfred Mann 1964) Key of E

I Fought The Law verse (Bobby Fuller Four 1966) Key of G

Substitute verse (The Who 1966) Key of D

Kentucky Woman verse (Neil Diamond 1967)Key of B - use capo on second fret and play Key of A chords

Mony, Mony verse (Tommy James & The Shodnells 1968) Key of Bb - use capo on first fret and play key of A chords

Dance To The Music verse (Sly & The Family Stones 1968) Key of G

Revolution verse (Beatles 1968) Key of B

Get Back verse (Beatles 1969) Key of A (A5, A6 and D5, D6)

Son Of A Preacher Man chorus (Dusty Springfield 1969) Key of E

I Can See Clearly Now verse (Johnny Nash 1972) Key of D

Rocket Man chorus (Elton John 1972) Key of Gm - use capo on third fret and play key of G chords

Anticipation verse (Carly Simon 1972) Key of D

Driving My Life Away verse (Eddie Rabbit 1980) Key of E

I Still Haven't Found What I'm Looking For verse (U2 1987) (I-IVsus2) Key of Db - use capo on first fret and play the key of C chords

Neon Moon verse (Brooks and Dunn 1991) Key of A

Relative Minor Substitutions

To build on what we have so far you can substitute the Major chord with its relative minor. The vi chord is the relative minor of the I chord and the ii chord is the relative minor of the IV. (I've put each Major chord's relative minor below it in the chord chart sheets to help with memorizing these chord relationships.) Here are some possible variations:

I-ii

vi-IV

vi-ii

Here are some songs using chord substitutions and extensions.

I-ii

Sweet City Woman verse/chorus (Stampeders 1971) Key of G

I-ii7

Just My Imagination (Running Away With Me) verse/chorus (Temptations 1971) Key of C

The Best Of My Love chorus (Eagles 1974) Key of C

Weekend In New England chorus (Barry Manilow 1976) Key of C

Smoke From A Distant Fire verse (Sandford/Townsend Band 1977) Key of A - use capo on second fret and play key of G chords

vi-IV

Listen To The Music chorus (Doobie Brothers 1972) Key of E

Show Me The Way chorus (Peter Frampton 1976) Key of D

vi-ii

Woman In Love verse (Barbara Streisand 1980) Key of Dm

You Belong To The City verse (Glenn Fry 1985) Key of Em

vi7-ii7

Legend In Your Own Time verse/chorus (Carly Simon 1971) Key of Am

You Belong To The City chorus (Glenn Fry 1985) Key of Em

vi-ii-vi

I Shot The Sheriff chorus (Eric Clapton 1974) Key of Gm

I-ii-IV

Blessed verse (Martina Mcbride 2001) key of G

A Broken Wing verse (Marina Mcbride 1997) Key of B - use capo on second fret and play key of G chords

Another popular variation on this is to make the ii minor chord into a II Major chord giving you the progression vi-II for a minor type Rock sound. In the minor key those chords would be i-IV.

DISPLACEMENT

Before we leave the I-IV progression there is another way to vary the progression and that's called displacement. Displacement means we start the progression at a different place or simply mix-up the chords into various combinations. For just a two chord progression that would mean in effect just playing it in reverse, but for other longer progressions you may decide to start the progression on the second chord in a four chord progression or the third, etc.. You may also just mix-up the chords into a variety of different combinations and see what you get. Here are a few songs with the I-VI chord progression reversed.

IV-I

Viva Las Vegas chorus (Elvis Presley 1964) Key of G

Won't Be Fooled Again chorus (The Who 1971) Key of A

Peaceful Easy Feeling chorus (Eagles 1973) Key of E

It's Only Rock 'N' Roll (But I Like It) chorus (Rolling Stones 1974) Key of E

Calypso chorus (John Denver 1975) Key of A

Take It To The Limit chorus (Eagles 1976) Key of E - use capo on the fourth fret and play key of G chords

Heart of Glass bridge (Blondie 1979) Key of E

Wild Wild West (Escape Club 1988) Key of B

FOLK I-V AND COMBINATION PROGRESSIONS I-V-vi-IV

Now that you have some ideas on how you can take a basic progression and transform it try it out on the I-V progression. This is called the folk progression and just like the I-IV thousands of songs have been constructed using this very basic progression. Use Extensions, Family Change chords, Relative Minors, Omission and Displacement for your variations on this progression. Then combine them with the I-IV progressions and see what you get. With some experimentation you should come across the very popular **I-V-vi-IV progression**. Check the internet out to learn the hundreds of songs based on this simple progression derived from combining the I-V and I-IV progressions.

I-V-vi-IV

You'll Think Of Me chorus (Keith Urban 2002) Key of A

Amazed verse (Lonestar 1999) Key of Ab - use capo on first fret and play key of G chords

D'yer Maker verse (Led Zeppelin 1973) Key of C

Love Hurts verse (Nazareth 1976) Key of G

Do That To Me One More Time verse (Captain & Tennille 1980) Key of C

I-V-IV

My Maria verse (Brooks and Dunn 1996) Key of Eb

I-V-IV-V

They Way You Love Me verse (Faith Hill 1999) Key of C chorus key of D same progression

Folk

50

IV-V-I

Brand New Man chorus (Brooks and Dunn 1991) Key of G

IV-V

She's Not The Cheatin' Kind verse (Brooks and Dunn 1994) Key of A

8, 12, 16 AND 24 BAR BLUES PROGRESSIONS

The 8 bar blues in its most basic form, with each bar getting 4 beats.

| I7 / / / | I7 / / / | IV7 / / / | IV7 / / / |
| I7 / / / | V7/ / / | I7 / / / | I7 / / / |

The 12 bar blues in its most basic form.

I / / /	I / / /	I / / /	I / / /
IV / / /	IV / / /	I / / /	I / / /
V / / /	IV / / /	I / / /	I / / /

The 16 bar blues in its most basic form.

I7 / / /	I7 / / /	I7 / / /	I7 / / /
I7 / / /	I7 / / /	I7 / / /	I7 / / /
IV7 / / /	IV7 / / /	I7 / / /	I7 / / /
V7 / / /	IV7 / / /	I7 / / /	I7 / / /

The 24 bar blues in its most basic form.

I7 / / /	I7 / / /	I7 / / /	I7 / / /
I7 / / /	I7 / / /	I7 / / /	I7 / / /
IV7 / / /	IV7 / / /	IV7 / / /	IV7/ / /
I7 / / /	I7 / / /	I7 / / /	I7 / / /
V7 / / /	V7 / / /	IV7/ / /	IV7/ / /
I7 / / /	I7 / / /	I7 / / /	I7 / / /

The 12 bar blues progression has made its way into just about every style of music. Hundreds of songs could be listed for this progression from Blues, Rock, Jazz, Folk and Country. To get every last drop of possibilities out of these progressions you really need to understand chord substitution principles. I've just given you the very basics. My suggestion is invest in some good books on this subject and really study how this progression can be transformed into hundreds of other possible progressions.

MINOR BLUES PROGRESSIONS

Use the Aeolian/Natural minor chord charts for these progressions.

The 8 bar blues in its most basic form, with each bar getting 4 beats.

| i / / / | i / / / | iv / / / | iv / / / |
| i / / / | v / / / | i / / / | i / / / |

The 12 bar blues in its most basic form.

i / / /	i / / /	i / / /	i / / /
iv / / /	iv / / /	i / / /	i / / /
v / / /	iv / / /	i / / /	i / / /

The 16 bar blues in its most basic form.

i / / /	i / / /	i / / /	i / / /
i / / /	i / / /	i / / /	i / / /
iv / / /	iv / / /	i / / /	i / / /
v / / /	iv / / /	i / / /	i / / /

In the Aeolian/Natural minor key the (i) is minor, the (iv) is minor and the (v) is minor.

In the Harmonic minor key the (i) is minor, the (iv) is minor and the (V7) is dominant.

In the Melodic minor key the (i) is minor, the (IV7) is dominant and (V7) is dominant.

Use these different keys for chord substitution possibilities along with all the other chord substitution choices.

Doo-Wop Progression I-vi-IV-V

The Doo-Wop Progression, also called the fifties cliché, is a I-vi-IV-V progression. Hundreds of songs have been written with this progression and its many variations. Again as you're working through this chord progression don't forget to use extensions, family change chords, omission and displacement to find different variations of this progression. It may be called the fifties cliché progression, but there are many new songs being written today that use this progression or a variation of it. Here are just a few examples of songs that use this progression in its basic form.

Do That To Me One More Time verse (Captain & Tennille 1980) Key of C

D'yer Maker verse (Led Zeppelin 1973) Key of C

If I Had A Hammer verse (Peter, Paul & Mary 1962) Key of A - use capo on second fret and play key of G chords

Just One Look verse (Doris Troy 1963) Key of F

Last Kiss chorus (Pearl Jam 2000) Key of G

Let's Twist Again verse (Chubby Checkers 1961) Key of Eb - use capo on first fret and play key of D chords

Love Hurts verse (Nazareth 1976) Key of G

Nothing's Gonna Stop Us chorus (Starship 1989) Key of F# - use capo on first fret and play key of F chords

Octopus's Garden verse (Beatles 1969) Key of E

Please Mr. Postman verse (Marvelettes 1961) Key of B

Runaround Sue verse/chorus (Dion 1961) Key of D

Where Have All The Flowers Gone verse (Kingston Trio 1962) Key of Bb - use capo on the first fret and play key of A chords

It Matters To Me chorus (Faith Hill 1995) key of Gb - use capo on second fret and play key of E chords

A few very popular variation of this progression can be found by omitting some of the chords. Here are just a few you should be able to play and have songs come to mind.

I-vi

One More Day (With You) verse (Diamond Rio 2000) Key E

I-vi-IV

I-vi-V

Just mix these chords up into as many variations as you can think of and you'll no doubt have a hit song progression.

Classic Rock Progression with the flat Majors bIII, bVI, bVII

When we talk about classic Rock we're talking about bands like the Rolling Stones, Beatles, Jimi Hendrix, Who, Led Zeppelin, Pink Floyd, Backman-Turner Overdrive, Fleetwood Mac, Bad Company, Eagles, ZZ Top, Cream, Boston, Doors, Queen and Lynyrd

Skynyrd. All these bands used the flat Majors to add more of a blues sound to there songs. Here are just a few examples of how these chords can be put together to create classic rock music.

I-bVII-IV

Last Time verse (Rolling Stones 1965) Key of E

Magic Bus verse (The Who 1968) Key of Ab - use capo on fourth fret and play key of E chords

Good Times, Bad Times chorus (Led Zeppelin 1969) Key of E

Living In The Past verse (Jethro Tull 1972) Key of C

Good Lovin' Gone Bad chorus (Bad Company 1975) Key of A

Back In Black verse (AC/DC 1981) Key of E

Centerfold chorus (J. Geils Band 1982) Key of G

Southern Cross verse (Crosby, Sill & Nash 1982) Key of A

Sharp Dressed Man verse (ZZ Top 1983) Key of F

The Way You Love Me verse (Faith Hill 2000) Key of C

I-bVII-IV-I

I Can't Explain verse (The Who 1965) Key of E

If I were A Carpenter verse (Bobby Darin 1966) Key of D

Sympathy For The Devil verse (Rolling Stones 1968) Key of E

Hey Jude outro (Beatles 1968) Key of F

Take A Letter Maria chorus (R. B. Greaves 1969) Key of A

Fortunate Son verse (Creedence Clearwater Revival 1969) Key of G

Good Times, Bad Times verse (Led Zeppelin 1969) Key of E

All Right Now chorus (Free 1970) Key of A

Rock'n Me verse (Steve Miller 1976) Key of B

Take The Money And Run verse (Steve Miller 1976) Key of G

Peace Of Mind verse (Boston 1977) Key of E

Addicted To Love verse (Robert Palmer 1986) Key of A

Sweet Child O' Mine verse (Guns N' Roses 1988) Key of Db - Use capo on first fret and play key of C chords, or tune down a half step and play the key of D chords.

You Got It verse (Roy Orbison 1989) Key of A

I-bVII

Fire chorus (Jimi Hendrix 1967) Key of D

Soul Man chorus (Sam & Dave 1967) Key of G

L.A. Woman verse (Doors 1968) Key of A

Whole Lotta Love chorus (Led Zeppelin 1969) Key of E

Here Comes That Rainy Day Feeling Again verse (Fortunes 1971) Key of C

Boogie Fever chorus (Sylvers 1976) Key of F

Cocaine verse (Eric Clapton 1980) Key of E

All Night Long (All Night) chorus (Lionel Richie 1983) Key of Ab - use capo on first fret and play key of G chords

I'll Be There For You (Theme from "Friends") verse (Rembrants 1995) Key of A

(The best way to vary these progression is with displacement. Just mix the Flat Majors in with the I, IV and V chords.)

I-bIII-IV

After Midnight verse (Eric Clapton 1970) Key of C

Back In The USSR chorus (Beatles 1068) Key of A

I-bIII-IV-I

Bang A Gong (get It On) chorus (T. Rex 1972) Key of E

Cats In The Cradle verse (Harry Chapin 1974) Key of F - use capo on first fret and play key of E chords

I-bIII-IV-V

Knock On Wood intro (Eddie Floyd 1966) Key of E

I-bIII-IV-bIII

Rikki Don't Lose That Number opening chorus(Steely Dan 1974) Key of E

I-bIII-IV-bVI

Gimme Some Lovin' chorus (Spencer Davis Group 1967) Key of G

I-bIII-bVII-IV

Old Man verse (Neil Young 1972) Key of D

I-bVII-bIII-I

Hello I Love You verse (Doors 1968) Key of A

I-bVI

Peggy Sue bridge (Buddy Holly 1957) Key of A

I-bVI-bVII

All I Want To Do verse/chorus (Sheryl Crow 1993) Key of E

I-bVII-bVI

Gimme Shelter chorus (Rolling Stones 1969) Key of Db

I-bVI-IV

Mamma Told Me (Not To Come) chorus (Three Dog Night 1970) Key of Ab

FLAMENCO PROGRESSION - *i-bVII-bVI-V*

Using the Major key sheets the progression would be i-bVII-bVI-V. Many hit songs were written in the sixties with this progression. It is still a progression that can be used today to create hit songs. Just like all the other examples use all the techniques I've shown you to find all the different variations of this progression as well. Here are just a few songs that have used the basic progression.

i-bVII-bVI-V

Walk, Don't Run verse (Ventures 1960) Key of A chords- or tune guitar down half step and play key of Bb chords

Hit The Road Jack verse (Ray Charles 1961) Key A chords

Wait A Million Years chorus (Grass Roots 1969) Key of B chords

Feels Like The First Time bridge (Foreigner 1977) Song is in key of G, but for bridge use Key of E chords

Happy Together verse (Turtles 1967) Key of F# chords

Maneater chorus (Daryl Hall & John Oats 1982) Key of B chords

Sultans Of Swing verse (Dire Straits 1979) Key of D chords

i-bVII-bVI-bVII

All Along The Watch Tower verse (Jimi Hendrix Experience 1968) Key of C chords

Stairway To Heaven final section (Led Zeppelin 1972) Key of A chords

Dream On chorus (Aerosmith 1976) Key of E chords

My Heart Will Go On chorus (Celine Dion 1997) Key of D chords

ROCK AND ROLL I-IV-V

Here are a few songs using the I-IV-V progression.

I-IV-V

Born To Run verse (Bruce Springsteen 1975) Key of E

Come And Get It verse (Badfinger 1970) Key of E

Dizzy chorus (Tommy Roe 1969) Key of Gb

Do You Love Me verse (Contours 1962) Key of F

Emotion In Motion verse (Ric Ocasck 1986) Key of C

Everyday verse (Buddy Holly 1957) Key of Eb - use capo on first fret and play key of D chords

Guitar Man verse (Bread 1972) Key of G

I'll Be There For You chorus (Rembrandts 1995) Key of A

Like A Rolling Stone chorus (Bob Dylan 1965) Key of C

Make Me Lose Control chorus (Eric Carmen 1988) Key of E

Mellow Yellow chorus (Donovan 1966) Key of D

Mr. Jones chorus (Counting Crows 1993) Key of Am

Rock And Roll All Night chorus (Kiss 1976) Key of Ab - or tune your guitar down a half step and play key of A chords

Stir It Up chorus (Johnny Nash 1973) Key of D Bob Marley Key of A

The River Of Dreams verse (Billy Joel 1993) Key of G

The Tide Is High verse/chorus (Blondie 1980) Key of B

Time Is On My Side chorus (Rolling Stones 1964) Key of F

Twist And Shout verse (Beatles 1964) Key of A

(You're My) Soul And Inspiration chorus (Righteous Brothers 1966) Key of B - use capo on second fret and play key of A chords

A couple of popular variations on this progression are I-IV-V-I and vi-IV-V. Really you can just mix-up the I, IV and V into about any combination you like and have a hit song written with it.

STANDARD PROGRESSION I-vi-ii-V

As you would imagine many of the old standards were written with this progression.

I-vi-ii-V

I Got Rhythm A section (from "Funny Girl" 1930)

Between The Devil And The Deep Blue Sea B section (from "Rhythmania" 1931)

Let's Call The Whole Thing Off A section (Standard 1936)

Have Yourself A Merry Little Christmas verse (Judy Garland 1944) Key of G

Beyond The Sea A section (Charles Trenet 1945) Key of F

(I Love You) For Sentimental Reasons A section (Nat King Cole 1945) Key of Db

Hey There A section (Standard 1954)

You Send Me verse (Sam Cooke 1957) Key of G

Put Your Head On My Shoulder verse (Paul Anka 1959) Key of G

Penny Lane verse (Beatles 1967) Key of B - use capo on second fret and play key of A chords

This Will Be (An Everlasting Love) verse (Natalie Cole 1975) Key of Bb

Don't It Make My Brown Eyes Blue verse (Crystal Gayle 1977) Key of Gb - use capo on second fret and play key of E chords

SINGLE CHORD PROGRESSIONS

You can even have chord progressions using a single chord by using extensions and family change techniques. Here are a few you can try.

I-IMaj7-I6-IMaj7

Gently On My Mind verse (Glen Campbell 1968)

Mandy verse (Barry Manilow 1975)

vi-viMaj7-vi7-vi6

In A Sentimental Mood A section (Standard 1935)

Summer Rain verse (Johnny Rivers 1968)

Cry Baby Cry verse (Beatles 1968)

Feelings verse (Morris Albert 1975)

Into The Great Wide Open verse (Tom Petty 1991)

I-I$^+$

Baby Hold On To Me verse (Eddie Money 1978)

I-I$^+$-I6

For Once In My Life verse (Stevie Wonder 1968)

I-I$^+$-I6-I7

The Greatest Love Of All verse (Whitney Houston 1986)

iv-iv#5-iv6-iv#5

Goldfinger D section (Shirley Bassey 1964)

Secret Agent Man intro (Johnny Rivers 1966)

Undun bridge (Guess Who 1969)

iv-iv#5-iv6-iv7

Cry Me A River A section (Standard 1953)

CONCLUSION

This is just a small sampling of chord progressions. There are still circle progressions, ascending and descending bass line progressions, the Jazz progression ii -V - I and more. All of these can be combined in a variety of ways and there are many more to be explored. I hope though I've given you some ideas about how learning the Roman numeral numbering system for chords can be useful.

If you'd like more information on chord progressions you should check-out Richard Scott's book, *Chord Progressions for songwriters* where much of this information came from and Rikky Rooksby's book, *How to Write Songs on Guitar*. Both these books are excellent sources on chord progressions for the guitar.

TWO NOTE CHORDS OR DYADS

POWER CHORDS 1 AND 5

Power chords contain only two different notes, the 1 and 5. The most common ones are based on an open A chord and an open E chord. These chords can be played with just the 1 and 5 or with the 1 doubled as shown below.

	C	C5	C5	A	A5	A5
	3rd	3rd	3rd	5th	5th	5th
Finger	X 1 3 3 3 1	X 1 3 X X X	X 1 3 3 X X	1 3 4 2 1 1	1 3 X X X X	1 3 3 X X X
Scale	X 1 5 1 3 5	X 1 5 X X X	X 1 5 1 X X	1 5 1 3 5 1	1 5 X X X X	1 5 1 X X X
Note	X C G C E G	X C G X X X	X C G C X X	A E A C# E A	A E X X X X	A E A X X X

You can also play the inversion of this chord where the 5 is in the bass and the 1 on top.

	C	C5	C5	A	A5
	3rd	3rd	3rd	5th	5th
Finger	X 1 3 3 3 1			1 3 4 2 1 1	X 3 3 X X X
Scale	X 1 5 1 3 5	5 1 X X X X	X X 5 1 X X	1 5 1 3 5 1	X 5 1 X X X
Note	X C G C E G	G C X X X X	X X G C X X	A E A C# E A	X E A X X X

Smoke On The Water by Deep Purple in the Key of Gm is a classic example of this power chord inversion.

	G5 (vi)	Bb5 (I)	C5 (ii)	Db5 (bIII)	or	G5 (vi)
	3rd		3rd	4th		3rd
Scale	X X 5 1 X X	X X 5 1 X X	X X 5 1 X X	X X 5 1 X X		X 5 1 X X X
Note	X X D G X X	X X F Bb X X	X X G C X X	X X Gb Db X X		X D G X X X

*Let me say something here about finding the key of a song when there are only power chords. Power chords are not minor or Major because they don't have the minor or Major 3rd in them. To determine the key of a song based on power chords you must look at the letter name of the chords and determine if they fit into the Major or minor key. In the case of *Smoke On The Water* their is no Db chord in the key of G Major, however there is a Db (bIII) in the key of Gm, so that's how I determined the key of the song. As a general rule use the first chord in the song to tell you the letter name of the key and then use the Quick Reference guide to determine the letter name of the power chords based on the letter names of the Major, minor and fat Major chords in the key.

You can also double up on the 1 and 5 to create monster power chords.

	C	C5	D (IV)	D5	A	A5
	3rd	3rd	7th	7th	7th	7th
Finger	X 1 3 3 3 1	1 1 3 4 X X	3 2 1 1 1 4	X X 1 1 4 4	X X 1 2 3 4	X 1 1 3 4 X
Scale	X 1 5 1 3 5	5 1 5 1 X X	1 3 5 1 3 1	X X 5 1 5 1	X X 1 5 1 3	X 5 1 5 1 X
Note	X C G C E G	G C G C X X	D F# A D F# D	X X A D A D	X X A E A C#	X E A E A X

57

Open chords can also be used as power chords.

C5 (I)	G5 (V)	D5 (IV)	E5 (V)	E5 (V)	A5 (I)
X X O	X O O	X O O X	O O O	O O O 7th	X O ⌐⌐
Finger X 3 X 0 1 4	Finger 3 X 0 0 4 4	Finger X 0 0 1 3 X	Finger 0 2 3 4 0 0	Finger 0 1 3 4 0 0	Finger X 0 1 1 4 4
Scale X 1 X 5 1 5	Scale 1 X 5 1 5 1	Scale X 5 1 5 1 X	Scale 1 5 1 5 5 1	Scale 1 1 5 1 5 1	Scale X 1 5 1 5 1
Note X C X G C G	Note G X D G D G	Note X A D A D X	Note E B E B B E	Note E E B E B E	Note X A E A E A

There are also passing chords that are used in Classic Rock you will want to know. The Dsus/F# or Dadd11 is one used by AC/DC and you can here a great example of the second chord shape in *Hold On Loosely* by Lover Boy.

G5 (V)	Dsus/F# or Dadd11	E5 (V)	G5	D Passing Chord	E5 (V)
X O O	X O O	O X X X	X X X 3rd	X X X	O X X X
Finger 2 X 0 0 3 4	Finger 1 0 0 2 3 0	Finger 0 1 2 X X X	Finger 1 4 4 X X X	Finger 1 4 3 X X X	Finger 0 1 2 X X X
Scale 1 X 5 1 5 1	Scale 3 5 1 5 1 2	Scale 1 5 1 X X X	Scale 1 5 1 X X X	Scale 3 1 3 X X X	Scale 1 5 1 X X X
Note G X D G D G	Note F# A D A D E	Note E B E X X X	Note G D G X X X	Note F# D F# X X X	Note E B E X X X

E5	B Passing Chord	D5	A Passing Chord	C5
X X X 7th	X X X 6th	X X X 5th	X X X 4th	X X X 3rd
Finger X 1 4 4 X X	Finger X 1 4 3 X X	Finger X 1 4 4 X X	Finger X 1 4 3 X X	Finger X 1 4 4 X X
Scale X 1 5 1 X X	Scale X 3 1 3 X X	Scale X 1 5 1 X X	Scale X 3 1 3 X X	Scale X 1 5 1 X X
Note X E B E X X	Note X D# B D# X X	Note X D A D X X	Note X E A E X X	Note X C G C X X

A good heavy metal type dyad is the flat six which has a very dark sound to it.

X X X X	X X X X
Scale 1 ♭6 X X X X	Scale X 1 ♭6 X X X

METAL

Rock-n-Roll 1, 6 and ♭7

The last group of Dyads are Rock and Roll type chords made famous by Chuck Berry.

A5 / A6 / A7	D5 / D6 / D7	G5 / G6 / G7
X X X X 5th	X X X X 5th	X X X X 5th
Scale 1 5 X X X X	Scale X 1 5 X X X	Scale X X 1 5 X X

DIMINISHED CHORDS

MOVE THE 1 UP 1 FRET

To make a diminished 7th chord all you need to do is move the root note of a dominant 7th chord up one fret.

One of the unique things about this chord is any note in can be considered the root note of the chord. The other unique thing is they repeat themselves as you move them up the fretboard every three frets. The only difference is the notes are re-arranged in the chord, but all the same notes are present. Because of this there are only three different chord shapes you need to know for making a Diminished 7th chord.

°7

F7

Finger	1	3	4	2	1	1
Scale	1	5	♭7	3	5	1
Note	F	C	E♭	A	C	F

B♭7

Finger	X	1	3	1	4	1
Scale	X	1	5	♭7	3	5
Note	X	B♭	F	A♭	D	F

D7

Finger	X	X	0	2	1	3
Scale	X	X	1	5	♭7	3
Note	X	X	D	A	C	F♯

F♯/G♭/D♯/E♭/A/C °7

Finger	2	X	1	3	1	X
Scale	1	X	♭♭7	♭3	♭5	X
Note	F♯	X	D♯	A	C	X

B/F/G♯/A♭/D °7

Finger	X	2	3	1	4	X
Scale	X	1	♭5	♭♭7	♭3	X
Note	X	B	F	G♯	D	X

D♯/E♭/A/C/F♯/G♭°7

Finger	X	X	1	3	2	4
Scale	X	X	1	♭5	♭♭7	♭3
Note	X	X	D♯	A	C	F♯

G/E/A♯/B♭/C♯/D♭ °7

Finger	2	X	1	3	1	X
Scale	1	X	♭♭7	♭3	♭5	X
Note	G	X	E	A♯	C♯	X

C/F♯/G♭/A/D♯/E♭°7

Finger	X	2	3	1	4	X
Scale	X	1	♭5	♭♭7	♭3	X
Note	X	C	F♯	A	D♯	X

E/A♯/B♭/C♯/D♭/G °7

Finger	X	X	1	3	2	4
Scale	X	X	1	♭5	♭♭7	♭3
Note	X	X	E	A♯	C♯	G

G♯/A♭/F/B/D °7

Finger	2	X	1	3	1	X
Scale	1	X	♭♭7	♭3	♭5	X
Note	G♯	X	F	B	D	X

C♯/D♭/G/A♯/B♭/E °7

Finger	X	2	3	1	4	X
Scale	X	1	♭5	♭♭7	♭3	X
Note	X	C♯	G	A♯	E	X

E/B/D/G♯/A♭ °7

Finger	X	X	1	3	2	4
Scale	X	X	1	♭5	♭♭7	♭3
Note	X	X	F	B	D	G♯

AUGMENTED CHORDS

MOVE THE 5 UP 1 FRET

To make an Augmented chord all you need to do is move the "5" of a Major chord up one fret. Make sure to move all the fives in the chord.

Like the Diminished 7th chord any note in the chord can be considered the root note or letter name of the chord. The other unique thing about an augmented chord is there is a universal shape that emerges when you start making these chords. You can choose any three notes out of this universal shape to make your augmented chord. Use the optional note technique of looking at what notes are in the chord and then seeing if you can add open strings to your chord for other ways to play these chords.

G

Finger	3	2	0	0	0	4
Scale	1	3	5	1	3	1
Note	G	B	D	G	B	G

C

Finger	X	3	2	0	1	0
Scale	X	1	3	5	1	3
Note	X	C	E	G	C	E

D

Finger	X	X	0	1	3	2
Scale	X	X	1	5	1	3
Note	X	X	D	A	D	F#

G+

Finger	3	2	1	0	0	4
Scale	1	3	#5	1	3	1
Note	G	B	D#	G	B	G

C+

Finger	X	3	2	1	1	X
Scale	X	1	3	#5	1	X
Note	X	C	E	G#	C	X

D+

Finger	X	X	0	2	3	1
Scale	X	X	1	#5	1	3
Note	X	X	D	A#	D	F#

F

Finger	1	3	4	2	1	1
Scale	1	5	1	3	5	1
Note	F	C	F	A	C	F

A

Finger	X	0	1	2	3	0
Scale	X	1	5	1	3	5
Note	X	A	E	A	C#	E

E

Finger	0	2	3	1	0	0
Scale	1	5	1	3	5	1
Note	E	B	E	G#	B	E

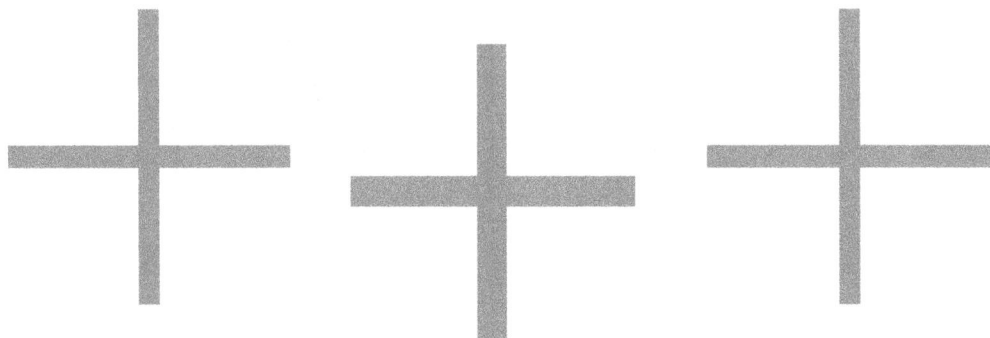

SLASH CHORDS

What Note is in the Bass?

Slash chords are chords that not only tell you what chord to play, but what note to play in the bass of the chord. Here's an example of how a D Major chord would be written if you wanted an F# in the bass - D/F#. This chord is called a D over F#. In this case the F# is the 3rd of the D Major chord. Many times slash chords are used to indicate the 3rd of a chord is to be played in the bass, but not always. Other notes outside the chord, or even outside the scale, can be used as bass notes.

I get excited every time I see a piece of music with slash chords because it means there is some kind of walking bass line to the chord progression. Understanding how to add ascending and descending bass lines to your playing will add a whole new dimension to your playing and can be quite fun. You can also use slash chords to add a pedal note to the bass of your chord progressions. A pedal note is a note that stays the same over several different chord changes. Adding these extra elements to your chord progressions can be one of the most rewarding and fun things you can do in your playing.

On the right are some common slash chord progressions. Try working out these progressions for the other keys as well. You can use the Slash Chord Worksheet to find your bass notes. This is just the tip of the iceberg. But hopefully you understand the principle and can use it to create ascending and descending bass lines as well as pedal note progressions. Also don't forget you can use this same principle up the neck. These are just a few possibilities in the key of A and E.

C (I)	G/B (V)	Am (vi)
Finger X 3 2 0 1 0	**Finger** X 2 0 0 0 4	**Finger** X 0 2 3 1 0
Scale X 1 3 5 1 3	**Scale** X 3 5 1 3 1	**Scale** X 1 5 1 ♭3 5
Note X C E G C E	**Note** X B D G B G	**Note** X A E A C E

G (I)	D/F# (V)	Em (vi)
Finger 3 2 0 0 0 4	**Finger** T X 0 1 3 2	**Finger** 0 2 3 0 0 0
Scale 1 3 5 1 3 1	**Scale** 3 X 1 5 1 3	**Scale** 1 5 1 ♭3 5 1
Note G B D G B G	**Note** F# X D A D F#	**Note** E B E G B E

D (I)	A/C# (V)	Bm (vi)
Finger X X 0 1 3 2	**Finger** X 3 1 1 1 X	**Finger** X 1 3 4 2 1
Scale X X 1 5 1 3	**Scale** X 3 5 1 3 X	**Scale** X 1 5 1 ♭3 5
Note X X D A D F#	**Note** X C# E A C# X	**Note** X B F# B D F#

Here are some common slash chord progressions with the 3rd of the chord in the bass.

A (I)	E/G# (V)	F#m (vi)
5th	X o o	
Finger 1 3 4 2 1 1	**Finger** 4 X 2 1 0 0	**Finger** 1 3 4 1 1 1
Scale 1 5 1 3 5 1	**Scale** 3 X 1 3 5 1	**Scale** 1 5 1 ♭3 5 1
Note A E A C# E A	**Note** G# X E G# B E	**Note** F# C# F# A C# F#

E (I)	B/D# (V)	C#m (vi)
X 7th	X X 4th	X 4th
Finger X 1 2 3 4 1	**Finger** X 3 1 1 1 X	**Finger** X 1 3 4 2 1
Scale X 1 5 1 3 5	**Scale** X 3 5 1 3 X	**Scale** X 1 5 1 ♭3 5
Note X E B E G# B	**Note** X D# F# B D# X	**Note** X C# G# C# E G#

61

Here are a few single chord progressions that can be written using slash chords. You can here these in songs like *Mr. Bojangles* by the Nitty Gritty Dirt Band, *America* - Simon and Garfunkel, *Our House* - Crosby , Stills & Nash, *Changes* - David Bowie and *Everything I own* - Bread. Don't forget to explore these progressions up the neck as well. The D is actually much easier to play up the neck than the first open position one.

D (I)
X X O
Finger	X X 0 1 3 2
Scale	X X 1 5 1 3
Note	X X D A D F♯

D/C♯ (I)
X   X
Finger	X 4 X 1 3 2
Scale	X 7 X 5 1 3
Note	X C♯ X A D F♯

D/B (I)
X   X
Finger	X 1 X 1 2 1
Scale	X 6 X 5 1 3
Note	X B X A D F♯

D/A (I)
X O X
Finger	X 0 X 1 3 1
Scale	X 5 X 5 1 3
Note	X A X A D F♯

D (I)
X   X   5th
Finger	X 1 4 4 4 X
Scale	X 1 5 1 3 X
Note	X D A D F♯ X

D/C♯ (I)
X   X   4th
Finger	X 1 4 4 4 X
Scale	X 7 5 1 3 X
Note	X C♯ A D F♯ X

D/B (I)
X   X   5th
Finger	3 X 4 4 4 X
Scale	6 X 5 1 3 X
Note	B X A D F♯ X

D/A (I)
X   X   5th
Finger	1 X 4 4 4 X
Scale	5 X 5 1 3 X
Note	A X A D F♯ X

G (I)
X X   3rd
Finger	X X 3 2 1 1
Scale	X X 1 3 5 1
Note	X X G B D G

G/F♯ (I)
X X   3rd
Finger	X X 2 3 1 1
Scale	X X 7 3 5 1
Note	X X F♯ B D G

G/E (I)
X X   2nd
Finger	X X 1 3 2 2
Scale	X X 6 3 5 1
Note	X X E B D G

G/D (I)
X X O
Finger	X X 0 3 2 2
Scale	X X 5 3 5 1
Note	X X D B D G

C (I)
X   O   O
Finger	X 3 2 0 1 0
Scale	X 1 3 5 1 3
Note	X C E G C E

C/B (I)
X   O   O
Finger	X 2 3 0 1 0
Scale	X 7 3 5 1 3
Note	X B E G C E

C/A (I)
X O   O
Finger	X 0 2 0 1 0
Scale	X 6 3 5 1 3
Note	X A E G C E

C/G (I)
X   O   O
Finger	3 X 2 0 1 0
Scale	5 X 3 5 1 3
Note	G X E G C E

Use the worksheet on the left to get started, but I've also included with each key another worksheet at the end of the triad section. You can use the fretboard to find your bass note and then use the triads to find the rest of the chord you want played on top of the bass. Often Slash Chords are just a bass note and a triad on top.

SLASH CHORD WORKSHEET

63

Diatonic and Secondary Dominant Chords

Key of **C Major** / **A minor**

C (I)
Finger	X	3	2	0	1	0
Scale	X	1	3	5	1	3
Note	X	C	E	G	C	E

F (IV)
Finger	1	3	4	2	1	1
Scale	1	5	1	3	5	1
Note	F	C	F	A	C	F

G (V)
Finger	3	2	0	0	0	4
Scale	1	3	5	1	3	1
Note	G	B	D	G	B	G

G7 (V7/I)
Finger	3	2	0	0	0	1
Scale	1	3	5	1	3	♭7
Note	G	B	D	G	B	F

C7 (V7/IV)
Finger	X	3	2	4	1	0
Scale	X	1	3	♭7	1	3
Note	X	C	E	B♭	C	E

D7 (V7/V)
Finger	X	X	0	2	1	3
Scale	X	X	1	5	♭7	3
Note	X	X	D	A	C	F♯

Am (vi)
Finger	X	0	2	3	1	0
Scale	X	1	5	1	♭3	5
Note	X	A	E	A	C	E

Dm (ii)
Finger	X	X	0	2	3	1
Scale	X	X	1	5	1	♭3
Note	X	X	D	A	D	F

Em (iii)
Finger	0	2	3	0	0	0
Scale	1	5	1	♭3	5	1
Note	E	B	E	G	B	E

E7 (V7/vi)
Finger	0	2	0	1	0	0
Scale	1	5	♭7	3	5	1
Note	E	B	D	G♯	B	E

A7 (V7/ii)
Finger	X	0	1	0	2	0
Scale	X	1	5	♭7	3	5
Note	X	A	E	G	C♯	E

B7 (V7/iii)
Finger	X	2	1	3	0	4
Scale	X	1	3	♭7	1	5
Note	X	B	D♯	A	B	F♯

Extensions

CMaj7 (I)
Finger	X	3	2	0	0	0
Scale	X	1	3	5	7	3
Note	X	C	E	G	B	E

FMaj7 (IV)
Finger	X	X	3	2	1	0
Scale	X	X	1	3	5	7
Note	X	X	F	A	C	E

G7 (V7)
Finger	3	2	0	0	0	1
Scale	1	3	5	1	3	♭7
Note	G	B	D	G	B	F

Am7 (vi)
Finger	X	0	2	0	1	0
Scale	X	1	5	♭7	3	5
Note	X	A	E	G	C	E

Dm7 (ii)
Finger	X	X	0	2	1	1
Scale	X	X	1	5	♭7	♭3
Note	X	X	D	A	C	F

Em7 (iii)
Finger	0	2	0	0	0	0
Scale	1	5	♭7	3	5	1
Note	E	B	D	G	B	E

Flat Majors

E♭ (♭III)
Finger	X	3	2	0	1	4
Scale	X	1	3	3	1	5
Note	X	E♭	G	G	E♭	B♭

A♭ (♭VI) 4th
Finger	1	3	4	2	1	1
Scale	1	5	1	3	5	1
Note	A♭	E♭	A♭	C	E♭	A♭

B♭ (♭VII)
Finger	X	1	2	3	4	1
Scale	X	1	5	1	3	5
Note	X	B♭	F	B♭	D	F

Suspended Chords

Csus (I)
Finger	X	3	4	0	1	1
Scale	X	1	4	5	1	4
Note	X	C	F	G	C	F

Csus2 (I)
Finger	X	2	0	0	3	4
Scale	X	1	2	5	2	5
Note	X	C	D	G	D	G

Fsus2 (IV)
Finger	X	X	3	0	1	1
Scale	X	X	1	2	5	1
Note	X	X	F	G	C	F

G7sus (V7)
Finger	3	X	0	0	1	1
Scale	1	X	5	1	4	♭7
Note	G	X	D	G	C	F

Gsus (V)
Finger	3	X	0	0	1	4
Scale	1	X	5	1	4	1
Note	G	X	D	G	C	G

Gsus2 (V)
Finger	3	X	0	2	4	4
Scale	1	X	5	2	5	1
Note	G	X	D	A	D	G

Add9 Chords

Cadd9 (I)
Finger	X	3	2	0	4	4
Scale	X	1	3	5	2	5
Note	X	C	E	G	D	G

Fadd9 (IV)
Finger	X	X	3	2	1	4
Scale	X	X	1	3	5	2
Note	X	X	F	A	C	G

Fadd9 (IV) 6th
Finger	X	3	2	0	1	4
Scale	X	1	3	2	1	5
Note	X	F	A	G	F	C

Gadd9 (V)
Finger	3	X	0	2	0	4
Scale	1	X	5	2	3	1
Note	G	X	D	A	B	G

Am Harmonic Chords

E (III)
Finger	0	2	3	1	0	0
Scale	1	5	1	3	5	1
Note	E	B	E	G♯	B	E

E7 (III7)
Finger	0	2	0	1	0	0
Scale	1	5	♭7	3	5	1
Note	E	B	D	G♯	B	E

Dominant 7th (Blues) Chords

C7 (I7)

Finger	X	3	2	4	1	0
Scale	X	1	3	♭7	1	3
Note	X	C	E	B♭	C	E

C7 (I7) — 3rd

Finger	X	1	3	1	4	1
Scale	X	1	5	♭7	3	5
Note	X	C	G	B♭	E	G

F7 (IV7)

Finger	1	3	1	2	1	1
Scale	1	5	♭7	3	5	1
Note	F	C	E♭	A	C	F

F7 (IV7) — 6th

Finger	X	3	2	4	1	X
Scale	X	1	3	♭7	1	X
Note	X	F	A	E♭	F	X

G7 (V7)

Finger	2	1	3	0	0	4
Scale	1	3	♭7	1	3	1
Note	G	B	F	G	B	G

G7 (V7) — 3rd

Finger	1	3	1	2	1	1
Scale	1	5	♭7	3	5	1
Note	G	D	F	B	D	G

Quality Change Chords

D (II) — V

Finger	X	X	0	1	3	2
Scale	X	X	1	5	1	3
Note	X	X	D	A	D	F#

Fm (iv) — I iv IV

Finger	1	3	4	1	1	1
Scale	1	5	1	♭3	5	1
Note	F	C	F	A♭	C	F

E (III) — vi

Finger	0	2	3	1	0	0
Scale	1	5	1	3	5	1
Note	E	B	E	G#	B	E

Gm (v) — I

Finger	2	X	0	3	3	3
Scale	1	X	5	♭3	5	1
Note	G	X	D	B♭	D	G

A (VI) — ii

Finger	X	0	1	2	3	0
Scale	X	1	5	1	3	5
Note	X	A	E	A	C#	E

Bm (vii) — iii

Finger	X	1	3	4	2	1
Scale	X	1	5	1	♭3	5
Note	X	B	F#	B	D	F#

B (VII) — iii

Finger	X	1	2	3	4	1
Scale	X	1	5	1	3	5
Note	X	B	F#	B	D#	F#

Cm (i) — 3rd

Finger	X	1	3	4	2	1
Scale	X	1	5	1	♭3	5
Note	X	C	G	C	E♭	G

Additional Diatonic Extensions

CMaj7add11 (I)

Finger	X	2	3	0	0	0
Scale	X	1	4	5	7	3
Note	X	C	F	G	B	E

C6 (I)

Finger	X	4	2	3	1	0
Scale	X	1	3	6	1	3
Note	X	C	E	A	C	E

CMaj9 (I)

Finger	X	2	1	4	3	0
Scale	X	1	3	7	2	3
Note	X	C	E	B	D	E

Dm6 (ii)

Finger	X	X	0	2	0	1
Scale	X	X	1	5	6	♭3
Note	X	X	D	A	B	F

Dm9 (ii) — 3rd

Finger	X	3	1	4	4	4
Scale	X	1	♭3	♭7	2	5
Note	X	D	F	C	E	A

Dm9 (ii) — 5th

Finger	X	X	0	2	3	0
Scale	X	X	1	♭7	3	2
Note	X	X	D	C	F	E

Em7/11 (iii)

Finger	0	0	0	0	0	0
Scale	1	4	♭7	♭3	5	1
Note	E	A	D	G	B	E

Emadd11 (iii)

Finger	0	0	3	0	0	0
Scale	1	4	1	♭3	5	1
Note	E	A	E	G	B	E

FMaj9 (IV)

Finger	1	0	3	0	2	0
Scale	1	3	7	2	5	7
Note	F	A	E	G	C	E

F6 (IV)

Finger	X	X	3	2	4	1
Scale	X	X	1	3	6	1
Note	X	X	F	A	D	F

F6/9 (IV)

Finger	X	X	2	1	3	3
Scale	X	X	1	3	6	2
Note	X	X	F	A	D	G

G9 (V7)

Finger	3	X	4	2	0	1
Scale	1	X	♭7	2	3	♭7
Note	G	X	F	A	B	F

G11 (V7)

Finger	3	X	4	0	1	1
Scale	1	X	5	2	4	♭7
Note	G	X	D	A	C	F

G7add13 (V7)

Finger	2	1	3	0	4	0
Scale	1	3	♭7	1	5	6
Note	G	B	F	G	D	E

Am9 (vi) — 5th

Finger	X	0	2	3	0	0
Scale	X	1	♭7	♭3	2	5
Note	X	A	G	C	B	E

Amadd9 (vi)

Finger	X	0	2	4	1	0
Scale	X	1	5	2	♭3	5
Note	X	A	E	B	C	E

Am11 (vi)

Finger	X	0	0	4	1	3
Scale	X	1	4	2	♭3	♭7
Note	X	A	D	B	C	G

Bm7♭5 (viiø7)

Finger	X	1	2	1	3	X
Scale	X	1	♭5	♭7	♭3	X
Note	X	B	F	A	D	X

Bm7♭5 (viiø7)

Finger	X	2	0	3	4	1
Scale	X	1	♭3	♭7	♭3	♭5
Note	X	B	D	A	D	F

B° (vii°)

Finger	X	1	2	4	3	X
Scale	X	1	♭5	1	♭3	X
Note	X	B	F	B	D	X

*The m7♭5 is also referred to as a half diminished chord and can be written as a degree symbol with a slash through it.

Chord Formula Worksheet Up The Neck - Key of C and Am

C (I) — 3rd
Finger X 1 2 3 4 1
Scale 5 1 5 1 3 5
Note G C G C E G

C (I) — 5th
Finger 3 2 1 1 1 4
Scale 1 3 5 1 3 1
Note C E G C E C

C (I) — 8th
Finger 1 3 4 2 1 1
Scale 1 5 1 3 5 1
Note C G C E G C

C (I) — 10th
Finger X X 1 2 4 3
Scale 3 5 1 5 1 3
Note E G C G C E

I - (1, 3, 5) Extensions - (2), (4), (6), (7)

F (IV) — 3rd
Finger X X 1 2 4 3
Scale 3 5 1 5 1 3
Note A C F C F A

F (IV) — 5th
Finger X 4 3 1 2 1
Scale 5 1 3 5 1 3
Note C F A C F A

F (IV) — 8th
Finger X 1 2 3 4 1
Scale 5 1 5 1 3 5
Note C F C F A C

F (IV) — 10th
Finger 3 2 1 1 1 4
Scale 1 3 5 1 3 1
Note F A C F A F

IV - (1, 3, 5) Extensions - (2), (#4), (6), (7)

G (V) — 3rd
Finger 1 3 4 2 1 1
Scale 1 5 1 3 5 1
Note G D G B D G

G (V) — 5th
Finger X X 1 2 4 3
Scale 3 5 1 5 1 3
Note B D G D G B

G (V) — 7th
Finger X 4 3 1 2 1
Scale 5 1 3 5 1 3
Note D G B D G B

G (V) — 10th
Finger X 1 2 3 4 1
Scale 5 1 5 1 3 5
Note D G D G B D

V - (1, 3, 5) Extensions - (2), (4), (6), (b7)

Am (vi)
Finger 4 2 1 1 X X
Scale 1 b3 5 1 b3 1
Note A C E A C A

Am (vi) — 5th
Finger 1 3 4 1 1 1
Scale 1 5 1 b3 5 1
Note A E A C E A

Am (vi) — 7th
Finger X X 1 3 4 2
Scale b3 5 1 5 1 b3
Note C E A E A C

Am (vi) — 8th
Finger X 4 2 1 3 X
Scale 5 1 b3 5 1 b3
Note E A C E A C

vi - (1, b3, 5) Extensions - (2), (4), (#5), (b7)

Dm (ii)
Finger X 4 2 1 3 X
Scale 5 1 b3 5 1 b3
Note A D F A D F

Dm (ii) — 5th
Finger X 1 3 4 2 1
Scale 5 1 5 1 b3 5
Note A D A D F A

Dm (ii) — 6th
Finger 4 2 1 1 X X
Scale 1 b3 5 1 b3 1
Note D F A D F D

Dm (ii) — 10th
Finger 1 3 4 1 1 1
Scale 1 5 1 b3 5 1
Note D A D F A D

ii - (1, b3, 5) Extensions - (2), (4), (6), (b7)

Em (iii)
Finger X X 1 3 4 2
Scale b3 5 1 5 1 b3
Note G B E B E G

Em (iii) — 3rd
Finger X 4 2 1 3 X
Scale 5 1 b3 5 1 b3
Note B E G B E G

Em (iii) — 7th
Finger X 1 3 4 2 1
Scale 5 1 5 1 b3 5
Note B E B E G B

Em (iii) — 8th
Finger 4 2 1 1 X X
Scale 1 b3 5 1 b3 1
Note E G B E G E

iii - (1, b3, 5) Extensions - (b2), (4), (#5), (b7)

* Order of notes as you move up and down a string.

1
b2 (b9)
2 (sus2, 9)
#2 (#9) / (b3 minor)
3
4 (sus, 11)
b5 (b5, #11)
5
#5 (#5, b13) / (+, aug)
6 (6, 13)
b7 (7) Dominant 7th
7 (Maj7)
1

E A D G B E
F · · · C F
· B E A · ·
G C F · D G   3rd

A D G C E A
· · · · F ·   5th

B E A D · B   7th
C F · · G C
· · B E · ·   9th
D G C F A D

E A D G B E   12th
F · · · C F

CHORD SUBSTITUTIONS - KEY OF C AND Am

1. CHORD EMBELLISHMENTS - EXTENSIONS AND ALTERATIONS

2. MAJOR, MINOR AND DOMINANT SUBSTITUTIONS

Major   **C (I)** Relative minor - **Am (vi)** or Common Tones - **Em (iii)**

           F (IV) Relative minor - **Dm (ii)** or Common Tones - **Am (vi)**

           G (V) Relative minor - **Em (iii)** or Common Tones - **Bm (vii)**

minor   **Am (vi)** Relative Major - **C (I)** or Common Tones - **F (IV)**

           Dm (ii) Relative Major - **F (IV)** or Common Tones - **Bb(bVII)**

           Em (iii) Relative Major - **G (V)** or Common Tones - **C (I)**

7th   **G7(V7)** Common Tones - **B°7 (VII°7)** or **Em (iii)** or Tritone - **Db7**

3. BACKCYCLING (CIRCLE OF 5THS)

(Em7-Am7-Dm7-G7) - C	**(Am7-Dm7-Gm7-C7) - F**	**(Bm7-Em7-Am7-D7) - G**
(C#m7-F#m7-Bm7-E7) - Am	**(F#m7-Bm7-Em7-A7) - Dm**	**(Abm7-C#m7-F#m7-B7) - Em**

Use the 5th of the chord you're going to to find the letter name of the chord that should proceed it. Here are a couple of variations on backcycling (E7, A7, D7, G7) - C or (Em7, A7, Dm7, G7) - C. The ii-V7 is a very common substitute for a V7 chord. Also don't forget you can just add the secondary dominants before a chord.

4. HALF STEP PROGRESSIONS

This is usually some type of dominant 7th chord.

Major	**B7-C**	**C#7-C**	**E7-F**	**F#7-F**	**Gb7-G**	**G#7-G**
minor	**Ab7-Am**	**A#7-Am**	**Db7-Dm**	**D#7-Dm**	**Eb7-Em**	**F7-Em**

5. PASSING CHORDS

°7   Diminished 7th chords can be used between diatonic chords to create a *chromatic* chord progression.

                 CMaj7(I)-C#°7-Dm7(ii)-D#°7-Em7(iii)-FMaj7(IV)-F#°7-G7(V7)-G#°7-Am7(vi)

Diatonic   You can also use diatonic chords to fill-in the gaps between chords.

                 Here is an example of a *diatonic* type passing chord progression:

                 original C(I)-C(I)-C(I)-F(IV) becomes C(I)-Dm(ii)-Em(iii)-F(IV).

6. TRITONE SUBSTITUTION

You can substitute a dominant 7th chord with another dominant 7th chord based on the flat five of the original dominant 7th chord. Below are the original 7th chords followed by their tritone substitution. You can also use these substitutions in your backcycling to create chromatic bass lines.

A7 to Eb7	Bb7 to E7	B7 to F7	C7 to Gb7	C#7 to G7	Db7 to G7	D7 to Ab7
Eb7 to A7	E7 to Bb7	F7 to B7	F#7 to C7	Gb7 to C7	G7 to Db7	Ab7 to D7

7. QUALITY CHANGE CHORDS

Majors - (minors, Dominant 7ths), Minors - (Majors, Dominant 7ths), Dominant 7ths - (Majors, minors)

Four Note Extensions Up The Neck - Key of C and Am

* Use the sections on *Bass Notes* and *Optional Notes* to find other notes you can add to these chords. Also don't forget you don't have to play every note in the chord, only the essential notes that convey the chords family and quality of sound.

CMaj7 (I) — 3rd
- Finger X 1 3 2 4 1
- Scale X 1 5 7 3 5
- Note X C G B E G

CMaj7 (I) — 5th
- Finger X X 1 1 1 4
- Scale X X 5 1 3 7
- Note X X G C E B

CMaj7 (I) — 8th
- Finger 1 X 3 4 2 X
- Scale 1 5 7 3 5 1
- Note C G B E G C

CMaj7 (I) — 7th
- Finger T X 4 3 2 1
- Scale 1 X 1 3 5 7
- Note C X C E G B

CMaj7 (I) — 10th
- Finger X X 1 4 4 4
- Scale X X 1 5 7 3
- Note X X C G B E

FMaj7 (IV)
- Finger 1 0 3 4 2 0
- Scale 1 3 7 3 5 7
- Note F A E A C E

FMaj7 (IV) — 3rd
- Finger X X 1 4 4 4
- Scale X X 1 5 7 3
- Note X X F C E A

FMaj7 (IV) — 5th
- Finger X 4 3 1 1 1
- Scale X 1 3 5 7 3
- Note X F A C E A

FMaj7 (IV) — 8th
- Finger X 1 3 2 4 1
- Scale X 1 5 7 3 5
- Note X F C E A C

FMaj7 (IV) — 10th
- Finger X X 1 1 1 4
- Scale X X 5 1 3 7
- Note X X C F A E

G7 (V7) — 3rd
- Finger 1 3 1 2 1 1
- Scale 1 5 ♭7 3 5 1
- Note G D F B D G

G7 (V7) — 5th
- Finger X X 1 3 2 4
- Scale X X 1 5 ♭7 3
- Note X X G D F B

G7 (V7) — 7th
- Finger X X X X X X
- Scale X 1 3 ♭7 1 3
- Note X G B F G B

G7 (V7) — 10th
- Finger X 1 2 1 4 1
- Scale X 1 5 ♭7 3 5
- Note X G D F B D

G7 (V7) — 12th
- Finger X X 1 1 1 2
- Scale X X 5 1 3 ♭7
- Note X X D G B F

Am7 (vi)
- Finger X 0 2 3 1 4
- Scale X 1 5 1 ♭3 ♭7
- Note X A E A C G

Am7 (vi) — 5th
- Finger 1 3 1 1 1 1
- Scale 1 5 ♭7 ♭3 5 1
- Note A E G C E A

Am7 (vi) — 7th
- Finger X X 1 3 2 2
- Scale X X 1 5 ♭7 ♭3
- Note X X A E G C

Am7 (vi) — 8th
- Finger X 0 3 2 1 0
- Scale X 1 ♭3 5 ♭7 5
- Note X A C E G E

Am7 (vi) — 10th
- Finger X 2 1 3 1 4
- Scale X 1 ♭3 ♭7 1 5
- Note X A C G A E

Dm7 (ii)
- Finger X 3 X 2 4 1
- Scale X ♭7 X 5 1 ♭3
- Note X C X A D F

Dm7 (ii) — 3rd
- Finger X 2 1 3 1 4
- Scale X 1 ♭3 ♭7 1 5
- Note X D F C D A

Dm7 (ii) — 5th
- Finger X 1 3 1 2 1
- Scale X 1 5 ♭7 ♭3 5
- Note X D A C F A

Dm (ii) — 6th
- Finger X X 2 3 1 4
- Scale X X 5 1 ♭3 ♭7
- Note X X A D F C

Dm7 (ii) — 10th
- Finger 1 3 1 1 1 1
- Scale 1 5 ♭7 ♭3 5 1
- Note D A C F A D

Em7 (iii)
- Finger 0 2 3 0 4 0
- Scale 1 5 1 ♭3 ♭7 1
- Note E B E G D E

Em7 (iii) — 5th
- Finger X X 1 3 2 2
- Scale X X 1 5 7 ♭3
- Note X X E B D G

Em7 (iii) — 5th
- Finger X 2 1 3 1 4
- Scale X 1 ♭3 ♭7 1 5
- Note X E G D E B

Em7 (iii) — 7th
- Finger X 1 3 1 2 1
- Scale X 1 5 ♭7 ♭3 5
- Note X E B D G B

Em7 (iii) — 8th
- Finger X X 2 3 1 4
- Scale X X 5 1 ♭3 ♭7
- Note X X B E G D

Classic Rock Power Chord & Rock-n-Roll Worksheet - Key of C and Am

I, IV & V Power Chords (1 and 5)

C5 (I)
x x o

Finger X 3 X 0 1 4
Scale X 1 X 5 1 5
Note X C X G C G

C5 (I)
x x
3rd

Scale 5 1 5 1 X X
Note G C G C X X

C5 (I)
x x x
8th

Scale 1 5 1 X X X
Note C G C X X X

F (IV)

Finger 1 3 4 2 1 1
Scale 1 5 1 3 5 1
Note F C F A C F

F5 (IV)
x x x

Scale 1 5 1 X X X
Note F C F X X X

F5 (IV)
x x
8th

Scale 5 1 5 1 X X
Note C F C F X X

G5 (V)
x o o

Finger 3 X 0 0 4 4
Scale 1 X 5 1 5 1
Note G X D G D G

G5 (V)
x x x
3rd

Scale 1 5 1 X X X
Note G D G X X X

G5 (V)
x x
10th

Scale 5 1 5 1 X X
Note D G D G X X

Flat Major Power Chords

E♭5 (♭III)
x x
6th

Scale 5 1 5 1 X X
Note B♭ E♭ B♭ E♭ X X

E♭5 (♭III)
x x x
11th

Scale 1 5 1 X X X
Note E♭ B♭ E♭ X X X

A♭5 (♭VI)
x x x
4th

Scale 1 5 1 X X X
Note A♭ E♭ A♭ X X X

A♭5 (♭VI)
x x
11th

Scale 5 1 5 1 X X
Note E♭ A♭ E♭ A♭ X X

B♭5 (♭VII)
x x

Scale 5 1 5 1 X X
Note F B♭ F B♭ X X

B♭5 (♭VII)
x x x
6th

Scale 1 5 1 X X X
Note B♭ F B♭ X X X

Combinations of notes that can be used to make Power Chords - 1, 5 or 1, 5, 1 called 1st Inversion Power Chords
5, 1 or 5, 1, 5 called 2nd Inversion Power Chords

ii, iii, vi Power Chords

D5 (ii)
x x
5th

Scale 5 1 5 1 X X
Note A D A D X X

D5 (ii)
x x x
10th

Scale 1 5 1 X X X
Note D A D X X X

E5 (iii)
o x x x

Scale 1 5 1 X X X
Note E B E X X X

E5 (iii)
x x
7th

Scale 5 1 5 1 X X
Note B E B E X X

A5 (vi)
o o x x

Scale 5 1 5 1 X X
Note E A E A X X

A5 (vi)
x x x
5th

Scale 1 5 1 X X X
Note A E A X X X

Other Power Chord Shapes

x x

Scale X X 5 1 5 1

x x

Scale X 5 1 5 1 X

X5add9
x x x

Scale 1 5 2 X X X

X5add9
x x

Scale X 1 5 2 X X

Csus 2 (IV)
x s o x

Finger X 2 X 0 3 X
Scale X 1 X 5 2 X
Note X C X G D X

Rock-n-Roll Chord Shapes for I, IV and V Chords

X5 / X6 / X7
x x x x

Scale 1 5 X X X X

X5 / X6 / X7
x x x x

Scale X 1 5 X X X

X5 / X6 / X7
x x x x

Scale X X 1 5 X X

Key of C and Am Triad Worksheet (1st, 2nd and 3rd strings)

Key of C and Am Triad Worksheet (2nd, 3rd and 4th strings)

Em (iii) — Scale 1 ♭3 5
C (I) — Scale 3 5 1
G (V) — Scale 5 1 3
A♭ (♭VI) — Scale 5 1 3
C (I) — Scale 3 5 1
C (I) 5th — Scale 5 1 3
C (I) 8th — Scale 1 3 5

F (IV) — Scale 1 3 5
Dm (ii) — Scale ♭3 5 1
Am (vi) — Scale 5 1 ♭3
B♭ (♭III) — Scale 5 1 3
F (IV) — Scale 1 3 5
F (IV) 5th — Scale 3 5 1
F (IV) 10th — Scale 5 1 3

G (V) 3rd — Scale 1 3 5
Em (iii) 4th — Scale ♭3 5 1
B° (vii°) 3rd — Scale ♭5 1 ♭3
E♭ (♭VI) 3rd — Scale 3 5 1
G (V) — Scale 5 1 3
G (V) 3rd — Scale 1 3 5
G (V) 7th — Scale 3 5 1

Am (vi) 5th — Scale 1 ♭3 5
F (IV) 5th — Scale 3 5 1
C (I) 5th — Scale 5 1 3
A♭ (♭VI) 4th — Scale 1 3 5

B° (vii°) 6th — Scale 1 ♭3 ♭5
G (V) 7th — Scale 3 5 1
Dm (ii) 6th — Scale 5 1 ♭3
B♭ (♭III) 6th — Scale 1 3 5
Am (vi) — Scale 5 1 ♭3
Am (vi) 5th — Scale 1 ♭3 5
Am (vi) 9th — Scale ♭3 5 1

C (I) 8th — Scale 1 3 5
Am (vi) 9th — Scale ♭3 5 1
Em (iii) 8th — Scale 5 1 ♭3
E♭ (♭VI) 8th — Scale 5 1 3
Dm (ii) — Scale ♭3 5 1
Dm (ii) 6th — Scale 5 1 ♭3
Dm (ii) 10th — Scale 1 ♭3 5

Dm (ii) 10th — Scale 1 ♭3 5
B° (vii°) 10th — Scale ♭3 ♭5 1
F (IV) 10th — Scale 5 1 3
A♭ (♭VI) 8th — Scale 3 5 1
Em (iii) — Scale 1 ♭3 5
Em (iii) 4th — Scale ♭3 5 1
Em (iii) 8th — Scale 5 1 ♭3

Em (iii) 12th — Scale 1 ♭3 5
C (I) 12th — Scale 3 5 1
G (V) 12th — Scale 5 1 3
B♭ (♭III) 10th — Scale 3 5 1

F (IV) 13th — Scale 1 3 5
Dm (ii) 14th — Scale ♭3 5 1
Am (vi) 13th — Scale 5 1 ♭3
E♭ (♭III) 11th — Scale 1 3 5
B° (vii°) 3rd — Scale ♭5 1 ♭3
B° (vii°) 6th — Scale 1 ♭3 ♭5
B° (vii°) 10th — Scale ♭3 ♭5 1

71

Key of C and Am Triad Worksheet (3rd, 4th and 5th strings)

Row 1:
- C (I) — Scale 1 3 5
- G (V) — Scale 3 5 1
- Em (iii) — Scale 5 1 ♭3
- A♭ (♭VI) — Scale 3 5 1
- C (I) — Scale 1 3 5
- C (I) 5th — Scale 3 5 1
- C (I) 9th — Scale 5 1 3

Row 2:
- Dm (ii) — Scale 1 ♭3 5
- Am (vi) — Scale ♭3 5 1
- F (IV) — Scale 5 1 3
- B♭ (♭III) 3rd — Scale 3 5 1
- F (IV) — Scale 5 1 3
- F (IV) 5th — Scale 1 3 5
- F (IV) 10th — Scale 3 5 1

Row 3:
- Em (iii) 4th — Scale 1 ♭3 5
- B° (vii°) 3rd — Scale ♭3 ♭5 1
- G (V) 4th — Scale 5 1 3
- E♭ (♭VI) 3rd — Scale 1 3 5
- G (V) — Scale 3 5 1
- G (V) 4th — Scale 5 1 3
- G (V) 7th — Scale 1 3 5

Row 4:
- F (IV) 5th — Scale 1 3 5
- C (I) 5th — Scale 3 5 1
- Am (vi) 5th — Scale 5 1 ♭3
- A♭ (♭VI) 5th — Scale 5 1 3

Row 5:
- G (V) 7th — Scale 1 3 5
- Dm (ii) 7th — Scale ♭3 5 1
- B° (vii°) 7th — Scale ♭5 1 ♭3
- B♭ (♭III) 7th — Scale 5 1 3
- Am (vi) — Scale ♭3 5 1
- Am (vi) 5th — Scale 5 1 ♭3
- Am (vi) 9th — Scale 1 ♭3 5

Row 6:
- Am (vi) 9th — Scale 1 ♭3 5
- Em (iii) 9th — Scale ♭3 5 1
- C (I) 9th — Scale 5 1 3
- E♭ (♭VI) 8th — Scale 3 5 1
- Dm (ii) — Scale 1 ♭3 5
- Dm (ii) 7th — Scale ♭3 5 1
- Dm (ii) 10th — Scale 5 1 ♭3

Row 7:
- B° (vii°) 10th — Scale 1 ♭3 ♭5
- F (IV) 10th — Scale 3 5 1
- Dm (ii) 10th — Scale 5 1 ♭3
- A♭ (♭VI) 8th — Scale 1 3 5
- Em (iii) — Scale 5 1 ♭3
- Em (iii) 4th — Scale 1 ♭3 5
- Em (iii) 9th — Scale ♭3 5 1

Row 8:
- C (I) 12th — Scale 1 3 5
- G (V) 12th — Scale 3 5 1
- Em (iii) 12th — Scale 5 1 ♭3
- B♭ (♭III) 10th — Scale 1 3 5

Row 9:
- Dm (ii) 14th — Scale 1 ♭3 5
- Am (vi) 14th — Scale ♭3 5 1
- F (IV) 14th — Scale 5 1 3
- E♭ (♭III) 12th — Scale 5 1 3
- B° (vii°) 3rd — Scale ♭3 ♭5 1
- B° (vii°) 7th — Scale ♭5 1 ♭3
- B° (vii°) 10th — Scale 1 ♭3 ♭5

72

Slash Chord Worksheet

Key of C and Am

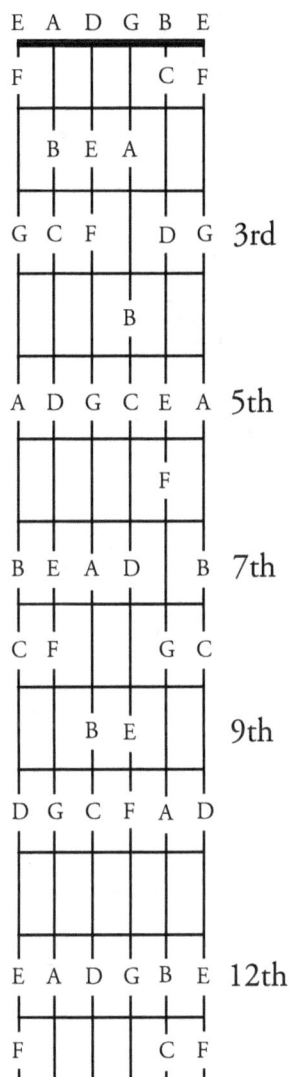

73

Diatonic and Secondary Dominant Chords

Key of G Major (with # sign)
(F#)

E minor

G (I)
Finger 3 2 0 0 0 4
Scale 1 3 5 1 3 1
Note G B D G B G

C (IV)
Finger X 3 2 0 1 0
Scale X 1 3 5 1 3
Note X C E G C E

D (V)
Finger X X 0 1 3 2
Scale X X 1 5 1 3
Note X X D A D F#

D7 (V7/I)
Finger X X 0 2 1 3
Scale X X 1 5 b7 3
Note X X D A C F#

G7 (V7/IV)
Finger 3 2 0 0 0 1
Scale 1 3 5 1 3 b7
Note G B D G B F

A7 (V7/V)
Finger X 0 1 0 2 0
Scale X 1 5 b7 3 5
Note X A E G C# E

Em (vi)
Finger 0 2 3 0 0 0
Scale 1 5 1 b3 5 1
Note E B E G B E

Am (ii)
Finger X 0 2 3 1 0
Scale X 1 5 1 b3 5
Note X A E A C E

Bm (iii)
Finger X 1 3 4 2 1
Scale X 1 5 1 b3 5
Note X B F# B D F#

B7 (V7/vi)
Finger X 2 1 3 0 4
Scale X 1 3 b7 1 5
Note X B D# A B F#

E7 (V7/ii)
Finger 0 2 0 1 0 0
Scale 1 5 b7 3 5 1
Note E B D G# B E

F#7 (V7/iii)
Finger 1 3 1 2 1 1
Scale 1 5 b7 3 5 1
Note F# C# E A# C# F#

Extensions

GMaj7 (I)
Finger 2 X 0 0 0 1
Scale 1 X 5 1 3 7
Note G X D G B F#

CMaj7 (IV)
Finger X 3 2 0 0 0
Scale X 1 3 5 7 3
Note X C E G B E

D7 (V7)
Finger X X 0 2 1 3
Scale X X 1 5 b7 3
Note X X D A C F#

Em7 (vi)
Finger 0 2 0 0 0 0
Scale 1 5 b7 b3 5 1
Note E B D G B E

Am7 (ii)
Finger X 0 2 0 1 0
Scale X 1 5 b7 b3 5
Note X A E G C E

Bm7 (iii)
Finger X 1 3 1 2 1
Scale X 1 5 b7 b3 5
Note X B F# A D F#

Flat Majors

Bb (bIII)
Finger X 1 2 3 4 1
Scale X 1 5 1 3 5
Note X Bb F Bb D F

Eb (bVI)
4th
Finger X 3 2 0 1 4
Scale X 1 3 3 1 5
Note X Eb G G Eb Bb

F (bVII)
Finger 1 3 4 2 1 1
Scale 1 5 1 3 5 1
Note F C F A C F

Suspended Chords

Gsus (I)
Finger 3 X 0 0 1 4
Scale 1 X 5 1 4 1
Note G X D G C G

Gsus2 (I)
Finger 2 X 0 1 3 4
Scale 1 X 5 2 5 1
Note G X D A D G

Csus2 (IV)
Finger X 2 0 0 4 4
Scale X 1 2 5 2 5
Note X C D G D G

D7sus (V7)
Finger X X 0 2 1 4
Scale X X 1 5 b7 4
Note X X D A C G

Dsus (V)
Finger X X 0 1 3 4
Scale X X 1 5 1 4
Note X X D A D G

Dsus2 (V)
Finger X X 0 1 3 0
Scale X X 1 5 1 2
Note X X D A D E

Add9 Chords

Gadd9 (I)
Finger 3 X 0 2 0 4
Scale 1 X 5 2 3 1
Note G X D A B G

Cadd9 (IV)
Finger X 3 2 0 4 0
Scale X 1 3 5 2 3
Note X C E G D E

Dadd9 (V)
Finger X X 0 1 4 1
Scale X X 1 5 2 3
Note X X D A E F#

Dadd9 (V)
7th
Finger X X 0 3 4 0
Scale X X 1 1 3 2
Note X X D D F# E

Em Harmonic Chords

B (III)
Finger X 1 3 4 2 1
Scale X 1 5 1 3 5
Note X B F# B D# F#

B7 (III7)
Finger X 2 1 3 0 4
Scale X 1 3 b7 1 5
Note X B D# A B F#

74

Dominant 7th (Blues) Chords

G7 (I7)
- Finger: 3 2 4 0 0 1
- Scale: 1 3 ♭7 1 3 ♭7
- Note: G B F G B F

G7 (I7) — 3rd
- Finger: 1 3 1 2 1 1
- Scale: 1 5 ♭7 3 5 1
- Note: G D F B D G

C7 (IV7)
- Finger: X 3 2 4 1 0
- Scale: X 1 3 ♭7 1 3
- Note: X C E B♭ C E

C7 (IV7) — 3rd
- Finger: X 1 3 1 4 1
- Scale: X 1 5 ♭7 3 5
- Note: X C G B♭ E G

D7 (V7)
- Finger: T X 0 1 3 2
- Scale: 3 X 1 5 ♭7 3
- Note: F# X D A C F#

D7 (V7) — 3rd
- Finger: X 3 2 4 1 X
- Scale: X 1 3 ♭7 1 X
- Note: X D F# C D X

Quality Change Chords

A (II) — V
- Finger: X 0 1 2 3 0
- Scale: X 1 5 1 3 5
- Note: X A E A C# E

Cm (iv) — I, iv, IV — 3rd
- Finger: X 1 3 4 2 1
- Scale: X 1 5 1 ♭3 5
- Note: X C G C E♭ G

B (III) — vi
- Finger: X 1 2 3 4 1
- Scale: X 1 5 1 3 5
- Note: X B F# B D# F#

Dm (v) — I
- Finger: X X 0 2 3 1
- Scale: X X 1 5 1 ♭3
- Note: X X D A D F

E (VI) — ii
- Finger: 0 2 3 1 0 0
- Scale: 1 5 1 3 5 1
- Note: E B E G# B E

F#m (vii) — iii
- Finger: 1 3 4 1 1 1
- Scale: 1 5 1 ♭3 5 1
- Note: F# C# F# A C# F#

F# (VII) — iii
- Finger: 1 3 4 2 1 1
- Scale: 1 5 1 3 5 1
- Note: F# C# F# A# C# F#

Gm (i) — 3rd
- Finger: 1 3 4 1 1 1
- Scale: 1 5 1 ♭3 5 1
- Note: G D G B♭ D G

Additional Diatonic Extensions

GMaj7 (I) — 3rd
- Finger: 1 X 3 4 2 X
- Scale: 1 X 7 3 5 X
- Note: G X F# B D X

G6 (I)
- Finger: 2 X 1 4 3 X
- Scale: 1 X 6 3 5 X
- Note: G X E B D X

G6/9 (I)
- Finger: 3 X 0 2 0 0
- Scale: 1 X 5 2 3 6
- Note: G X D A B E

Am6 (ii) — 4th
- Finger: X 0 1 3 3 3
- Scale: X 1 6 ♭3 5 1
- Note: X A F# C E A

Amadd9 (ii)
- Finger: X 0 2 4 1 0
- Scale: X 1 5 2 ♭3 5
- Note: X A E B C E

Am9 (ii) — 5th
- Finger: X 0 2 3 0 0
- Scale: X 1 ♭7 3 2 5
- Note: X A G C B E

Bm7/11 (iii)
- Finger: 0 0 1 3 2 1
- Scale: 4 ♭7 4 1 ♭3 5
- Note: E A E B D F#

Bmadd11 (iii)
- Finger: 0 1 1 3 2 1
- Scale: 4 1 4 1 ♭3 5
- Note: E B E B D F#

CMaj7 (IV) — 3rd
- Finger: X 1 3 2 4 1
- Scale: X 1 5 7 3 5
- Note: X C G B E G

C6 (IV)
- Finger: X 4 2 3 1 0
- Scale: X 1 3 6 1 3
- Note: X C E A C E

CMaj9 (IV)
- Finger: X 2 1 4 3 0
- Scale: X 1 3 7 2 3
- Note: X C E B D E

D9 (V7) — 4th
- Finger: X 2 1 3 3 3
- Scale: X 1 3 ♭7 2 5
- Note: X D F# C E A

D7/11 (V7) — 5th
- Finger: X 1 1 1 3 1
- Scale: X 1 4 ♭7 3 5
- Note: X D G C F# A

D13 (V7) — 4th
- Finger: X 2 1 3 3 4
- Scale: X 1 3 ♭7 2 6
- Note: X D F# C E B

Em9 (vi)
- Finger: 0 1 2 0 4 3
- Scale: 1 5 1 ♭3 ♭7 2
- Note: E B E G D F#

Emadd9 (vi)
- Finger: 0 2 3 0 0 4
- Scale: 1 5 1 ♭3 5 2
- Note: E B E G B F#

Emadd9 (vi)
- Finger: 0 1 4 0 0 0
- Scale: 1 5 2 ♭3 5 1
- Note: E B F# G B E

F#m7♭5 (viiø7) — 4th
- Finger: X X 1 3 3 3
- Scale: X X 1 ♭5 ♭7 ♭3
- Note: X X F# C E A

F#m7♭5 (viiø7)
- Finger: X X 1 3 3 3
- Scale: X X 1 ♭3 ♭5 ♭7
- Note: X X F# A C E

F#°(vii°)
- Finger: T X 4 2 1 X
- Scale: 1 X 1 ♭3 ♭5 X
- Note: F# X F# A C X

*The m7♭5 is also referred to as a half diminished chord and can be written as a degree symbol with a slash through it.

Chord Formula Worksheet Up The Neck - Key of G and Em

G (I) — 3rd
Finger 1 3 4 2 1 1
Scale 1 5 1 3 5 1
Note G D G B D G

G (I) — 5th
Finger X X 1 2 4 3
Scale 3 5 1 5 1 3
Note B D G D G B

G (I) — 7th
Finger X 4 3 1 2 1
Scale 5 1 3 5 1 3
Note D G B D G B

G (I) — 10th
Finger X 1 2 3 4 1
Scale 5 1 5 1 3 5
Note D G D G B D

I - (1, 3, 5) Extensions - (2), (4), (6), (7)

C (IV) — 3rd
Finger X 1 2 3 4 1
Scale 5 1 5 1 3 5
Note G C G C E G

C (IV) — 5th
Finger 3 2 1 1 1 4
Scale 1 3 5 1 3 1
Note C E G C E C

C (IV) — 8th
Finger 1 3 4 2 1 1
Scale 1 5 1 3 5 1
Note C G C E G C

C (IV) — 10th
Finger X X 1 2 4 3
Scale 3 5 1 5 1 3
Note E G C G C E

IV - (1, 3, 5) Extensions - (2), (b5), (6), (7)

D (V) — 3rd
Finger X 4 3 1 2 1
Scale 5 1 3 5 1 3
Note A D F# A D F#

D (V) — 5th
Finger X 1 2 3 4 1
Scale 5 1 1 3 5
Note A D A D F# A

D (V) — 7th
Finger 3 2 1 1 1 4
Scale 1 3 5 1 3 1
Note D F# A D F# D

D (V) — 10th
Finger 1 3 4 2 1 1
Scale 1 5 1 3 5 1
Note D A D F# A D

V - (1, 3, 5) Extensions - (2), (4), (6), (b7)

Em (vi)
Finger X X 1 3 4 2
Scale b3 5 1 5 1 b3
Note G B E B E G

Em (vi) — 3rd
Finger X 4 2 1 3 X
Scale 5 1 b3 5 1 b3
Note B E G B E G

Em (vi) — 7th
Finger X 1 3 4 2 1
Scale 5 1 5 1 b3 5
Note B E B E G B

Em (vi) — 8th
Finger 4 2 1 1 X X
Scale 1 b3 5 1 b3 1
Note E G B E G E

vi - (1, b3, 5) Extensions - (2), (4), (#5), (b7)

Am (ii)
Finger 4 2 1 1 X X
Scale 1 b3 5 1 b3 1
Note A C E A C A

Am (ii) — 5th
Finger 1 3 4 1 1 1
Scale 1 5 1 b3 5 1
Note A E A C E A

Am (ii) — 7th
Finger X X 1 3 4 2
Scale b3 5 1 5 1 b3
Note C E A E A C

Am (ii) — 8th
Finger X 4 2 1 3 X
Scale 5 1 b3 5 1 b3
Note E A C E A C

ii - (1, b3, 5) Extensions - (2), (4), (6), (b7)

Bm (iii) — 3rd
Finger 4 2 1 1 X X
Scale 1 b3 5 1 b3 1
Note B D F# B D B

Bm (iii) — 7th
Finger 1 3 4 1 1 1
Scale 1 5 1 b3 5 1
Note B F# B D F# B

Bm (iii) — 9th
Finger X X 1 3 4 2
Scale b3 5 1 5 1 b3
Note D F# B F# B D

Bm (iii) — 10th
Finger X 4 2 1 3 X
Scale 5 1 b3 5 1 b3
Note F# B D F# B D

iii - (1, b3, 5) Extensions - (b2), (4), (#5), (b7)

* Order of notes as you move up and down a string.

1
b2 (b9)
2 (sus2, 9)
#2 (#9) / (b3 minor)
3
4 (sus, 11)
b5 (b5, #11)
5
#5 (#5, b13) / (+, aug)
6 (6, 13)
b7 (7) Dominant 7th
7 (Maj7)
1

E A D G B E

| | | | C | | |
| F# | B | E | A | | F# |
| G | C | | | D | G | 3rd
| | | F# | B | | |
| A | D | G | C | E | A | 5th
| B | E | A | D | F# | B | 7th
| C | | | | G | C |
| | F# | B | E | | | 9th
| D | G | C | | A | D |
| | | F# | | | |
| E | A | D | G | B | E | 12th
| | | | C | | |

CHORD SUBSTITUTIONS - KEY OF G AND Em

1. CHORD EMBELLISHMENTS - EXTENSIONS AND ALTERATIONS

2. MAJOR, MINOR AND DOMINANT SUBSTITUTIONS

Major   **G (I)** Relative minor - **Em (vi)** or Common Tones - **Bm (iii)**

          C (IV) Relative minor - **Am (ii)** or Common Tones - **Em (vi)**

          D (V) Relative minor - **Bm (iii)** or Common Tones - **F#m (vii)**

minor   **Em (vi)** Relative Major - **G (I)** or Common Tones - **C (IV)**

          Am (ii) Relative Major - **C (IV)** or Common Tones - **F (bVII)**

          Bm (iii) Relative Major - **D (V)** or Common Tones - **G (I)**

7th   **D7(V7)** Common Tones - **F#°7 (VII°7)** or **Bm (iii)** or Tritone - **Ab7**

3. BACKCYCLING (CIRCLE OF 5THS)

(Bm7-Em7-Am7-D7) - G	**(Em7-Am7-Dm7-G7) - C**	**(F#m7-Bm7-Em7-A7) - D**
(Abm7-C#m7-F#m7-B7) - Em	**(C#m7-F#m7-Bm7-E7) - Am**	**(Ebm7-Abm7-C#m7-F#7) - Bm**

Use the 5th of the chord you're going to to find the letter name of the chord that should proceed it. Here are a couple of variations on backcycling (B7, E7, A7, D7) - G or (Bm7, E7, Am7, D7) - G. The ii-V7 is a very common substitute for a V7 chord. Also don't forget you can just add the secondary dominants before a chord.

4. HALF STEP PROGRESSIONS

This is usually some type of dominant 7th chord.

Major	**Gb7-G**	**G#7-G**	**B7-C**	**C#7-C**	**Db7-D**	**D#7-D**
minor	**Eb7-Em**	**F7-Em**	**Ab7-Am**	**A#7-Am**	**Bb7-Bm**	**C7-Bm**

5. PASSING CHORDS

°7   Diminished 7th chords can be used between diatonic chords to create a *chromatic* chord progression.

          GMaj7(I)-G#°7-Am7(ii)-A#°7-Bm7(iii)-CMaj7(IV)-C#°7-D7(V7)-D#°7-Em7(vi)

Diatonic   You can also use diatonic chords to fill-in the gaps between chords.

          Here is an example of a *diatonic* type passing chord progression:

          original G(I)-G(I)-G(I)-C(IV) becomes G(I)-Am(ii)-Bm(iii)-C(IV).

6. TRITONE SUBSTITUTION

You can substitute a dominant 7th chord with another dominant 7th chord based on the flat five of the original dominant 7th chord. Below are the original 7th chords followed by their tritone substitution. You can also use these substitutions in your backcycling to create chromatic bass lines.

A7 to Eb7	Bb7 to E7	B7 to F7	C7 to Gb7	C#7 to G7	Db7 to G7	D7 to Ab7
Eb7 to A7	E7 to Bb7	F7 to B7	F#7 to C7	Gb7 to C7	G7 to Db7	Ab7 to D7

7. QUALITY CHANGE CHORDS

Majors - (minors, Dominant 7ths), Minors - (Majors, Dominant 7ths), Dominant 7ths - (Majors, minors)

Four Note Extensions Up The Neck - Key of G and Em

* Use the sections on *Bass Notes* and *Optional Notes* to find other notes you can add to these chords. Also don't forget you don't have to play every note in the chord, only the essential notes that convey the chords family and quality of sound.

GMaj7 (I) — 3rd
Finger	1	X	3	4	2	X
Scale	1	5	7	3	5	1
Note	G	D	F#	B	D	G

GMaj7 (I)
Finger	T	X	4	3	2	1
Scale	1	X	1	3	5	7
Note	G	X	G	B	D	F#

GMaj7 (I) — 5th
Finger	X	X	1	4	4	4
Scale	X	X	1	5	7	3
Note	X	X	G	D	F#	B

GMaj7 (I) — 7th
Finger	X	4	3	1	1	1
Scale	X	1	3	5	7	3
Note	X	G	B	D	F#	B

GMaj7 (I) — 10th
Finger	X	1	3	2	4	1
Scale	X	1	5	7	3	5
Note	X	B	D	F#	B	D

CMaj7 (IV) — 3rd
Finger	X	1	3	2	4	1
Scale	X	1	5	7	3	5
Note	X	C	G	B	E	G

CMaj7 (IV) — 5th
Finger	X	X	1	1	1	4
Scale	X	X	5	1	3	7
Note	X	X	G	C	E	B

CMaj7 (IV) — 8th
Finger	1	X	3	4	2	X
Scale	1	5	7	3	5	1
Note	C	G	B	E	G	C

CMaj7 (IV) — 7th
Finger	T	X	4	3	2	1
Scale	1	X	1	3	5	7
Note	C	X	C	E	G	B

CMaj7 (IV) — 10th
Finger	X	X	1	4	4	4
Scale	X	X	1	5	7	3
Note	X	X	C	G	B	E

D7 (V7)
Finger	X	3	2	4	1	X
Scale	X	1	3	b7	1	3
Note	X	D	F#	C	D	F#

D7 (V7) — 5th
Finger	X	1	2	1	4	1
Scale	X	1	5	b7	3	5
Note	X	D	A	C	F#	A

D7 (V7) — 7th
Finger	X	X	1	1	1	2
Scale	X	X	5	1	3	b7
Note	X	X	A	D	F#	C

D7 (V7) — 10th
Finger	1	3	1	2	1	1
Scale	1	5	b7	3	5	1
Note	D	A	C	F#	A	D

D7 (V7) — 12th
Finger	X	X	1	3	2	4
Scale	X	X	1	5	b7	3
Note	X	X	D	A	C	F#

Em7 (vi)
Finger	0	2	3	0	4	0
Scale	1	5	1	b3	b7	1
Note	E	B	E	G	D	E

Em7 (vi)
Finger	X	X	1	3	2	2
Scale	X	X	1	5	b7	b3
Note	X	X	E	B	D	G

Em7 (vi) — 5th
Finger	X	2	1	3	1	4
Scale	X	1	b3	b7	1	5
Note	X	E	G	D	E	B

Em7 (vi) — 7th
Finger	X	1	3	1	2	1
Scale	X	1	5	b7	b3	5
Note	X	E	B	D	G	B

Em7 (vi) — 8th
Finger	X	X	2	3	1	4
Scale	X	X	5	1	b3	b7
Note	X	X	B	E	G	D

Am7 (ii)
Finger	X	0	2	3	1	4
Scale	X	1	5	1	b3	b7
Note	X	A	E	A	C	G

Am7 (ii) — 5th
Finger	1	3	1	1	1	1
Scale	1	5	b7	b3	5	1
Note	A	E	G	C	E	A

Am7 (ii) — 7th
Finger	X	X	1	3	2	2
Scale	X	X	1	5	b7	b3
Note	X	X	A	E	G	C

Am7 (ii) — 8th
Finger	X	0	3	2	1	0
Scale	X	1	b3	5	b7	5
Note	X	A	C	E	G	E

Am7 (ii) — 10th
Finger	X	2	1	3	1	4
Scale	X	1	b3	b7	1	5
Note	X	A	C	G	A	E

Bm7 (iii)
Finger	X	1	0	2	0	3
Scale	X	1	b3	b7	1	5
Note	X	B	D	A	B	F#

Bm7 (iii) — 3rd
Finger	X	X	2	3	1	4
Scale	X	X	5	1	b3	b7
Note	X	X	F#	B	D	A

Bm7 (iii) — 7th
Finger	1	3	1	1	1	1
Scale	1	5	b7	b3	5	1
Note	B	F#	A	D	F#	B

Bm7 (iii) — 9th
Finger	X	X	1	3	2	2
Scale	X	X	1	5	b7	b3
Note	X	X	B	F#	A	D

Bm7 (iii) — 12th
Finger	X	2	1	3	1	4
Scale	X	1	b3	b7	1	5
Note	X	B	D	A	B	F#

Classic Rock Power Chord & Rock-n-Roll Worksheet - Key of G and Em

I, IV & V Power Chords (1 and 5)

G5 (I)
X O O

Finger 3 X 0 0 4 4
Scale 1 X 5 1 5 1
Note G X D G D G

G5 (I)
X X X — 3rd

Scale 1 5 1 X X X
Note G D G X X X

G5 (I)
X X — 10th

Scale 5 1 5 1 X X
Note D G D G X X

Flat Major Power Chords

B♭5 (♭III)
X X

Scale 5 1 5 1 X X
Note F B♭ F B♭ X X

B♭5 (♭III)
X X X — 6th

Scale 1 5 1 X X X
Note B♭ F B♭ X X X

C5 (IV)
X X O

Finger X 3 X 0 1 4
Scale X 1 X 5 1 5
Note X C X G C G

C5 (IV)
X X — 3rd

Scale 5 1 5 1 X X
Note G C G C X X

C5 (IV)
X X X — 8th

Scale 1 5 1 X X X
Note C G C X X X

E♭5 (♭VI)
X X — 6th

Scale 5 1 5 1 X X
Note B♭ E♭ B♭ E♭ X X

E♭5 (♭VI)
X X X — 11th

Scale 1 5 1 X X X
Note E♭ B♭ E♭ X X X

D5 (V)
X O O X

Finger X 0 0 1 3 X
Scale X 5 1 5 1 X
Note X A D A D X

D5 (V)
X X — 5th

Scale 5 1 5 1 X X
Note A D A D X X

D5 (V)
X X X — 10th

Scale 1 5 1 X X X
Note D A D X X X

F5 (♭VII)
X X

Scale 1 5 1 X X X
Note F C F X X X

F5 (♭VII)
X X — 8th

Scale 5 1 5 1 X X
Note C F C F X X

Combinations of notes that can be used to make Power Chords - 1, 5 or 1, 5, 1 called 1st Inversion Power Chords
5, 1 or 5, 1, 5 called 2nd Inversion Power Chords

ii, iii, vi Power Chords

A5 (ii)
O O X X

Scale 5 1 5 1 X X
Note E A E A X X

A5 (ii)
X X X — 5th

Scale 1 5 1 X X X
Note A E A X X X

Csus2 (IV)
X X O X

Finger X 2 X 0 3 X
Scale X 1 X 5 2 X
Note X C X G D X

Other Power Chord Shapes

X X

Scale X X 5 1 5 1

X X

Scale X 5 1 5 1 X

B5 (iii)
X X

Scale 5 1 5 1 X X
Note F♯ B F♯ B X X

B5 (iii)
X X X — 7th

Scale 1 5 1 X X X
Note B F♯ B X X X

Dsus2 (V)
X O

Finger T X 0 1 3 0
Scale 3 X 1 5 1 2
Note X X D A D X

X5add9
X X X

Scale 1 5 2 X X X

X5add9
X X X

Scale X 1 5 2 X X

E5 (vi)
O X X X

Scale 1 5 1 X X X
Note E B E X X X

E5 (vi)
X X — 7th

Scale 5 1 5 1 X X
Note B E B E X X

Rock-n-Roll Chord Shapes for I, IV and V Chords

X5 / X6 / X7
X X X X

Scale 1 5 X X X X

X5 / X6 / X7
X X X X

Scale X 1 5 X X X

X5 / X6 / X7
X X X X

Scale X X 1 5 X X

Key of G and Em Triad Worksheet (1st, 2nd and 3rd strings)

Key of G and Em Triad Worksheet (2nd, 3rd and 4th strings)

Key of G and Em Triad Worksheet (3rd, 4th and 5th strings)

C (IV) — Scale 1 3 5
G (I) — Scale 3 5 1
Em (vi) — Scale 5 1 ♭3
F (♭VII) — Scale 5 1 3
G (I) — Scale 3 5 1
G (I) 4th — Scale 5 1 3
G (I) 7th — Scale 1 3 5

D (V) — Scale 1 3 5
Am (ii) — Scale ♭3 5 1
F#o (viio) — Scale ♭5 1 ♭3
B♭ (♭III) 3rd — Scale 3 5 1
C (IV) — Scale 1 3 5
C (IV) 5th — Scale 3 5 1
C (IV) 9th — Scale 5 1 3

Em(vi) 4th — Scale 1 ♭3 5
Bm (iii) 4th — Scale ♭3 5 1
G (I) 4th — Scale 5 1 3
E♭ (♭VI) 3rd — Scale 1 3 5
D (V) — Scale 1 3 5
D (V) 7th — Scale 3 5 1
D (V) 11th — Scale 5 1 3

F#o (viio) 5th — Scale 1 ♭3 ♭5
C (IV) 5th — Scale 3 5 1
Am (ii) 5th — Scale 5 1 ♭3
F (♭VII) 5th — Scale 1 3 5

G (I) 7th — Scale 1 3 5
D (V) 7th — Scale 3 5 1
Bm (iii) 7th — Scale 5 1 ♭3
B♭ (♭III) 7th — Scale 5 1 3
Em (vi) — Scale 5 1 ♭3
Em(vi) 4th — Scale 1 ♭3 5
Em (vi) 9th — Scale ♭3 5 1

Am(ii) 9th — Scale 1 ♭3 5
Em (vi) 9th — Scale ♭3 5 1
C (IV) 9th — Scale 5 1 3
E♭ (♭VI) 8th — Scale 3 5 1
Am (ii) — Scale ♭3 5 1
Am (ii) 5th — Scale 5 1 ♭3
Am(ii) 9th — Scale 1 ♭3 5

Bm(iii) 11th — Scale 1 ♭3 5
F#o (viio) 10th — Scale ♭3 ♭5 1
D (V) 11th — Scale 5 1 3
F (♭VII) 10th — Scale 3 5 1
Bm (iii) 4th — Scale ♭3 5 1
Bm (iii) 7th — Scale 5 1 ♭3
Bm(iii) 11th — Scale 1 ♭3 5

C (IV) 12th — Scale 1 3 5
G (I) 12th — Scale 3 5 1
Em (vi) 12th — Scale 5 1 ♭3
B♭ (♭III) 10th — Scale 1 3 5

D (V) 14th — Scale 1 3 5
Am (ii) 14th — Scale ♭3 5 1
F#o (viio) 14th — Scale ♭5 1 ♭3
E♭ (♭VI) 12th — Scale 5 1 3
F#o (viio) — Scale ♭5 1 ♭3
F#o (viio) 5th — Scale 1 ♭3 ♭5
F#o (viio) 10th — Scale ♭3 ♭5 1

Slash Chord Worksheet

Key of G and Em

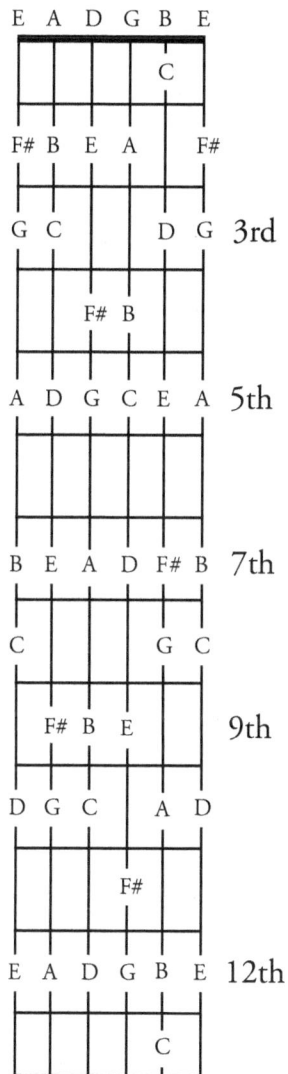

E	A	D	G	B	E	
				C		
F#	B	E	A		F#	
G	C			D	G	3rd
		F#	B			5th
A	D	G	C	E	A	5th
B	E	A	D	F#	B	7th
C				G	C	
		F#	B	E		9th
D	G	C		A	D	
			F#			
E	A	D	G	B	E	12th
				C		

Diatonic and Secondary Dominant Chords

D (I) — X X O
Finger X X 0 1 3 2
Scale X X 1 5 1 3
Note X X D A D F#

G (IV) — O O O
Finger 3 2 0 0 0 4
Scale 1 3 5 1 3 1
Note G B D G B G

A (V) — X O O
Finger X 0 1 2 3 0
Scale X 1 5 1 3 5
Note X A E A C# E

A7 (V7/I) — X O O O
Finger X 0 1 0 2 0
Scale X 1 5 ♭7 3 5
Note X A E G C# E

D7 (V7/IV) — X X O
Finger X X 0 2 1 3
Scale X X 1 5 ♭7 3
Note X X D A C F#

E7 (V7/V) — O O O
Finger 0 2 0 1 0 0
Scale 1 5 ♭7 3 5 1
Note E B D G# B E

Bm (vi) — X
Finger X 1 3 4 2 1
Scale X 1 5 1 ♭3 5
Note X B F# B D F#

Em (ii) — O O O
Finger 0 2 3 0 0 0
Scale 1 5 1 ♭3 5 1
Note E B E G B E

F#m (iii)
Finger 1 3 4 1 1 1
Scale 1 5 1 ♭3 5 1
Note F# C# F# A C# F#

F#7 (V7/vi) — X
Finger X 3 4 2 1 0
Scale X 5 1 3 5 ♭7
Note X C# F# A# C# E

B7 (V7/ii) — X O
Finger X 2 1 3 0 4
Scale X 1 3 ♭7 1 5
Note X B D# A B F#

C#7 (V7/iii) — X X
Finger X 3 2 4 1 X
Scale X 1 3 ♭7 1 X
Note X C# F B C# X

Extensions

DMaj7 (I) — X X O
Finger X X 0 1 2 3
Scale X X 1 5 7 3
Note X X D A C# F#

GMaj7 (IV) — X O O O
Finger 3 X 0 0 0 2
Scale 1 X 5 1 3 7
Note G X D G B F#

A7 (V7) — X O O O
Finger X 0 1 0 2 0
Scale X 1 5 ♭7 3 5
Note X A E G C# E

Bm7 (vi) — X
Finger X 1 3 1 2 1
Scale X 1 5 ♭7 ♭3 5
Note X B F# A D F#

Em7 (ii) — O O O O O
Finger 0 2 0 0 0 0
Scale 1 5 ♭7 ♭3 5 1
Note E B D G B E

F#m7 (iii)
Finger 1 3 1 1 1 1
Scale 1 5 ♭7 ♭3 5 1
Note F# C# E A C# F#

Flat Majors

F (♭III)
Finger 1 3 4 2 1 1
Scale 1 5 1 3 5 1
Note F C F A C F

B♭ (♭VI) — X
Finger X 1 2 3 4 1
Scale X 1 5 1 3 5
Note X B♭ F B♭ D F

C (♭VII) — X O O
Finger X 3 2 0 1 0
Scale X 1 3 5 1 3
Note X C E G C E

Suspended Chords

Dsus (I) — X X O
Finger X X 0 1 3 4
Scale X X 1 5 1 4
Note X X D A D G

Dsus2 (I) — X X O
Finger X X 0 1 3 0
Scale X X 1 5 1 2
Note X X D A D E

Gsus2 (IV) — X O
Finger 2 X 0 1 3 3
Scale 1 X 5 2 5 1
Note G X D A D G

A7sus (V7) — X O O
Finger X 0 1 0 3 0
Scale X 1 5 ♭7 4 5
Note X A E G D E

Asus (V) — X O
Finger X 0 1 2 3 0
Scale X 1 5 1 4 5
Note X A E A D E

Asus2 (V) — X O O
Finger X 0 1 2 0 0
Scale X 1 5 1 2 5
Note X A E A B E

Add9 Chords

Dadd9 (I) — X X O O — 7th
Finger X X 0 3 4 0
Scale X X 1 1 3 2
Note X X D D F# E

Gadd9 (IV) — X O
Finger 2 X 0 1 0 3
Scale 1 X 5 2 3 1
Note G X D A B G

Aadd9 (V) — X O O
Finger X 0 1 4 2 0
Scale X 1 5 2 3 5
Note X A E B C# E

Aadd9 (V) — X O O O — 6th
Finger X 0 2 1 0 0
Scale X 1 1 3 2 5
Note X A A C# B E

Bm Harmonic Chords

F# (III)
Finger 1 3 4 2 1 1
Scale 1 5 1 3 5 1
Note F# C# F# A# C# F#

F#7 (III7)
Finger 1 3 1 2 1 1
Scale 1 5 ♭7 3 5 1
Note F# C# E A# C# F#

Dominant 7th (Blues) Chords

D7 (I7)
Finger X X 0 2 1 3
Scale X X 1 5 ♭7 3
Note X X D A C F♯

D7 (I7) 5th
Finger X 1 3 1 4 1
Scale X 1 5 ♭7 3 5
Note X D A C F♯ A

G7 (IV7)
Finger 3 2 0 0 0 1
Scale 1 3 5 1 3 ♭7
Note G B D G B F

G7 (IV7) 3rd
Finger 1 3 1 2 1 1
Scale 1 5 ♭7 3 5 1
Note G D F B D G

A7 (V7)
Finger X 0 1 0 2 0
Scale X 1 5 ♭7 3 5
Note X A E G C♯ E

A7 (V7) 5th
Finger 1 3 1 2 1 1
Scale 1 5 ♭7 3 5 1
Note A E G C♯ E A

Quality Change Chords

E (II) V
Finger 0 2 3 1 0 0
Scale 1 5 1 3 5 1
Note E B E G♯ B E

Gm (iv) I iv IV 3rd
Finger 1 3 4 1 1 1
Scale 1 5 1 ♭3 5 1
Note G D G B♭ D G

F♯ (III) vi
Finger 1 3 4 2 1 1
Scale 1 5 1 3 5 1
Note F♯ C♯ F♯ A♯ C♯ F♯

Am (v) I
Finger X 0 2 3 1 0
Scale X 1 5 1 ♭3 5
Note X A E A C E

B (VI) ii
Finger X 1 2 3 4 1
Scale X 1 5 1 3 5
Note X B F♯ B D♯ F♯

C♯m (vii) iii 4th
Finger X 1 3 4 2 1
Scale X 1 5 1 ♭3 5
Note X C♯ G♯ C♯ E G♯

C♯ (VII) iii 4th
Finger X 1 2 3 4 1
Scale X 1 5 1 3 5
Note X C♯ G♯ C♯ F G♯

Dm (i)
Finger X X 0 2 3 1
Scale X X 1 5 1 ♭3
Note X X D A D F

Additional Diatonic Extensions

D6 (I)
Finger X X 0 1 0 2
Scale X X 1 5 6 3
Note X X D A B F♯

DMaj9 (I) 4th
Finger X 2 1 4 3 X
Scale X 1 3 7 2 X
Note X D F♯ C♯ E X

DMaj9add13 (I) 4th
Finger X 2 1 4 0 0
Scale X 1 3 7 6 2
Note X D F♯ C♯ B E

Em7 (ii)
Finger 0 1 2 0 3 0
Scale 1 5 1 ♭3 ♭7 1
Note E B E G D E

Em6 (ii)
Finger 0 1 2 0 3 0
Scale 1 5 1 ♭3 6 1
Note E B E G C♯ E

Em9 (ii)
Finger 0 1 2 0 4 3
Scale 1 5 1 ♭3 ♭7 2
Note E B E G D F♯

F♯m7/11 (iii)
Finger X 3 4 1 0 0
Scale X 5 1 ♭3 4 ♭7
Note X C♯ F♯ A B E

F♯madd11 (iii)
Finger 1 1 3 1 1 1
Scale 1 4 1 ♭3 5 1
Note F♯ B F♯ A C♯ F♯

GMaj7 (IV) 3rd
Finger 1 X 3 4 2 X
Scale 1 X 7 3 5 X
Note G X F♯ B D X

G6 (IV)
Finger 2 X 1 4 3 X
Scale 1 X 6 3 5 X
Note G X E B D X

G6/9 (IV)
Finger 3 X 0 1 0 0
Scale 1 X 5 2 3 6
Note G X D A B E

A9 (V7)
Finger X 0 4 3 1 0
Scale X 1 ♭7 2 3 5
Note X A G B C♯ E

A11 (V7)
Finger X 0 0 3 1 2
Scale X 1 4 2 3 ♭7
Note X A D B C♯ G

A7add13 (V7)
Finger X 0 1 0 2 3
Scale X 1 5 ♭7 3 6
Note X A E G C♯ F♯

Bm9 (vi)
Finger X 2 0 3 3 3
Scale X 1 ♭3 ♭7 2 5
Note X B D A C♯ F♯

Bm11 (vi)
Finger X 1 0 2 3 0
Scale X 1 ♭3 ♭7 2 4
Note X B D A C♯ E

Bm7add11 (vi) 7th
Finger 1 X 2 3 0 0
Scale 1 X ♭7 ♭3 1 4
Note B X A D B E

C♯m7♭5 (vii∅7) 4th
Finger X 1 3 2 4 X
Scale X 1 ♭5 ♭7 ♭3 X
Note X C♯ G B E X

C♯m7♭5 (vii∅7)
Finger X 3 1 0 0 0
Scale X 1 ♭3 ♭5 ♭7 ♭3
Note X C♯ E G B E

C♯o (viio) 4th
Finger X 1 2 0 3 0
Scale X 1 ♭5 ♭5 ♭3 ♭3
Note X C♯ G G E E

*The m7♭5 is also referred to as a half diminished chord and can be written as a degree symbol with a slash through it.

Chord Formula Worksheet Up The Neck - Key of D and Bm

D (I)
Finger	X	4	3	1	2	1
Scale	5	1	3	5	1	3
Note	A	D	F#	A	D	F#

D (I) 5th
Finger	X	1	2	3	4	1
Scale	5	1	5	1	3	5
Note	A	D	A	D	F#	A

D (I) 7th
Finger	3	2	1	1	1	4
Scale	1	3	5	1	3	1
Note	D	F#	A	D	F#	D

D (I) 10th
Finger	1	3	4	2	1	1
Scale	1	5	1	3	5	1
Note	D	A	D	F#	A	D

I - (1, 3, 5) Extensions - (2), (4), (6), (7)

G (IV) 3rd
Finger	1	3	4	2	1	1
Scale	1	5	1	3	5	1
Note	G	D	G	B	D	G

G (IV) 5th
Finger	X	X	1	2	4	3
Scale	3	5	1	5	1	3
Note	B	D	G	D	G	B

G (IV) 7th
Finger	X	4	3	1	2	1
Scale	5	1	3	5	1	3
Note	D	G	B	D	G	B

G (IV) 10th
Finger	X	1	2	3	4	1
Scale	5	1	5	1	3	5
Note	D	G	D	G	B	D

IV - (1, 3, 5) Extensions - (2), (b5), (6), (7)

A (V)
Finger	3	2	1	1	1	4
Scale	1	3	5	1	3	1
Note	A	C#	E	A	C#	A

A (V) 5th
Finger	1	3	4	2	1	1
Scale	1	5	1	3	5	1
Note	A	E	A	C#	E	A

A (V) 7th
Finger	X	X	1	2	4	3
Scale	3	5	1	5	1	3
Note	C#	E	A	E	A	C#

A (V) 9th
Finger	X	4	3	1	2	1
Scale	5	1	3	5	1	3
Note	E	A	C#	E	A	C#

V - (1, 3, 5) Extensions - (2), (4), (6), (b7)

Bm (vi) 3rd
Finger	4	2	1	1	X	X
Scale	1	b3	5	1	b3	1
Note	B	D	F#	B	D	B

Bm (vi) 7th
Finger	1	3	4	1	1	1
Scale	1	5	1	b3	5	1
Note	B	F#	B	D	F#	B

Bm (vi) 9th
Finger	X	X	1	3	4	2
Scale	b3	5	1	5	1	b3
Note	D	F#	B	F#	B	D

Bm (vi) 10th
Finger	X	4	2	1	3	X
Scale	5	1	b3	5	1	b3
Note	F#	B	D	F#	B	D

vi - (1, b3, 5) Extensions - (2), (4), (#5), (b7)

Em (ii)
Finger	X	X	1	3	4	2
Scale	b3	5	1	5	1	b3
Note	G	B	E	B	E	G

Em (ii) 3rd
Finger	X	4	2	1	3	X
Scale	5	1	b3	5	1	b3
Note	B	E	G	B	E	G

Em (ii) 7th
Finger	X	1	3	4	2	1
Scale	5	1	5	1	b3	5
Note	B	E	B	E	G	B

Em (ii) 8th
Finger	4	2	1	1	X	X
Scale	1	b3	5	1	b3	1
Note	E	G	B	E	G	E

ii - (1, b3, 5) Extensions - (2), (4), (6), (b7)

F#m (iii) 4th
Finger	X	X	1	3	4	2
Scale	b3	5	1	5	1	b3
Note	A	C#	F#	C#	F#	A

F#m (iii) 5th
Finger	X	4	2	1	3	X
Scale	5	1	b3	5	1	b3
Note	C#	F#	A	C#	F#	A

F#m (iii) 9th
Finger	X	1	3	4	2	1
Scale	5	1	5	1	b3	5
Note	C#	F#	C#	F#	A	C#

F#m (iii) 10th
Finger	4	2	1	1	X	X
Scale	1	b3	5	1	b3	1
Note	F#	A	C#	F#	A	F#

iii - (1, b3, 5) Extensions - (b2), (4), (#5), (b7)

* Order of notes as you move up and down a string.

1
b2 (b9)
2 (sus2, 9)
#2 (#9) / (b3 minor)
3
4 (sus, 11)
b5 (b5, #11)
5
#5 (#5, b13) / (+, aug)
6 (6, 13)
b7 (7) Dominant 7th
7 (Maj7)
1

E	A	D	G	B	E

| F# | B | E | A | C# | F# |
| G | | | | D | G | 3rd
| | C# | F# | B | | |
| A | D | G | | E | A | 5th
| | | C# | | | |
| B | E | A | D | F# | B | 7th
| | | | G | | |
| C# | F# | B | E | | C# | 9th
| D | G | | | A | D |
| | | C# | F# | | |
| E | A | D | G | B | E | 12th

86

CHORD SUBSTITUTIONS - KEY OF D AND Bm

1. CHORD EMBELLISHMENTS - EXTENSIONS AND ALTERATIONS

2. MAJOR, MINOR AND DOMINANT SUBSTITUTIONS

Major   **D (I)** Relative minor - **Bm (vi)** or Common Tones - **F#m (iii)**

         G (IV) Relative minor - **Em (ii)** or Common Tones - **Bm (vi)**

         A (V)   Relative minor - **F#m (iii)** or Common Tones - **C#m (vii)**

minor   **Bm (vi)** Relative Major - **D (I)** or Common Tones - **G (IV)**

         Em (ii) Relative Major - **G (IV)** or Common Tones - **C (bVII)**

         F#m (iii) Relative Major - **A (V)** or Common Tones - **D (I)**

7th   **A7(V7)** Common Tones - **C#^{o}7 (VII°7)** or **F#m (iii)** or Tritone - **Eb7**

3. BACKCYCLING (CIRCLE OF 5THS)

(F#m7-Bm7-Em7-A7) - D	(Bm7-Em7-Am7-D7) - G	(C#m7-F#m7-Bm7-E7) - A
(Ebm7-Abm7-C#m7-F#7) - Bm	(Abm7-C#m7-F#m7-B7) - Em	(Bbm7-Ebm7-Abm7-C#7) - F#m

Use the 5th of the chord you're going to to find the letter name of the chord that should proceed it. Here are a couple of variations on backcycling (F#7, B7, E7, A7) - D or (F#m7, B7, Em7, A7) - D. The ii-V7 is a very common substitute for a V7 chord. Also don't forget you can just add the secondary dominants before a chord.

4. HALF STEP PROGRESSIONS

This is usually some type of dominant 7th chord.

Major	Db7-D	D#7-D	Gb7-G	G#7-G	Ab7-A	A#7-A
minor	Bb7-Bm	C7-Bm	Eb7-Em	F7-Em	F7-F#m	G7-F#m

5. PASSING CHORDS

^{o}7   Diminished 7th chords can be used between diatonic chords to create a *chromatic* chord progression.

                 DMaj7(I)-D#^{o}7-Em7(ii)-F^{o}7-F#m7(iii)-GMaj7(IV)-G#^{o}7-A7(V7)-A#^{o}7-Bm7(vi)

Diatonic   You can also use diatonic chords to fill-in the gaps between chords.

                 Here is an example of a *diatonic* type passing chord progression:

                 original D(I)-D(I)-D(I)-G(IV) becomes D(I)-Em(ii)-F#m(iii)-G(IV).

6. TRITONE SUBSTITUTION

You can substitute a dominant 7th chord with another dominant 7th chord based on the flat five of the original dominant 7th chord. Below are the original 7th chords followed by their tritone substitution. You can also use these substitutions in your backcycling to create chromatic bass lines.

A7 to Eb7	Bb7 to E7	B7 to F7	C7 to Gb7	C#7 to G7	Db7 to G7	D7 to Ab7
Eb7 to A7	E7 to Bb7	F7 to B7	F#7 to C7	Gb7 to C7	G7 to Db7	Ab7 to D7

7. QUALITY CHANGE CHORDS

Majors - (minors, Dominant 7ths), Minors - (Majors, Dominant 7ths), Dominant 7ths - (Majors, minors)

Four Note Extensions Up The Neck - Key of D and Bm

* Use the sections on *Bass Notes* and *Optional Notes* to find other notes you can add to these chords. Also don't forget you don't have to play every note in the chord, only the essential notes that convey the chords family and quality of sound.

DMaj7 (I)

Finger	X	4	3	1	1	1
Scale	X	1	3	5	7	3
Note	X	D	F#	A	C#	F#

DMaj7 (I) — 5th

Finger	X	1	3	2	4	1
Scale	X	1	5	7	3	5
Note	X	D	A	C#	F#	A

DMaj7 (I) — 7th

Finger	X	X	1	1	1	2
Scale	X	X	5	1	3	7
Note	X	X	A	D	F#	C#

DMaj7 (I) — 10th

Finger	1	X	3	4	2	X
Scale	1	5	7	3	5	1
Note	D	A	C#	F#	A	D

DMaj7 (I) — 9th

Finger	T	X	4	3	2	1
Scale	1	X	1	3	5	7
Note	D	X	D	F#	A	C#

GMaj7 (IV) — 3rd

Finger	1	X	3	4	2	X
Scale	1	5	7	3	5	1
Note	G	D	F#	B	D	G

GMaj7 (IV)

Finger	T	X	4	3	2	1
Scale	1	X	1	3	5	7
Note	G	X	G	B	D	F#

GMaj7 (IV) — 5th

Finger	X	X	1	4	4	4
Scale	X	X	1	5	7	3
Note	X	X	G	D	F#	B

GMaj7 (IV) — 7th

Finger	X	4	3	1	1	1
Scale	X	1	3	5	7	3
Note	X	G	B	D	F#	B

GMaj7 (IV) — 10th

Finger	X	1	3	2	4	1
Scale	X	1	5	7	3	5
Note	X	B	D	F#	B	D

A7 (V7)

Finger	X	0	1	1	1	2
Scale	X	1	5	1	3	♭7
Note	X	A	E	A	C#	G

A7 (V7)

Finger	X	2	3	1	4	X
Scale	X	3	♭7	1	5	X
Note	X	C#	G	A	E	X

A7 (V7) — 5th

Finger	1	3	1	2	1	1
Scale	1	5	♭7	3	5	1
Note	A	E	G	C#	E	A

A7 (V7) — 7th

Finger	X	X	1	3	2	4
Scale	X	X	1	5	♭7	3
Note	X	X	A	E	G	C#

A7 (V7) — 9th

Finger	X	3	2	4	1	X
Scale	5	1	3	♭7	1	3
Note	E	A	C#	G	A	C#

Bm7 (vi)

Finger	X	1	0	2	0	3
Scale	X	1	♭3	♭7	1	5
Note	X	B	D	A	B	F#

Bm7 (vi) — 3rd

Finger	X	X	2	3	1	4
Scale	X	X	5	1	♭3	♭7
Note	X	X	F#	B	D	A

Bm7 (vi) — 7th

Finger	1	3	1	1	1	1
Scale	1	5	♭7	♭3	5	1
Note	B	F#	A	D	F#	B

Bm7 (vi) — 9th

Finger	X	X	1	3	2	2
Scale	X	X	1	5	♭7	♭3
Note	X	X	B	F#	A	D

Bm7 (vi) — 12th

Finger	X	2	1	3	1	4
Scale	X	1	♭3	♭7	1	5
Note	X	B	D	A	B	F#

Em7 (ii)

Finger	0	2	3	0	4	0
Scale	1	5	1	♭3	♭7	1
Note	E	B	E	G	D	E

Em7 (ii)

Finger	X	X	1	3	2	2
Scale	X	X	1	5	♭7	♭3
Note	X	X	E	B	D	G

Em7 (ii) — 5th

Finger	X	2	1	3	1	4
Scale	X	1	♭3	♭7	1	5
Note	X	E	G	D	E	B

Em7 (ii) — 7th

Finger	X	1	3	1	2	1
Scale	X	1	5	♭7	♭3	5
Note	X	E	B	D	G	B

Em7 (ii) — 8th

Finger	X	X	2	3	1	4
Scale	X	X	5	1	♭3	♭7
Note	X	X	B	E	G	D

F#m7 (iii)

Finger	X	0	4	1	2	0
Scale	X	♭3	1	♭3	5	♭7
Note	X	A	F#	A	C#	E

F#m7 (iii) — 4th

Finger	X	X	1	3	2	2
Scale	X	X	1	5	♭7	♭3
Note	X	X	F#	C#	E	A

F#m7 (iii) — 7th

Finger	X	2	1	3	1	4
Scale	X	1	♭3	♭7	1	5
Note	X	F#	A	E	F#	C#

F#m7 (iii) — 9th

Finger	X	1	3	1	2	1
Scale	X	1	5	♭7	♭3	5
Note	X	F#	C#	E	A	C#

F#m7 (iii) — 10th

Finger	X	X	2	3	1	4
Scale	X	X	5	1	♭3	♭7
Note	X	X	C#	F#	A	E

Classic Rock Power Chord & Rock-n-Roll Worksheet - Key of D and Bm

I, IV & V Power Chords (1 and 5)

D5 (I)
X O O   X
Finger X 0 0 1 3 X
Scale X 5 1 5 1 X
Note X A D A D X

D5 (I)
X X   5th
Scale 5 1 5 1 X X
Note A D A D X X

D5 (I)
X X X 10th
Scale 1 5 1 X X X
Note D A D X X X

G5 (IV)
X O O
Finger 2 X 0 0 3 3
Scale 1 X 5 1 5 1
Note G X D G D G

G5 (IV)
X X X 3rd
Scale 1 5 1 X X X
Note G D G X X X

G5 (IV)
X X 10th
Scale 5 1 5 1 X X
Note D G D G X X

A5 (V)
X O
Finger X 0 1 1 4 4
Scale X 1 5 1 5 1
Note X A E A E A

A5 (V)
O O X X
Scale 5 1 5 1 X X
Note E A E A X X

A5 (V)
X X X 5th
Scale 1 5 1 X X X
Note A E A X X X

Flat Major Power Chords

F5 (♭III)
X X X
Scale 1 5 1 X X X
Note F C F X X X

F5 (♭III)
X X 8th
Scale 5 1 5 1 X X
Note C F C F X X

B♭5 (♭VI)
X X
Scale 5 1 5 1 X X
Note F B♭ F B♭ X X

B♭5 (♭VI)
X X X 6th
Scale 1 5 1 X X X
Note B♭ F B♭ X X X

C5 (♭VII)
X X 3rd
Scale 5 1 5 1 X X
Note G C G C X X

C5 (♭VII)
X X X 8th
Scale 1 5 1 X X X
Note C G C X X X

Combinations of notes that can be used to make Power Chords - 1, 5 or 1, 5, 1 called 1st Inversion Power Chords
5, 1 or 5, 1, 5 called 2nd Inversion Power Chords

ii, iii, vi Power Chords

E5 (ii)
O   X X X
Scale 1 5 1 X X X
Note E B E X X X

E5 (ii)
X X 7th
Scale 5 1 5 1 X X
Note B E B E X X

F#5 (ii)
X X X
Scale 1 5 1 X X X
Note F#C#F#X X X

F#5 (iii)
X X 9th
Scale 5 1 5 1 X X
Note C#F#C#F#X X

B5 (vi)
X X
Scale 5 1 5 1 X X
Note F#B F#B X X

B5 (vi)
X X X 7th
Scale 1 5 1 X X X
Note B F#B X X X

Other Power Chord Shapes

X X
Scale X X 5 1 5 1

X   X
Scale X 5 1 5 1 X

X5add9
X X X
Scale 1 5 2 X X X

X5add9
X X
Scale X 1 5 2 X X

Dsus2 (I)
X O   O
Finger T X 0 1 3 0
Scale 3 X 1 5 1 2
Note X X D A D X

Rock-n-Roll Chord Shapes for I, IV and V Chords

X5 / X6 / X7
X X X X
Scale 1 5 X X X X

X5 / X6 / X7
X X X X
Scale X 1 5 X X X

X5 / X6 / X7
X X X X
Scale X X 1 5 X X

Key of D and Bm Triad Worksheet (1st, 2nd and 3rd strings)

Key of D and Bm Triad Worksheet (2nd, 3rd and 4th strings)

Em (ii)	C#o (viio)	G (IV)	C (♭VII)	D (I)	D (I)	D (I)
Scale 1 ♭3 5	Scale ♭3 5 1	Scale 5 1 3	Scale 3 5 1	Scale 3 5 1	Scale 5 1 3 (7th)	Scale 1 3 5 (10th)

F#m (iii)	D (I)	A (V)	F (♭III)	G (IV)	G (IV)	G (IV)
Scale 1 ♭3 5	Scale 3 5 1	Scale 5 1 3	Scale 1 3 5	Scale 5 1 3	Scale 1 3 5 (3rd)	Scale 3 5 1 (7th)

G (IV)	Em (ii)	Bm (vi)	B♭ (♭VI)	A (V)	A (V)	A (V)
Scale 1 3 5 (3rd)	Scale ♭3 5 1 (4th)	Scale 5 1 ♭3 (3rd)	Scale 5 1 3	Scale 5 1 3	Scale 1 3 5 (5th)	Scale 3 5 1 (9th)

A (V)	F#m (iii)	C#o (viio)	C (♭VII)
Scale 1 3 5 (5th)	Scale ♭3 5 1 (6th)	Scale 5 1 ♭3 (5th)	Scale 5 1 3 (5th)

Bm (vi)	G (IV)	D (I)	F (♭III)	Bm (vi)	Bm (vi)	Bm(vi)
Scale 1 ♭3 5 (7th)	Scale 3 5 1 (7th)	Scale 5 1 3 (7th)	Scale 3 5 1 (5th)	Scale 5 1 ♭3 (3rd)	Scale 1 ♭3 5 (7th)	Scale ♭3 5 1 (11th)

C#o (viio)	A (V)	Em (ii)	B♭ (♭VI)	Em (ii)	Em(ii)	Em (ii)
Scale 1 ♭3 ♭5 (8th)	Scale 3 5 1 (9th)	Scale 5 1 ♭3 (8th)	Scale 1 3 5 (6th)	Scale 1 ♭3 5	Scale ♭3 5 1 (4th)	Scale 5 1 ♭3 (8th)

D (I)	Bm(vi)	F#m (iii)	C (♭VII)	F#m (iii)	F#m(iii)	F#m (iii)
Scale 1 3 5 (10th)	Scale ♭3 5 1 (11th)	Scale 5 1 ♭3 (10th)	Scale 1 3 5 (8th)	Scale 1 ♭3 5	Scale ♭3 5 1 (6th)	Scale 5 1 ♭3 (10th)

Em (ii)	C#o (viio)	G (IV)	F (♭III)
Scale 1 ♭3 5 (12th)	Scale ♭3 5 1 (12th)	Scale 5 1 3 (12th)	Scale 5 1 3 (10th)

F#m (iii)	D (I)	A (V)	B♭ (♭VI)	C#o (viio)	C#o (viio)	C#o (viio)
Scale 1 ♭3 5 (14th)	Scale 3 5 1 (14th)	Scale 5 1 3 (14th)	Scale 3 5 1 (10th)	Scale ♭3 5 1	Scale 5 1 ♭3 (5th)	Scale 1 ♭3 ♭5 (8th)

91

Key of D and Bm Triad Worksheet (3rd, 4th and 5th strings)

Slash Chord Worksheet

Key of D and Bm

Diatonic and Secondary Dominant Chords

A (I)
Finger X 0 1 2 3 0
Scale X 1 5 1 3 5
Note X A E A C#E

D (IV)
Finger X X 0 1 3 2
Scale X X 1 5 1 3
Note X X D A D F#

E (V)
Finger 0 2 3 1 0 0
Scale 1 5 1 3 5 1
Note E B E G#B E

E7 (V7/I)
Finger 0 2 0 1 0 0
Scale 1 5 ♭7 3 5 1
Note E B D G#B E

A7 (V7/IV)
Finger X 0 1 0 2 0
Scale X 1 5 ♭7 3 5
Note X A E G C#E

B7 (V7/V)
Finger X 2 1 3 0 4
Scale X 1 3 ♭7 1 5
Note X B D#A B F#

F#m (vi)
Finger 1 3 4 1 1 1
Scale 1 5 1 ♭3 5 1
Note F#C#F# A C#F#

Bm (ii)
Finger X 1 3 4 2 1
Scale X 1 5 1 ♭3 5
Note X B F#B D F#

C#m (iii)
4th
Finger X 1 3 4 2 1
Scale X 1 5 1 ♭3 5
Note X C#G#C#E G#

C#7 (V7/vi)
4th
Finger X 1 3 1 4 1
Scale X 1 5 ♭7 3 5
Note X C#G#B F G#

F#7 (V7/ii)
Finger 1 3 1 2 1 1
Scale 1 5 ♭7 3 5 1
Note F#C#E A#C#F#

G#7 (V7/iii)
4th
Finger 1 3 1 2 1 1
Scale 1 5 ♭7 3 5 1
Note G#D#F#B#D#G#

Extensions

AMaj7 (I)
Finger X 0 2 1 3 0
Scale X 1 5 7 3 5
Note X A E G#C#E

DMaj7 (IV)
Finger X X 0 1 2 3
Scale X X 1 5 7 3
Note X X D A C#F#

E7 (V7)
Finger 0 2 0 1 0 0
Scale 1 5 ♭7 3 5 1
Note E B D G#B E

F#m7 (vi)
Finger 1 3 1 1 1 1
Scale 1 5 ♭7 ♭3 5 1
Note F#C#E A C#F#

Bm7 (ii)
Finger X 1 3 1 2 1
Scale X 1 5 ♭7 ♭3 5
Note X B F#A D F#

C#m7 (iii)
4th
Finger X 1 3 1 2 1
Scale X 1 5 ♭7 ♭3 5
Note X C#G#B E G#

Flat Majors

C (♭III)
Finger X 3 2 0 1 0
Scale X 1 3 5 1 3
Note X C E G C E

F (♭VI)
Finger 1 3 4 2 1 1
Scale 1 5 1 3 5 1
Note F C F A C F

G (♭VII)
Finger 3 2 0 0 0 4
Scale 1 3 5 1 3 1
Note G B D G B G

Suspended Chords

Asus (I)
Finger X 0 1 2 3 0
Scale X 1 5 1 4 5
Note X A E A D E

Asus2 (I)
Finger X 0 1 2 0 0
Scale X 1 5 1 2 5
Note X A E A B E

Dsus2 (IV)
Finger X X 0 1 3 0
Scale X X 1 5 1 2
Note X X D A D E

E7sus (V7)
Finger 0 2 0 3 0 0
Scale 1 5 ♭7 4 5 1
Note E B D A B E

Esus (V)
Finger 0 1 2 3 0 0
Scale 1 5 1 4 5 1
Note E B E A B E

Esus2 (V)
Finger 0 1 3 4 0 0
Scale 1 5 2 5 5 1
Note E B F#B B E

Add9 Chords

Aadd9 (I)
6th
Finger X 0 2 1 0 0
Scale X 1 1 3 2 5
Note X A A C#B E

Aadd9 (I)
Finger X 0 1 4 2 0
Scale X 1 5 2 3 5
Note X A E B C#E

Dadd9 (IV)
7th
Finger X X 0 3 4 0
Scale X X 1 1 3 2
Note X X D D F#E

Eadd9 (V)
Finger 0 2 4 1 0 0
Scale 1 5 2 3 5 1
Note E B F#G#B E

F#m Harmonic chords

C# (III)
4th
Finger X 1 3 4 2 1
Scale X 1 5 1 3 5
Note X C#G#C#F G#

C#7 (III7)
Finger X 3 2 4 1 X
Scale X 1 3 ♭7 1 X
Note X C#F B C#X

94

Dominant 7th (Blues) Chords

A7 (I7)
X O O O
Finger X 0 1 0 2 0
Scale X 1 5 ♭7 3 5
Note X A E G C# E

A7 (I7) — 5th
Finger 1 3 1 2 1 1
Scale 1 5 ♭7 3 5 1
Note A E G C# E A

D7 (IV7)
X X
Finger X X 0 2 1 3
Scale X X 1 5 ♭7 3
Note X X D A C F#

D7 (IV7) — 5th
X
Finger X 1 3 1 4 1
Scale X 1 5 ♭7 3 5
Note X D A C F# A

E7 (V7)
O O O
Finger 0 2 0 1 0 0
Scale 1 5 ♭7 3 5 1
Note E B D G# B E

E7 (V7) — 7th
X
Finger X 1 3 1 4 1
Scale X 1 5 ♭7 3 5
Note X E B D G# B

Quality Change Chords

B (II) — V
X
Finger X 1 2 3 4 1
Scale X 1 5 1 3 5
Note X B F# B D# F#

Dm (iv) — I, iv, IV
X X O
Finger X X 0 2 3 1
Scale X X 1 5 1 ♭3
Note X X D A D F

C# (III) — vi — 4th
Finger X 1 2 3 4 1
Scale X 1 5 1 3 5
Note X C# G# C# F G#

Em (v) — I
O O O O
Finger 0 2 3 0 0 0
Scale 1 5 1 ♭3 5 1
Note E B E G B E

F# (VI) — ii
Finger 1 3 4 2 1 1
Scale 1 5 1 3 5 1
Note F# C# F# A# C# F#

G#m (vii) — iii — 4th
Finger 1 3 4 1 1 1
Scale 1 5 1 ♭3 5 1
Note G# D# G# B D# G#

G# (VII) — iii — 4th
Finger 1 3 4 2 1 1
Scale 1 5 1 3 5 1
Note G# D# G# C D# G#

Am (i)
X O O
Finger X 0 2 3 1 0
Scale X 1 5 1 ♭3 5
Note X A E A C E

Additional Diatonic Extensions

A6 (I)
X O
Finger X 0 1 1 1 1
Scale X 1 5 1 3 6
Note X A E A C# F#

AMaj9 (I)
X O
Finger X 0 1 3 1 4
Scale X 1 5 2 3 7
Note X A E B C# G#

AMaj7add11 (I)
X O O
Finger X 0 0 1 3 0
Scale X 1 4 7 3 5
Note X A D G# C# E

Bm6 (ii)
X O O
Finger X 2 0 1 0 3
Scale X 1 ♭3 6 1 5
Note X B D G# B F#

Bm9 (ii)
X O
Finger X 2 0 3 3 3
Scale X 1 ♭3 ♭7 2 5
Note X B D A C# F#

Bm11 (ii)
X O O
Finger X 1 0 2 3 0
Scale X 1 ♭3 ♭7 2 4
Note X B D A C# E

C#m7/11 (iii) — 4th
X
Finger X 1 1 1 2 1
Scale X 1 4 ♭7 ♭3 5
Note X C# F# B E G#

C#madd11 (iii) — 4th
X
Finger X 1 1 3 2 1
Scale X 1 4 1 ♭3 5
Note X C# F# C# E G#

D6 (IV)
X X O
Finger X X 0 1 0 2
Scale X X 1 5 6 3
Note X X D A B F#

DMaj9 (IV) — 4th
X
Finger X 2 1 4 3 X
Scale X 1 3 7 2 X
Note X D F# C# E X

DMaj9add13 (IV) — 4th
X O O
Finger X 2 1 4 0 0
Scale X 1 3 7 6 2
Note X D F# C# B E

E9 (V7)
O O
Finger 0 2 0 1 0 3
Scale 1 5 ♭7 3 5 2
Note E B D G# B F#

E11 (V7)
O O
Finger 0 0 2 1 4 3
Scale 1 4 1 3 ♭7 2
Note E A E G# D F#

E13 (V7)
O O
Finger 0 2 0 1 3 4
Scale 1 5 ♭7 3 6 2
Note E B D G# C# F#

F#m9 (vi)
Finger 1 3 1 1 1 4
Scale 1 5 ♭7 ♭3 5 2
Note F# C# E A C# G#

F#m9 (vi)
O O
Finger 2 0 3 1 4 0
Scale 1 ♭3 ♭7 2 5 ♭7
Note F# A E G# C# E

F#m7add11 (vi) — 6th
X O O
Finger X 4 2 1 0 0
Scale X 1 ♭3 5 4 ♭7
Note X F# A C# B E

G#m7♭5 (vii∅7)
X X
Finger 1 X 2 3 4 X
Scale 1 X ♭7 ♭3 ♭5 X
Note G# X F# B D X

G#m7♭5 (vii∅7)
X O O
Finger 3 X 0 4 0 1
Scale 1 X ♭5 ♭3 1 ♭7
Note G# X D B B F#

G#o (viio)
X O O
Finger 2 X 0 3 0 4
Scale 1 X ♭5 ♭3 ♭3 1
Note G# X D B B G#

*The m7♭5 is also referred to as a half diminished chord and can be written as a degree symbol with a slash through it.

95

Chord Formula Worksheet Up The Neck - Key of A and F#m

A (I)
Finger 3 2 1 1 4
Scale 1 3 5 1 3 1
Note A C# E A C# A

A (I) 5th
Finger 1 3 4 2 1 1
Scale 1 5 1 3 5 1
Note A E A C# E A

A (I) 7th
Finger X X 1 2 4 3
Scale 3 5 1 5 1 3
Note C# E A E A C#

A (I) 9th
Finger X 4 3 1 2 1
Scale 5 1 3 5 1 3
Note E A C# E A C#

I - (1, 3, 5) Extensions - (2), (4), (6), (7)

D (IV)
Finger X 4 3 1 2 1
Scale 5 1 3 5 1 3
Note A D F# A D F#

D (IV) 5th
Finger X 1 2 3 4 1
Scale 5 1 5 1 3 5
Note A D A D F# A

D (IV) 7th
Finger 3 2 1 1 1 4
Scale 1 3 5 1 3 1
Note D F# A D F# D

D (IV) 10th
Finger 1 3 4 2 1 1
Scale 1 5 1 3 5 1
Note D A D F# A D

IV - (1, 3, 5) Extensions - (2), (b5), (6), (7)

E (V)
Finger X X 1 2 4 3
Scale 3 5 1 5 1 3
Note G# B E B E G#

E (V) 4th
Finger X 4 3 1 2 1
Scale 5 1 3 5 1 3
Note B E G# B E G#

E (V) 7th
Finger X 1 2 3 4 1
Scale 5 1 5 1 3 5
Note B E B E G# B

E (V) 9th
Finger 3 2 1 1 1 4
Scale 1 3 5 1 3 1
Note E G# B E G# E

V - (1, 3, 5) Extensions - (2), (4), (6), (b7)

F#m (vi) 4th
Finger X X 1 3 4 2
Scale b3 5 1 5 1 b3
Note A C# F# C# F# A

F#m (vi) 5th
Finger X 4 2 1 3 X
Scale 5 1 b3 5 1 b3
Note C# F# A C# F# A

F#m (vi) 9th
Finger X 1 3 4 2 1
Scale 5 1 5 1 b3 5
Note C# F# C# F# A C#

F#m (vi) 10th
Finger 4 2 1 1 X X
Scale 1 b3 5 1 b3 1
Note F# A C# F# A F#

vi - (1, b3, 5) Extensions - (2), (4), (#5), (b7)

Bm (ii) 3rd
Finger 4 2 1 1 X X
Scale 1 b3 5 1 b3 1
Note B D F# B D B

Bm (ii) 7th
Finger 1 3 4 1 1 1
Scale 1 5 1 b3 5 1
Note B F# B D F# B

Bm (ii) 9th
Finger X X 1 3 4 2
Scale b3 5 1 5 1 b3
Note D F# B F# B D

Bm (ii) 10th
Finger X 4 2 1 3 X
Scale 5 1 b3 5 1 b3
Note F# B D F# B D

ii - (1, b3, 5) Extensions - (2), (4), (6), (b7)

C#m (iii)
Finger X 4 2 1 3 0
Scale 5 1 b3 5 1 b3
Note G# C# E G# C# E

C#m (iii) 5th
Finger 4 2 1 1 X X
Scale 1 b3 5 1 b3 1
Note C# E G# C# E C#

C#m (iii) 9th
Finger 1 3 4 1 1 1
Scale 1 5 1 b3 5 1
Note C# G# C# E G# C#

C#m (iii) 11th
Finger X X 1 3 4 2
Scale b3 5 1 5 1 b3
Note E G# C# G# C# E

iii - (1, b3, 5) Extensions - (b2), (4), (#5), (b7)

* Order of notes as you move up and down a string.

1
b2 (b9)
2 (sus2, 9)
#2 (#9) / (b3 minor)
3
4 (sus, 11)
b5 (b5, #11)
5
#5 (#5, b13) / (+, aug)
6 (6, 13)
b7 (7) Dominant 7th
7 (Maj7)
1

E A D B E
G#
F# B E A C# F#
D 3rd
G# C# F# B G#
A D E A 5th
G# C#
B E A D F# B 7th
C# F# B E G# C# 9th
D A D
G# C# F#
E A D B E 12th
G#

CHORD SUBSTITUTIONS - KEY OF A AND F#m

1. CHORD EMBELLISHMENTS - EXTENSIONS AND ALTERATIONS

2. MAJOR, MINOR AND DOMINANT SUBSTITUTIONS

Major   **A (I)** Relative minor - **F#m (vi)** or Common Tones - **C#m (iii)**

            D (IV) Relative minor - **Bm (ii)** or Common Tones - **F#m (vi)**

            E (V) Relative minor - **C#m (iii)** or Common Tones - **G#m (vii)**

minor   **F#m (vi)** Relative Major - **A (I)** or Common Tones - **D (IV)**

            Bm (ii) Relative Major - **D (IV)** or Common Tones - **G (bVII)**

            C#m (iii) Relative Major - **E (V)** or Common Tones - **A (I)**

7th   **E7(V7)** Common Tones - **G#^{o}7 (VII°7)** or **C#m (iii)** or Tritone - **Bb7**

3. BACKCYCLING (CIRCLE OF 5THS)

(C#m7-F#m7-Bm7-E7) - A   **(F#m7-Bm7-Em7-A7) - D**   **(G#m7-C#m7-F#m7-B7) - E**

(Bbm7-Ebm7-G#m7-C#7) - F#m   **(Ebm7-G#m7-C#m7-F#7) - Bm**   **(Fm7-Bbm7-Ebm7-G#7) - C#m**

Use the 5th of the chord you're going to to find the letter name of the chord that should proceed it. Here are a couple of variations on backcycling (C#7, F#7, B7, E7) - A or (C#m7, F#7, Bm7, E7) - A. The ii-V7 is a very common substitute for a V7 chord. Also don't forget you can just add the secondary dominants before a chord.

4. HALF STEP PROGRESSIONS

This is usually some type of dominant 7th chord.

Major	**Ab7-A**	**A#7-A**	**Db7-D**	**D#7-D**	**Eb7-E**	**F7-E**
minor	**F7-F#m**	**G7-F#m**	**Bb7-Bm**	**C7-Bm**	**C7-C#m**	**D7-C#m**

5. PASSING CHORDS

^{o}7   Diminished 7th chords can be used between diatonic chords to create a *chromatic* chord progression.

                      AMaj7(I)-A#^{o}7-Bm7(ii)-C^{o}7-C#m7(iii)-DMaj7(IV)-D#^{o}7-E7(V7)-F^{o}7-F#m7(vi)

Diatonic   You can also use diatonic chords to fill-in the gaps between chords.

                      Here is an example of a *diatonic* type passing chord progression:

                      original A(I)-A(I)-A(I)-D(IV) becomes A(I)-Bm(ii)-C#m(iii)-D(IV).

6. TRITONE SUBSTITUTION

You can substitute a dominant 7th chord with another dominant 7th chord based on the flat five of the original dominant 7th chord. Below are the original 7th chords followed by their tritone substitution. You can also use these substitutions in your backcycling to create chromatic bass lines.

A7 to Eb7	Bb7 to E7	B7 to F7	C7 to Gb7	C#7 to G7	Db7 to G7	D7 to Ab7
Eb7 to A7	E7 to Bb7	F7 to B7	F#7 to C7	Gb7 to C7	G7 to Db7	Ab7 to D7

7. QUALITY CHANGE CHORDS

Majors - (minors, Dominant 7ths), Minors - (Majors, Dominant 7ths), Dominant 7ths - (Majors, minors)

Four Note Extensions Up The Neck - Key of A and F#m

* Use the sections on Bass Notes and Optional Notes to find other notes you can add to these chords. Also don't forget you don't have to play every note in the chord, only the essential notes that convey the chords family and quality of sound.

AMaj7 (I)
Finger X 0 1 1 1 2
Scale X 1 5 1 3 7
Note X A E A C# G#

AMaj7 (I) 5th
Finger 1 X 3 4 2 X
Scale 1 5 7 3 5 1
Note A E G# C# E A

AMaj7 (I) 4th
Finger T X 4 3 2 1
Scale 1 X 1 3 5 7
Note A X A C# E G#

AMaj7 (I) 7th
Finger X X 1 4 4 4
Scale X X 1 5 7 3
Note X X A E G# C#

AMaj7 (I) 9th
Finger X 4 3 1 1 1
Scale X 1 3 5 7 3
Note X A C# E G# C#

DMaj7 (IV)
Finger X 4 3 1 1 1
Scale X 1 3 5 7 3
Note X D F# A C# F#

DMaj7 (IV) 5th
Finger X 1 3 2 4 1
Scale X 1 5 7 3 5
Note X D A C# F# A

DMaj7 (IV) 7th
Finger X X 1 1 1 2
Scale X X 5 1 3 7
Note X X A D F# C#

DMaj7 (IV) 10th
Finger 1 X 3 4 2 X
Scale 1 5 7 3 5 1
Note D A C# F# A D

DMaj7 (IV) 9th
Finger T X 4 3 2 1
Scale 1 X 1 3 5 7
Note D X D F# A C#

E (V)
Finger 0 2 3 1 4 0
Scale 1 5 1 3 7 1
Note E B E G# D E

E7 (V7)
Finger X X 1 3 2 4
Scale X X 1 5 b7 3
Note X X E B D G#

E7 (V7) 4th
Finger X 3 2 4 1 X
Scale 5 1 3 b7 1 3
Note B E G# D E G#

E7 (V7) 7th
Finger X 1 2 1 4 1
Scale X 1 5 b7 3 5
Note X E B D G# B

E7 (V7) 9th
Finger X X 1 1 1 2
Scale X X 5 1 3 b7
Note X X B E G# D

F#m7 (vi)
Finger X 0 4 1 2 0
Scale X b3 1 b3 5 b7
Note X A F# A C# E

F#m7 (vi) 4th
Finger X X 1 3 2 2
Scale X X 1 5 b7 b3
Note X X F# C# E A

F#m7 (vi) 7th
Finger X 2 1 3 1 4
Scale X 1 b3 b7 1 5
Note X F# A E F# C#

F#m7 (vi) 9th
Finger X 1 3 1 2 1
Scale X 1 5 b7 b3 5
Note X F# C# E A C#

F#m7 (vi) 10th
Finger X X 2 3 1 4
Scale X X 5 1 b3 b7
Note X X C# F# A E

Bm7 (ii)
Finger X 1 0 2 0 3
Scale X 1 b3 b7 1 5
Note X B D A B F#

Bm7 (ii) 3rd
Finger X X 2 3 1 4
Scale X X 5 1 b3 b7
Note X X F# B D A

Bm7 (ii) 7th
Finger 1 3 1 1 1 1
Scale 1 5 b7 3 5 1
Note B F# A D F# B

Bm7 (ii) 9th
Finger X X 1 3 2 2
Scale X X 1 5 b7 b3
Note X X B F# A D

Bm7 (ii) 12th
Finger X 2 1 3 1 4
Scale X 1 b3 b7 1 5
Note X B D A B F#

C#m7 (iii)
Finger X 4 2 1 0 0
Scale X 1 b3 5 b7 b3
Note X C# E G# B E

C#m7 (iii) 2nd
Finger X 2 1 3 1 4
Scale X 1 b3 b7 1 5
Note X C# E B C# G#

C#m7 (iii) 5th
Finger X X 2 3 1 4
Scale X X 5 1 b3 b7
Note X X G# C# E B

C#m7 (iii) 9th
Finger 1 3 1 1 1 1
Scale 1 5 b7 b3 5 1
Note C# G# B E G# C#

C#m7 (iii) 11th
Finger X X 1 3 2 2
Scale X X 1 5 b7 b3
Note X X C# G# B E

Classic Rock Power Chord & Rock-n-Roll Worksheet - Key of A and F#m

I, IV & V Power Chords (1 and 5)

A5 (I)
X O
Finger	X 0 1 1 4 4
Scale	X 1 5 1 5 1
Note	X A E A E A

A5 (I)
O O   X X
| Scale | 5 1 5 1 X X |
| Note | E A E A X X |

A5 (I) 5th
X X X
| Scale | 1 5 1 X X X |
| Note | A E A X X X |

D5 (IV)
X O O   X
Finger	X 0 0 1 3 X
Scale	X 5 1 5 1 X
Note	X A D A D X

D5 (IV) 5th
X X
| Scale | 5 1 5 1 X X |
| Note | A D A D X X |

D5 (IV) 10th
X X X
| Scale | 1 5 1 X X X |
| Note | D A D X X X |

E5 (V)
O   O O
Finger	0 2 3 4 0 0
Scale	1 5 1 5 5 1
Note	E B E B B E

E5 (V)
O X X X
| Scale | 1 5 1 X X X |
| Note | E B E X X X |

E5 (V) 7th
X X
| Scale | 5 1 5 1 X X |
| Note | B E B E X X |

Flat Major Power Chords

C5 (♭III) 3rd
X X
| Scale | 5 1 5 1 X X |
| Note | G C G C X X |

C5 (♭III) 8th
| Scale | 1 5 1 X X X |
| Note | C G C X X X |

F5 (♭VI)
X X X
| Scale | 1 5 1 X X X |
| Note | F C F X X X |

F5 (♭VI) 8th
X X
| Scale | 5 1 5 1 X X |
| Note | C F C F X X |

G5 (♭VII) 3rd
| Scale | 1 5 1 X X X |
| Note | G D G X X X |

G5 (♭VII) 10th
X X
| Scale | 5 1 5 1 X X |
| Note | D G D G X X |

Combinations of notes that can be used to make Power Chords - 1, 5 or 1, 5, 1 called 1st Inversion Power Chords
5, 1 or 5, 1, 5 called 2nd Inversion Power Chords

ii, iii, vi Power Chords

B5 (ii)
X X
| Scale | 5 1 5 1 X X |
| Note | F#B F#B X X |

B5 (ii) 7th
X X X
| Scale | 1 5 1 X X X |
| Note | B F#B X X X |

C#5 (iii) 4th
X X
| Scale | 5 1 5 1 X X |
| Note | G#C#G#C#X X |

C#5 (iii) 9th
X X X
| Scale | 1 5 1 X X X |
| Note | C#G#C#X X X |

F#5 (vi)
X X X
| Scale | 1 5 1 X X X |
| Note | F#C#F#X X X |

F#5 (vi) 9th
X X
| Scale | 5 1 5 1 X X |
| Note | C#F#C#F#X X |

Dsus2 (I)
X O   O
Finger	T X 0 1 3 0
Scale	3 X 1 5 1 2
Note	X X D A D X

E5 (V) 7th
O   O O
Finger	0 1 3 4 0 0
Scale	1 1 5 1 5 1
Note	E E B E B E

Other Power Chord Shapes

X X
| Scale | X X 5 1 5 1 |

X   X
| Scale | X 5 1 5 1 X |

X5add9
X X X
| Scale | 1 5 2 X X X |

X5add9
X   X X
| Scale | X 1 5 2 X X |

Rock-n-Roll Chord Shapes for I, IV and V Chords

X5 / X6 / X7
X X X X
| Scale | 1 5 X X X X |

X5 / X6 / X7
X X X X
| Scale | X 1 5 X X X |

X5 / X6 / X7
X X   X X
| Scale | X X 1 5 X X |

Key of A and F#m Triad Worksheet (1st, 2nd and 3rd strings)

Key of A and F#m Triad Worksheet (2nd, 3rd and 4th strings)

E (V) — Scale 1 3 5

C#m(iii) — Scale ♭3 5 1

G#o (viio) — Scale ♭5 1 ♭3

G (♭VII) — Scale 5 1 3

A (I) — Scale 5 1 3

A (I) 5th — Scale 1 3 5

A (I) 9th — Scale 3 5 1

F#m (vi) — Scale 1 ♭3 5

D (IV) — Scale 3 5 1

A (I) — Scale 5 1 3

C (♭III) — Scale 3 5 1

D (IV) — Scale 3 5 1

D (IV) 7th — Scale 5 1 3

D (IV) 10th — Scale 1 3 5

G#o (viio) 3rd — Scale 1 ♭3 ♭5

E (V) 4th — Scale 3 5 1

Bm (ii) 3rd — Scale 5 1 ♭3

F (♭VI) — Scale 1 3 5

E (V) — Scale 1 3 5

E (V) 4th — Scale 3 5 1

E (V) 9th — Scale 5 1 3

A (I) 5th — Scale 1 3 5

F#m(vi) 6th — Scale ♭3 5 1

C#m (iii) 5th — Scale 5 1 ♭3

G (♭VII) 3rd — Scale 1 3 5

Bm (ii) 7th — Scale 1 ♭3 5

G#o (viio) 7th — Scale ♭3 ♭5 1

D (IV) 7th — Scale 5 1 3

C (♭III) 5th — Scale 5 1 3

F#m (vi) — Scale 1 ♭3 5

F#m(vi) 6th — Scale ♭3 5 1

F#m (vi) 10th — Scale 5 1 ♭3

C#m (iii) 9th — Scale 1 ♭3 5

A (I) 9th — Scale 3 5 1

E (V) 9th — Scale 5 1 3

F (♭VI) 5th — Scale 3 5 1

Bm (ii) 3rd — Scale 5 1 ♭3

Bm (ii) 7th — Scale 1 ♭3 5

Bm(ii) 11th — Scale ♭3 5 1

D (IV) 10th — Scale 1 3 5

Bm(ii) 11th — Scale ♭3 5 1

F#m (vi) 10th — Scale 5 1 ♭3

G (♭VII) 7th — Scale 3 5 1

C#m(iii) — Scale ♭3 5 1

C#m (iii) 5th — Scale 5 1 ♭3

C#m (iii) 9th — Scale 1 ♭3 5

E (V) 12th — Scale 1 3 5

C#m(iii) 13th — Scale ♭3 5 1

G#o (viio) 12th — Scale ♭5 1 ♭3

C (♭III) 8th — Scale 1 3 5

F#m (vi) 14th — Scale 1 ♭3 5

D (IV) 14th — Scale 3 5 1

A (I) 14th — Scale 5 1 3

F (♭VI) 10th — Scale 5 1 3

G#o (viio) — Scale ♭5 1 ♭3

G#o (viio) 3rd — Scale 1 ♭3 ♭5

G#o (viio) 7th — Scale ♭3 ♭5 1

101

Key of A and F#m Triad Worksheet (3rd, 4th and 5th strings)

C#m(iii)
Scale 1 ♭3 5

G#o (viio)
Scale ♭3 ♭5 1

E (V)
Scale 5 1 3

G (♭VII)
Scale 3 5 1

A (I)
Scale 3 5 1

A (I) 6th
Scale 5 1 3

A (I) 9th
Scale 1 3 5

D (IV)
Scale 1 3 5

A (I)
Scale 3 5 1

F#m (vi)
Scale 5 1 ♭3

C (♭III)
Scale 1 3 5

D (IV)
Scale 1 3 5

D (IV) 7th
Scale 3 5 1

D (IV) 11th
Scale 5 1 3

E (V) 4th
Scale 1 3 5

Bm (ii) 4th
Scale ♭3 5 1

G#o (viio) 4th
Scale ♭5 1 ♭3

F (♭VI)
Scale 5 1 3

E (V)
Scale 5 1 3

E (V) 4th
Scale 1 3 5

E (V) 9th
Scale 3 5 1

F#m(vi) 6th
Scale 1 ♭3 5

C#m (iii) 6th
Scale ♭3 5 1

A (I) 6th
Scale 5 1 3

G (♭VII) 4th
Scale 5 1 3

G#o (viio) 7th
Scale 1 ♭3 ♭5

D (IV) 7th
Scale 3 5 1

Bm (ii) 7th
Scale 5 1 ♭3

C (♭III) 5th
Scale 3 5 1

F#m (vi)
Scale 5 1 ♭3

F#m(vi) 6th
Scale 1 ♭3 5

F#m (vi) 11th
Scale ♭3 5 1

A (I) 9th
Scale 1 3 5

E (V) 9th
Scale 3 5 1

C#m (iii) 9th
Scale 5 1 ♭3

F (♭VI) 5th
Scale 1 3 5

Bm (ii) 4th
Scale ♭3 5 1

Bm (ii) 7th
Scale 5 1 ♭3

Bm(ii) 11th
Scale 1 ♭3 5

Bm(ii) 11th
Scale 1 ♭3 5

F#m (vi) 11th
Scale ♭3 5 1

D (IV) 11th
Scale 5 1 3

G (♭VII) 7th
Scale 1 3 5

C#m(iii) 4th
Scale 1 ♭3 5

C#m (iii) 6th
Scale ♭3 5 1

C#m (iii) 9th
Scale 5 1 ♭3

C#m(iii) 13th
Scale 1 ♭3 5

G#o (viio) 12th
Scale ♭3 ♭5 1

E (V) 13th
Scale 5 1 3

C (♭III) 9th
Scale 5 1 3

D (IV) 14th
Scale 1 3 5

A (I) 14th
Scale 3 5 1

F#m (vi) 14th
Scale 5 1 ♭3

F (♭VI) 10th
Scale 3 5 1

G#o (viio)
Scale ♭3 ♭5 1

G#o (viio) 4th
Scale ♭5 1 ♭3

G#o (viio) 7th
Scale 1 ♭3 ♭5

102

Slash Chord Worksheet

Key of A and F#m

103

Diatonic and Secondary Dominant Chords

E (I)
Finger 0 2 3 1 0 0
Scale 1 5 1 3 5 1
Note E B E G# B E

A (IV)
Finger X 0 1 2 3 0
Scale X 1 5 1 3 5
Note X A E A C# E

B (V)
Finger X 1 2 3 4 1
Scale X 1 5 1 3 5
Note X B F# B D F#

B7 (V7/I)
Finger X 2 1 3 0 4
Scale X 1 3 ♭7 1 5
Note X B D# A B F#

E7 (V7/IV)
Finger 0 2 0 1 0 0
Scale 1 5 ♭7 3 5 1
Note E B D G# B E

F#7 (V7/V)
Finger 1 3 1 2 1 1
Scale 1 5 ♭7 3 5 1
Note F# C# E A# C# F#

C#m (vi)
4th
Finger X 1 3 4 2 1
Scale X 1 5 ♭3 5
Note X C# G# C# E G#

F#m (ii)
Finger 1 3 4 1 1 1
Scale 1 5 1 ♭3 5 1
Note F# C# F# A C# F#

G#m (iii)
4th
Finger 1 3 4 1 1 1
Scale 1 5 1 ♭3 5 1
Note G# D# G# B D# G#

G#7 (V7/vi)
4th
Finger 1 3 1 2 1 1
Scale 1 5 ♭7 3 5 1
Note G# D# F# C D# G#

C#7 (V7/ii)
Finger X 3 2 4 1 X
Scale X 1 3 ♭7 1 X
Note X C# F B C# X

D#7 (V7/iii)
4th
Finger X 3 2 4 1 X
Scale X 1 3 ♭7 1 X
Note X D# G C# D# X

Extensions

EMaj7 (I)
Finger 0 3 1 2 0 0
Scale 1 5 7 3 5 1
Note E B D# G# B E

AMaj7 (IV)
Finger X 0 2 1 3 0
Scale X 1 5 7 3 5
Note X A E G# C# E

B7 (V7)
Finger X 2 1 3 0 4
Scale X 1 3 ♭7 1 5
Note X B D# A B F#

C#m7 (vi)
4th
Finger X 1 3 1 2 1
Scale X 1 5 ♭7 ♭3 5
Note X C# G# B E G#

F#m7 (ii)
Finger 1 3 1 1 1 1
Scale 1 5 ♭7 ♭3 5 1
Note F# C# E A C# F#

G#m7 (iii)
4th
Finger 1 3 1 1 1 1
Scale 1 5 ♭7 ♭3 5 1
Note G# D# F# B D# G#

Flat Majors

G (♭III)
Finger 3 2 0 0 0 4
Scale 1 3 5 1 3 1
Note G B D G B G

C (♭VI)
Finger X 3 2 0 1 0
Scale X 1 3 5 1 3
Note X C E G C E

D (♭VII)
Finger X X 0 1 3 2
Scale X X 1 5 1 3
Note X X D A D F#

Suspended Chords

Esus (I)
Finger 0 1 2 3 0 0
Scale 1 5 1 4 5 1
Note E B E A B E

Esus2 (I)
Finger 0 1 3 4 0 0
Scale 1 5 2 5 5 1
Note E B F# B B E

Asus2 (IV)
Finger X 0 1 2 0 0
Scale X 1 5 1 2 5
Note X A E A B E

B7sus (V7)
Finger X 1 3 1 4 1
Scale X 1 5 ♭7 4 5
Note X B F# A E F#

Bsus (V)
Finger X 1 3 4 0 0
Scale X 1 5 1 1 4
Note X B F# B B E

Bsus2 (V)
Finger X 1 3 4 1 1
Scale X 1 5 1 2 5
Note X B F# B C# F#

Add9 Chords

Eadd9 (I)
Finger 0 2 4 1 0 0
Scale 1 5 2 3 5 1
Note E B F# G# B E

Aadd9 (IV)
Finger X 0 1 4 2 0
Scale X 1 5 2 3 5
Note X A E B C# E

Aadd9 (IV)
6th
Finger X 0 2 1 0 0
Scale X 1 1 3 2 5
Note X A A C# B E

Badd9 (V)
4th
Finger 3 X 1 2 1 4
Scale 1 X 5 2 3 1
Note B X F# C# D# B

C#m Harmonic chords

G# (III)
4th
Finger 1 3 4 2 1 1
Scale 1 5 1 3 5 1
Note G# D# G# C D# G#

G#7 (III7)
4th
Finger 1 3 4 2 1 1
Scale 1 5 ♭7 3 5 1
Note G# D# F# C D# G#

104

Dominant 7th (Blues) Chords

E7 (I7)

Finger	0	2	0	1	0	0
Scale	1	5	♭7	3	5	1
Note	E	B	D	G#	B	E

E7 (I7) — 7th

Finger	X	1	3	1	4	1
Scale	X	1	5	♭7	3	5
Note	X	E	B	D	G#	B

A7 (IV7)

Finger	X	0	1	0	2	0
Scale	X	1	5	♭7	3	5
Note	X	A	E	G	C#	E

A7 (IV7) — 5th

Finger	1	3	1	2	1	1
Scale	1	5	♭7	3	5	1
Note	A	E	G	C#	E	A

B7 (V7)

Finger	X	2	1	3	0	4
Scale	X	1	3	♭7	1	5
Note	X	B	D#	A	B	F#

B7 (V7)

Finger	X	1	3	1	4	1
Scale	X	1	5	♭7	3	5
Note	X	B	F#	A	D#	F#

Quality Change Chords

F# (II) — V

Finger	1	3	4	2	1	1
Scale	1	5	1	3	5	1
Note	F#	C#	F#	A#	C#	F#

Am (iv) — I, iv, IV

Finger	X	0	2	3	1	0
Scale	X	1	5	1	♭3	5
Note	X	A	E	A	C	E

G# (III) — vi — 4th

Finger	1	3	4	2	1	1
Scale	1	5	1	3	5	1
Note	G#	D#	G#	C	D#	G#

Bm (v) — I

Finger	X	1	3	4	2	1
Scale	X	1	5	1	♭3	5
Note	X	B	F#	B	D	F#

C# (VI) — ii — 4th

Finger	X	1	2	3	4	1
Scale	X	1	5	1	3	5
Note	X	C#	G#	C#	F	G#

D#m (vii) — iii

Finger	X	X	1	3	4	2
Scale	X	X	1	5	1	♭3
Note	X	X	D#	A#	D#	F#

D# (VII) — iii — 3rd

Finger	X	4	3	1	2	1
Scale	X	1	3	5	1	3
Note	X	D#	G	A#	D#	G

Em (i)

Finger	0	2	3	0	0	0
Scale	1	5	1	♭3	5	1
Note	E	B	E	G	B	E

Additional Diatonic Extensions

EMaj7 (I)

Finger	0	3	1	2	0	0
Scale	1	5	7	3	5	1
Note	E	B	D#	G#	B	E

E6 (I)

Finger	0	2	3	1	4	0
Scale	1	5	1	3	6	1
Note	E	B	E	G#	C#	E

EMaj9 (I)

Finger	0	3	1	2	0	4
Scale	1	5	7	3	5	2
Note	E	B	D#	G#	B	F#

F#m6 (ii)

Finger	2	X	1	3	3	3
Scale	1	X	6	♭3	5	1
Note	F#	X	D	A	C	F#

F#m9 (ii)

Finger	1	3	1	1	1	4
Scale	1	5	♭7	♭3	5	2
Note	F#	C#	E	A	C	G#

F#m7add11 (ii) — 6th

Finger	X	4	2	1	0	0
Scale	X	1	♭3	5	4	♭7
Note	X	F#	A	C#	B	E

G#m7/11 (iii)

Finger	X	2	1	1	3	4
Scale	X	♭3	5	1	4	♭7
Note	X	B	D#	G#	C#	F#

G#madd11 (iii) — 4th

Finger	1	1	3	1	1	1
Scale	1	4	1	♭3	5	1
Note	G#	C#	G#	B	D#	G#

A6 (IV)

Finger	X	0	1	1	1	1
Scale	X	1	5	1	3	6
Note	X	A	E	A	C#	F#

AMaj9 (IV)

Finger	X	0	1	3	1	4
Scale	X	1	5	2	3	7
Note	X	A	E	B	C#	G#

AMaj7add13 (IV)

Finger	X	0	2	1	3	3
Scale	X	1	5	7	3	6
Note	X	A	E	G#	C#	F#

B9 (V7)

Finger	X	2	1	3	3	3
Scale	X	1	3	♭7	2	5
Note	X	B	D#	A	C#	F#

B11 (V7)

Finger	X	2	1	3	4	0
Scale	X	1	3	♭7	2	4
Note	X	B	D#	A	C#	E

B13 (V7)

Finger	X	2	1	3	3	4
Scale	X	1	3	♭7	2	6
Note	X	B	D#	A	C#	G#

C#m9 (vi)

Finger	X	3	1	4	4	4
Scale	X	1	♭3	♭7	2	5
Note	X	C#	E	B	D#	G#

C#m9 (vi) — 4th

Finger	X	1	2	4	0	0
Scale	X	1	5	2	♭7	♭3
Note	X	C#	G#	D#	B	E

C#madd9 (vi)

Finger	X	2	X	3	4	0
Scale	X	1	X	♭7	2	♭3
Note	X	C#	X	B	D#	E

D#m7♭5 (viiø7)

Finger	X	X	1	3	3	3
Scale	X	X	1	♭5	♭7	♭3
Note	X	X	D#	A	C	F#

D#º (viiº)

Finger	X	X	3	1	4	1
Scale	X	X	♭3	♭5	1	♭3
Note	X	X	F#	A	D#	F#

*The m7♭5 is also referred to as a half diminished chord and can be written as a degree symbol with a slash through it.

105

Chord Formula Worksheet Up The Neck - Key of E and C#m

E (I)
Finger X X 1 2 4 3	**Finger** X 4 3 1 2 1	**Finger** X 1 2 3 4 1	**Finger** 3 2 1 1 1 4
Scale 3 5 1 5 1 3	**Scale** 5 1 3 5 1 3	**Scale** 5 1 5 1 3 5	**Scale** 1 3 5 1 3 1
Note G# B E B E G#	**Note** B E G# B E G#	**Note** B E B E C# B	**Note** E G# B E G# E

I - (1, 3, 5) Extensions - (2), (4), (6), (7)

A (IV)
Finger 3 2 1 1 1 4	**Finger** 1 3 4 2 1 1	**Finger** X X 1 2 4 3	**Finger** X 4 3 1 2 1
Scale 1 3 5 1 3 1	**Scale** 1 5 1 3 5 1	**Scale** 3 5 1 5 1 3	**Scale** 5 1 3 5 1 3
Note A C# E A C# A	**Note** A E A C# E A	**Note** C# E A E A C#	**Note** E A C# E A C#

IV - (1, 3, 5) Extensions - (2), (b5), (6), (7)

B (V)
Finger 3 2 1 1 1 4	**Finger** 1 3 4 2 1 1	**Finger** X X 1 2 4 3	**Finger** X 4 3 1 2 1
Scale 1 3 5 1 3 1	**Scale** 1 5 1 3 5 1	**Scale** 3 5 1 5 1 3	**Scale** 5 1 3 5 1 3
Note B D# F# B D# B	**Note** B F# B D# F# B	**Note** D# F# B F# B D#	**Note** F# B D# F# B D#

V - (1, 3, 5) Extensions - (2), (4), (6), (b7)

C#m (vi)
Finger X 4 2 1 3 0	**Finger** 4 2 1 1 X X	**Finger** 1 3 4 1 1 1	**Finger** X X 1 3 4 2
Scale 5 1 b3 5 1 b3	**Scale** 1 b3 5 1 b3 1	**Scale** 1 5 1 b3 5 1	**Scale** b3 5 1 5 1 b3
Note G# C# E G# C# E	**Note** C# E G# C# E C#	**Note** C# G# C# E G# C#	**Note** E G# C# G# C# E

vi - (1, b3, 5) Extensions - (2), (4), (#5), (b7)

F#m (ii)
Finger X X 1 3 4 2	**Finger** X 4 2 1 3 X	**Finger** X 1 3 4 2 1	**Finger** 4 2 1 1 X X
Scale b3 5 1 5 1 b3	**Scale** 5 1 b3 5 1 b3	**Scale** 5 1 5 1 b3 5	**Scale** 1 b3 5 1 b3 1
Note A C# F# C# F# A	**Note** C# F# A C# F# A	**Note** C# F# C# F# A C#	**Note** F# A C# F# A F#

ii - (1, b3, 5) Extensions - (2), (4), (6), (b7)

G#m (iii)
Finger X 3 1 2 0 X	**Finger** X X 1 3 4 2	**Finger** X 4 2 1 3 X	**Finger** X 1 3 4 2 1
Scale 1 b3 5 1 b3 1	**Scale** b3 5 1 5 1 b3	**Scale** 5 1 b3 5 1 b3	**Scale** 5 1 5 1 b3 5
Note G# B D# G# B G#	**Note** B D# G# D# G# B	**Note** D# G# B D# G# B	**Note** D# G# D# G# B D#

iii - (1, b3, 5) Extensions - (b2), (4), (#5), (b7)

* Order of notes as you move up and down a string.

1
b2 (b9)
2 (sus2, 9)
#2 (#9) / (b3 minor)
3
4 (sus, 11)
b5 (b5, #11)
5
#5 (#5, b13) / (+, aug)
6 (6, 13)
b7 (7) Dominant 7th
7 (Maj7)
1

CHORD SUBSTITUTIONS - KEY OF E AND C#m

1. CHORD EMBELLISHMENTS - EXTENSIONS AND ALTERATIONS

2. MAJOR, MINOR AND DOMINANT SUBSTITUTIONS

Major   **E (I** Relative minor - **C#m (vi)** or Common Tones - **G#m (iii)**

              A (IV) Relative minor - **F#m (ii)** or Common Tones - **C#m (vi)**

              B (V) Relative minor - **G#m (iii)** or Common Tones - **D#m (vii)**

minor   **C#m (vi)** - Relative Major - **E (I)** or Common Tones - **A (IV)**

              F#m (ii) - Relative Major - **A (IV)** or Common Tones - **D (bVII)**

              G#m (iii) - Relative Major - **B (V)** or Common Tones - **E (I)**

7th   **B7(V7)** Common Tones - **D#°7 (VII°7)** or **G#m (iii)** or Tritone - **F7**

3. BACKCYCLING (CIRCLE OF 5THS)

(G#m7-C#m7-F#m7-B7) - E   **(C#m7-F#m7-Bm7-E7) - A**   **(Ebm7-G#m7-C#m7-F#7) - B**

(Fm7-Bbm7-Ebm7-G#7) - C#m   **(Bbm7-Ebm7-G#m7-C#7) - F#m** **(Cm7-Fm7-Bbm7-Eb7) - G#m**

Use the 5th of the chord you're going to to find the letter name of the chord that should proceed it. Here are a couple of variations on backcycling (G#7, C#7, F#7, B7) - E or (G#m7, C#7, F#m7, B7) - E. The ii-V7 is a very common substitute for a V7 chord. Also don't forget you can just add the secondary dominants before a chord.

4. HALF STEP PROGRESSIONS

This is usually some type of dominant 7th chord.

Major	**Eb7-E**	**F7-E**	**Ab7-A**	**A#7-A**	**Bb7-B**	**C7-B**
minor	**C7-C#m**	**D7-C#m**	**F7-F#m**	**G7-F#m**	**G7-G#m**	**A7-G#m**

5. PASSING CHORDS

°7   Diminished 7th chords can be used between diatonic chords to create a *chromatic* chord progression.

              EMaj7(I)-F°7-F#m7(ii)-G°7-G#m7(iii)-AMaj7(IV)-A#°7-B7(V7)-C°7-C#m7(vi)

Diatonic   You can also use diatonic chords to fill-in the gaps between chords.

              Here is an example of a *diatonic* type passing chord progression:

              original E(I)-E(I)-E(I)-A(IV) becomes E(I)-F#m(ii)-G#m(iii)-A(IV).

6. TRITONE SUBSTITUTION

You can substitute a dominant 7th chord with another dominant 7th chord based on the flat five of the original dominant 7th chord. Below are the original 7th chords followed by their tritone substitution. You can also use these substitutions in your backcycling to create chromatic bass lines.

A7 to Eb7	Bb7 to E7	B7 to F7	C7 to Gb7	C#7 to G7	Db7 to G7	D7 to Ab7
Eb7 to A7	E7 to Bb7	F7 to B7	F#7 to C7	Gb7 to C7	G7 to Db7	Ab7 to D7

7. QUALITY CHANGE CHORDS

Majors - (minors, Dominant 7ths), Minors - (Majors, Dominant 7ths), Dominant 7ths - (Majors, minors)

Four Note Extensions Up The Neck - Key of E and C#m

* Use the sections on *Bass Notes* and *Optional Notes* to find other notes you can add to these chords. Also don't forget you don't have to play every note in the chord, only the essential notes that convey the chords family and quality of sound.

EMaj7 (I)

Finger	X	X	1	4	4 4
Scale	X	X	1	5	7 3
Note	X	X	E	B	D# G#

EMaj7 (I) — 4th

Finger	X	4	3	1	1 1
Scale	X	1	3	5	7 3
Note	X	E	G#	B	D# G#

EMaj7 (I) — 7th

Finger	X	1	3	2	4 1
Scale	X	1	5	7	3 5
Note	X	E	B	D#	G# B

EMaj7 (I) — 9th

Finger	X	0	1	1	1 2
Scale	X	1	5	1	3 7
Note	X	E	B	E	G# D#

EMaj7 (I) — 11th

Finger	X	X	4	3	2 1
Scale	X	X	1	3	5 7
Note	X	X	E	G#	B D#

AMaj7 (IV)

Finger	X	0	1	1	1 2
Scale	X	1	5	1	3 7
Note	X	A	E	A	C# G#

AMaj7 (IV) — 5th

Finger	1	X	3	4	2 X
Scale	1	5	7	3	5 1
Note	A	E	G#	C#	E A

AMaj7 (IV) — 4th

Finger	T	X	4	3	2 1
Scale	1	X	1	3	5 7
Note	A	X	A	C#	E G#

AMaj7 (IV) — 7th

Finger	X	X	1	4	4 4
Scale	X	X	1	5	7 3
Note	X	X	A	E	G# C#

AMaj7 (IV) — 9th

Finger	X	4	3	1	1 1
Scale	X	1	3	5	7 3
Note	X	A	C#	E	G# C#

B7 (V7)

Finger	X	1	2	1	4 1
Scale	X	1	5	b7	3 5
Note	X	B	F#	A	D# F#

B7 (V7) — 4th

Finger	X	X	1	1	1 2
Scale	X	X	5	1	3 b7
Note	X	X	F#	B	D# A

B7 (V7) — 7th

Finger	1	3	1	2	1 1
Scale	1	5	b7	3	5 1
Note	B	F#	A	D#	F# B

B7 (V7) — 8th

Finger	X	2	3	1	4 X
Scale	X	5	1	3	b7 X
Note	X	F#	B	D#	A X

B7 (V7) — 9th

Finger	X	X	1	3	2 4
Scale	X	X	1	5	b7 3
Note	X	X	B	F#	A D#

C#m7 (vi)

Finger	X	4	2	1	0 0
Scale	X	1	b3	5	b7 b3
Note	X	C#	E	G#	B E

C#m7 (vi) — 2nd

Finger	X	2	1	3	1 4
Scale	X	1	b3	b7	1 5
Note	X	C#	E	B	C# G#

C#m7 (vi) — 5th

Finger	X	X	2	3	1 4
Scale	X	X	5	1	b3 b7
Note	X	X	G#	C#	E B

C#m7 (vi) — 9th

Finger	1	3	1	1	1 1
Scale	1	5	b7	b3	5 1
Note	C#	G#	B	E	G# C#

C#m7 (vi) — 11th

Finger	X	X	1	3	2 2
Scale	X	X	1	5	b7 b3
Note	X	X	C#	G#	B E

F#m7 (ii)

Finger	X	0	4	1	2 0
Scale	X	b3	1	b3	5 b7
Note	X	A	F#	A	C# E

F#m7 (ii) — 4th

Finger	X	X	1	3	2 2
Scale	X	X	1	5	b7 b3
Note	X	X	F#	C#	E A

F#m7 (ii) — 7th

Finger	X	2	1	3	1 4
Scale	X	1	b3	b7	1 5
Note	X	F#	A	E	F# C#

F#m7 (ii) — 9th

Finger	X	1	3	1	2 1
Scale	X	1	5	b7	b3 5
Note	X	F#	C#	E	A C#

F#m7 (ii) — 10th

Finger	X	X	2	3	1 4
Scale	X	X	5	1	b3 b7
Note	X	X	C#	F#	A E

G#m7 (iii)

Finger	X	3	1	2	0 4
Scale	X	b3	5	1	b3 b7
Note	X	B	D#	G#	B F#

G#m7 (iii) — 6th

Finger	X	X	1	3	2 2
Scale	X	X	1	5	b7 b3
Note	X	X	G#	D#	F# B

G#m7 (iii) — 9th

Finger	X	2	1	3	1 4
Scale	X	1	b3	b7	1 5
Note	X	G#	B	F#	G# D#

G#m7 (iii) — 11th

Finger	X	1	3	1	2 1
Scale	X	1	5	b7	b3 5
Note	X	G#	D#	F#	B D#

G#m7 (iii) — 12th

Finger	X	X	2	3	1 4
Scale	X	X	5	1	b3 b7
Note	X	X	D#	G#	B F#

Classic Rock Power Chord & Rock-n-Roll Worksheet - Key of E and C#m

I, IV & V Power Chords (1 and 5)

E5 (I)
Finger 0 2 3 4 0 0
Scale   1 5 1 5 5 1
Note   E B E B B E

E5 (I)
Scale   1 5 1 X X X
Note   E B E X X X

E5 (I) — 7th
Scale   5 1 5 1 X X
Note   B E B E X X

A5 (IV)
Finger X 0 1 1 4 4
Scale   X 1 5 1 5 1
Note   X A E A E A

A5 (IV)
Scale   5 1 5 1 X X
Note   E A E A X X

A5 (IV) — 5th
Scale   1 5 1 X X X
Note   A E A X X X

B (V)
Finger X 1 2 3 4 1
Scale   X 1 5 1 3 5
Note   X B F# B D# F#

B5 (V)
Scale   5 1 5 1 X X
Note   F# B F# B X X

B5 (V) — 7th
Scale   1 5 1 X X X
Note   B F# B X X X

Flat Major Power Chords

G5 (♭III) — 3rd
Scale   1 5 1 X X X
Note   G D G X X X

G5 (♭III) — 10th
Scale   5 1 5 1 X X
Note   D G D G X X

C5 (♭VI) — 3rd
Scale   5 1 5 1 X X
Note   G C G C X X

C5 (♭VI) — 8th
Scale   1 5 1 X X X
Note   C G C X X X

D5 (♭VII) — 5th
Scale   5 1 5 1 X X
Note   A D A D X X

D5 (♭VII) — 10th
Scale   1 5 1 X X X
Note   D A D X X X

Combinations of notes that can be used to make Power Chords - 1, 5 or 1, 5, 1 called 1st Inversion Power Chords
5, 1 or 5, 1, 5 called 2nd Inversion Power Chords

ii, iii, vi Power Chords

F#5 (ii)
Scale   1 5 1 X X X
Note   F# C# F# X X X

F#5 (ii) — 9th
Scale   5 1 5 1 X X
Note   C# F# C# F# X X

G#5 (iii) — 4th
Scale   1 5 1 X X X
Note   G# D# G# X X X

G#5 (iii) — 11th
Scale   5 1 5 1 X X
Note   D# G# D# G# X X

C#5 (vi) — 4th
Scale   5 1 5 1 X X
Note   G# C# G# C# X X

C#5 (vi) — 9th
Scale   1 5 1 X X X
Note   C# G# C# X X X

Other Power Chord Shapes

Scale   X X 5 1 5 1

Scale   X 5 1 5 1 X

X5add9
Scale   1 5 2 X X X

X5add9
Scale   X 1 5 2 X X

E5 (I) — 7th
Finger 0 1 3 4 0 0
Scale   1 1 5 1 5 1
Note   E E B E B E

Rock-n-Roll Chord Shapes for I, IV and V Chords

X5 / X6 / X7
Scale   1 5 X X X X

X5 / X6 / X7
Scale   X 1 5 X X X

X5 / X6 / X7
Scale   X X 1 5 X X

Key of E and C#m Triad Worksheet (1st, 2nd and 3rd strings)

A (IV) — Scale 1 3 5
E (I) — Scale 3 5 1
C#m (vi) — Scale 5 1 ♭3
C (♭VI) — Scale 5 1 3
E (I) — Scale 3 5 1
E (I) 4th — Scale 5 1 3
E (I) 7th — Scale 1 3 5

B (V) — Scale 1 3 5
F#m (ii) — Scale ♭3 5 1
D#o (viio) — Scale ♭5 1 ♭3
D (♭VII) — Scale 5 1 3
A (IV) — Scale 1 3 5
A (IV) 5th — Scale 3 5 1
A (IV) 9th — Scale 5 1 3

C#m (vi) 4th — Scale 1 ♭3 5
G#m (iii) 4th — Scale ♭3 5 1
E (I) 4th — Scale 5 1 3
G (♭III) 3rd — Scale 3 5 1
B (V) — Scale 1 3 5
B (V) 7th — Scale 3 5 1
B (V) 11th — Scale 5 1 3

D#o (viio) 5th — Scale 1 ♭3 ♭5
A (IV) 5th — Scale 3 5 1
F#m (ii) 5th — Scale 5 1 ♭3
C (♭VI) 3rd — Scale 1 3 5

E (I) 7th — Scale 1 3 5
B (V) 7th — Scale 3 5 1
G#m (iii) 7th — Scale 5 1 ♭3
D (♭VII) 5th — Scale 1 3 5
C#m (vi) — Scale 5 1 ♭3
C#m (vi) 4th — Scale 1 ♭3 5
C#m (vi) 9th — Scale ♭3 5 1

F#m (ii) 9th — Scale 1 ♭3 5
C#m (vi) 9th — Scale ♭3 5 1
A (IV) 9th — Scale 5 1 3
G (♭III) 7th — Scale 5 1 3
F#m (ii) — Scale ♭3 5 1
F#m (ii) 5th — Scale 5 1 ♭3
F#m (ii) 9th — Scale 1 ♭3 5

G#m (iii) 11th — Scale 1 ♭3 5
D#o (viio) 10th — Scale ♭3 ♭5 1
B (V) 11th — Scale 5 1 3
C (♭VI) 8th — Scale 3 5 1
G#m (iii) 4th — Scale ♭3 5 1
G#m (iii) 7th — Scale 5 1 ♭3
G#m (iii) 11th — Scale 1 ♭3 5

A (IV) 12th — Scale 1 3 5
E (I) 12th — Scale 3 5 1
C#m (vi) 12th — Scale 5 1 ♭3
D (♭VII) 10th — Scale 3 5 1

B (V) 14th — Scale 1 3 5
F#m (ii) 14th — Scale ♭3 5 1
D#o (viio) 14th — Scale ♭5 1 ♭3
G (♭III) 10th — Scale 1 3 5
D#o (viio) — Scale ♭5 1 ♭3
D#o (viio) 5th — Scale 1 ♭3 ♭5
D#o (viio) 10th — Scale ♭3 5 1

110

Key of E and C#m Triad Worksheet (2nd, 3rd and 4th strings)

Row 1:

E (I) — Scale 1 3 5
C#m (vi) — Scale ♭3 5 1
G#m (iii) — Scale 5 1 ♭3
G (♭III) — Scale 5 1 3
E (I) — Scale 1 3 5
E (I), 4th — Scale 3 5 1
E (I), 9th — Scale 5 1 3

Row 2:

F#m (ii) — Scale 1 ♭3 5
D#o (viio) — Scale ♭3 ♭5 1
A (IV) — Scale 5 1 3
C (♭VI) — Scale 3 5 1
A (IV) — Scale 5 1 3
A (IV), 5th — Scale 1 3 5
A (IV), 9th — Scale 3 5 1

Row 3:

G#m (iii), 4th — Scale 1 ♭3 5
E (I), 4th — Scale 3 5 1
B (V), 4th — Scale 5 1 3
D (♭VII) — Scale 3 5 1
B (V), 4th — Scale 5 1 3
B (V), 7th — Scale 1 3 5
B (V), 11th — Scale 3 5 1

Row 4:

A (IV), 5th — Scale 1 3 5
F#m (ii), 6th — Scale ♭3 5 1
C#m (vi), 5th — Scale 5 1 ♭3
G (♭III), 3rd — Scale 1 3 5

Row 5:

B (V), 7th — Scale 1 3 5
G#m (iii), 8th — Scale ♭3 5 1
D#o (viio), 7th — Scale 5 1 ♭3
C (♭VI), 5th — Scale 5 1 3
C#m (vi) — Scale ♭3 5 1
C#m (vi), 5th — Scale 5 1 ♭3
C#m (vi), 9th — Scale 1 ♭3 5

Row 6:

C#m (vi), 9th — Scale 1 ♭3 5
A (IV), 9th — Scale 3 5 1
E (I), 9th — Scale 5 1 3
D (♭VII), 7th — Scale 5 1 3
F#m (ii) — Scale 1 ♭3 5
F#m (ii), 6th — Scale ♭3 5 1
F#m (ii), 10th — Scale 5 1 ♭3

Row 7:

D#o (viio), 10th — Scale 1 ♭3 ♭5
B (V), 11th — Scale 3 5 1
F#m (ii), 10th — Scale 5 1 ♭3
G (♭III), 7th — Scale 3 5 1
G#m (iii) — Scale 5 1 ♭3
G#m (iii), 4th — Scale 1 ♭3 5
G#m (iii), 8th — Scale ♭3 5 1

Row 8:

E (I), 12th — Scale 1 3 5
C#m (vi), 13th — Scale ♭3 5 1
G#m (iii), 12th — Scale 5 1 ♭3
C (♭VI), 8th — Scale 1 3 5

Row 9:

F#m (ii), 14th — Scale 1 ♭3 5
D#o (viio), 14th — Scale ♭3 ♭5 1
A (IV), 14th — Scale 5 1 3
D (♭VII), 10th — Scale 1 3 5
D#o (viio) — Scale ♭3 ♭5 1
D#o (viio), 7th — Scale 5 1 ♭3
D#o (viio), 10th — Scale 1 ♭3 ♭5

111

Key of E and C#m Triad Worksheet (3rd, 4th and 5th strings)

C#m(vi) — Scale 1 ♭3 5	**G#m (iii)** — Scale ♭3 5 1	**E (I)** — Scale 5 1 3	**G (♭III)** — Scale 3 5 1	**E (I)** — Scale 5 1 3	**E (I)** 4th — Scale 1 3 5	**E (I)** 9th — Scale 3 5 1
D#o (viio) 2nd — Scale 1 ♭3 ♭5	**A (IV)** — Scale 3 5 1	**F#m (ii)** — Scale 5 1 ♭3	**C (♭VI)** — Scale 1 3 5	**A (IV)** — Scale 3 5 1	**A (IV)** 6th — Scale 5 1 3	**A (IV)** 9th — Scale 1 3 5
E (I) 4th — Scale 1 3 5	**B (V)** 4th — Scale 3 5 1	**G#m (iii)** 4th — Scale 5 1 ♭3	**D (♭VII)** — Scale 1 3 5	**B (V)** 4th — Scale 3 5 1	**B (V)** 8th — Scale 5 1 3	**B (V)** 11th — Scale 1 3 5
F#m(ii) 6th — Scale 1 ♭3 5	**C#m (vi)** 6th — Scale ♭3 5 1	**A (IV)** 6th — Scale 5 1 3	**G (♭III)** 4th — Scale 5 1 3			
G#m(iii) 8th — Scale 1 ♭3 5	**D#o (viio)** 7th — Scale ♭3 5 1	**B (V)** 8th — Scale 5 1 3	**C (♭VI)** 5th — Scale 3 5 1	**C#m(vi)** — Scale 1 ♭3 5	**C#m (vi)** 6th — Scale ♭3 5 1	**C#m (vi)** 9th — Scale 5 1 ♭3
A (IV) 9th — Scale 1 3 5	**E (I)** 9th — Scale 3 5 1	**C#m (vi)** 9th — Scale 5 1 ♭3	**D (♭VII)** 7th — Scale 3 5 1	**F#m (ii)** 9th — Scale 5 1 ♭3	**F#m(ii)** 6th — Scale 1 ♭3 5	**F#m (ii)** 11th — Scale ♭3 5 1
B (V) 11th — Scale 1 3 5	**F#m (ii)** 11th — Scale ♭3 5 1	**D#o (viio)** 11th — Scale ♭5 1 ♭3	**G (♭III)** 7th — Scale 1 3 5	**G#m (iii)** — Scale ♭3 5 1	**G#m (iii)** 4th — Scale 5 1 ♭3	**G#m(iii)** 8th — Scale 1 ♭3 5
C#m(vi) 13th — Scale 1 ♭3 5	**G#m (iii)** 13th — Scale ♭3 5 1	**E (I)** 13th — Scale 5 1 3	**C (♭VI)** 9th — Scale 5 1 3			
D#o (viio) 14th — Scale 1 ♭3 ♭5	**A (IV)** 14th — Scale 3 5 1	**F#m (ii)** 14th — Scale 5 1 ♭3	**D (♭VII)** 11th — Scale 5 1 3	**D#o (viio)** 2nd — Scale 1 ♭3 ♭5	**D#o (viio)** 7th — Scale ♭3 5 1	**D#o (viio)** 11th — Scale ♭5 1 ♭3

Slash Chord Worksheet

Key of E and C#m

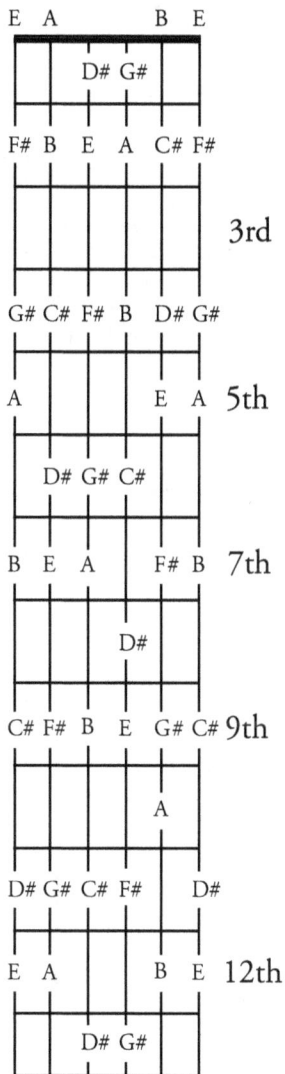

E A   B E

      D# G#

F# B E A C# F#

                    3rd

G# C# F# B D# G#

A   E A   5th

      D# G# C#

B E A   F# B   7th

            D#

C# F# B E G# C#   9th

                A

D# G# C# F#   D#

E A   B E   12th

      D# G#

Diatonic and Secondary Dominant Chords

F Major

Key of (Bb)

D minor

F (I)
Finger 1 3 4 2 1 1
Scale 1 5 1 3 5 1
Note F C F A C F

Bb (IV)
Finger X 1 2 3 4 1
Scale X 1 5 1 3 5
Note X Bb F Bb D F

C (V)
Finger X 3 2 0 1 0
Scale X 1 3 5 1 3
Note X C E G C E

C7 (V7/I)
Finger X 3 2 4 1 0
Scale X 1 3 b7 1 3
Note X C E Bb C E

F7 (V7/IV)
Finger 1 3 1 2 1 1
Scale 1 5 b7 3 5 1
Note F C Eb A C F

G7 (V7/V)
Finger 3 2 0 0 0 1
Scale 1 3 5 1 3 b7
Note G B D G B F

Dm (vi)
Finger X X 0 2 3 1
Scale X X 1 5 1 b3
Note X X D A D F

Gm (ii)
Finger 1 3 4 1 1 1
Scale 1 5 1 b3 5 1
Note G D G Bb D G

Am (iii)
Finger X 0 2 3 1 0
Scale X 1 5 1 b3 5
Note X A E A C E

A7 (V7/vi)
Finger X 0 1 0 2 0
Scale X 1 5 b7 3 5
Note X A E G C# E

D7 (V7/ii)
Finger X X 0 2 1 3
Scale X X 1 5 b7 3
Note X X D A C F#

E7 (V7/iii)
Finger 0 2 0 1 0 0
Scale 1 5 b7 3 5 1
Note E B D G# B E

Extensions

FMaj7 (I)
Finger X X 3 2 1 0
Scale X X 1 3 5 7
Note X X F A C E

BbMaj7 (IV)
Finger X 1 3 2 4 1
Scale X 1 5 7 3 5
Note X Bb F A D F

C7 (V7)
Finger X 3 2 4 1 0
Scale X 1 3 b7 1 3
Note X C E Bb C E

Dm7 (vi)
Finger X X 0 2 1 1
Scale X X 1 5 b7 b3
Note X X D A C F

Gm7 (ii)
Finger 1 3 1 1 1 1
Scale 1 5 b7 b3 5 1
Note G D F Bb D G

Am7 (iii)
Finger X 0 2 0 1 0
Scale X 1 5 b7 b3 5
Note X A E G C E

Flat Majors

Ab (bIII)
Finger 1 3 4 2 1 1
Scale 1 5 1 3 5 1
Note Ab Eb Ab C Eb Ab

Db (bVI)
Finger X 1 2 3 4 1
Scale X 1 5 1 3 5
Note X Db Ab Db F Ab

Eb (bVII)
Finger X 1 2 3 4 1
Scale X 1 5 1 3 5
Note X Eb Bb Eb G Bb

Suspended Chords

Fsus (I)
Finger X X 3 4 1 1
Scale X X 1 4 5 1
Note X X F A# C F

Fsus2 (I)
Finger X X 3 0 1 1
Scale X X 1 2 5 1
Note X X F G C F

Bbsus2 (IV)
Finger X 1 2 3 1 1
Scale X 1 5 1 2 5
Note X Bb F Bb C F

C7sus (V7)
Finger X 2 3 4 1 X
Scale X 1 4 b7 1 X
Note X C F Bb C X

Csus (V)
Finger X 3 4 0 1 1
Scale X 1 4 5 1 4
Note X C F G C F

Csus2 (V)
Finger X 2 0 0 4 4
Scale X 1 2 5 2 5
Note X C D G D G

Add9 Chords

Fadd9 (I)
Finger X X 3 2 1 4
Scale X X 1 3 5 2
Note X X F A C G

Fadd9 (I)
Finger X 3 2 0 1 4
Scale X 1 3 2 1 5
Note X F A G F C

Bbadd9 (IV)
Finger X X 0 3 1 1
Scale X X 3 1 2 5
Note X X D Bb C F

Cadd9 (V)
Finger X 3 2 0 4 0
Scale X 1 3 5 2 3
Note X C E G D E

Dm Harmonic chords

A (III)
Finger X 0 1 2 3 0
Scale X 1 5 1 3 5
Note X A E A C# E

A7 (III7)
Finger X 0 1 0 2 0
Scale X 1 5 b7 3 5
Note X A E G C# E

114

Dominant 7th (Blues) Chords

F7 (I7)
Finger 1 3 1 2 1 1
Scale 1 5 ♭7 3 5 1
Note F C E♭ A C F

F7 (I7) — 8th
Finger X 1 3 1 4 1
Scale X 1 5 ♭7 3 5
Note X F C E♭ A C

B♭7 (IV7)
Finger X 1 3 1 4 1
Scale X 1 5 ♭7 3 5
Note X B♭ F A♭ D F

B♭7 (IV7) — 6th
Finger 1 3 1 2 1 1
Scale 1 5 ♭7 3 5 1
Note B♭ F A♭ D F B♭

C7 (V7)
Finger X 3 2 4 1 0
Scale X 1 3 ♭7 1 3
Note X C E B♭ C E

C7 (V7) — 3rd
Finger X 1 3 1 4 1
Scale X 1 5 ♭7 3 5
Note X C G B♭ E G

Quality Change Chords

G (II) — V
Finger 3 2 0 0 0 4
Scale 1 3 5 1 3 1
Note G B D G B G

B♭m (iv) — I iv IV
Finger X 1 3 4 2 1
Scale X 1 5 1 ♭3 5
Note X B♭ F B♭ D♭ F

A (III) — vi
Finger X 0 1 2 3 0
Scale X 1 5 1 3 5
Note X A E A C# E

Cm (v) — I — 3rd
Finger X 1 3 4 2 1
Scale X 1 5 1 ♭3 5
Note X C G C E♭ G

D (VI) — ii
Finger X X 0 1 3 2
Scale X X 1 5 1 3
Note X X D A D F#

Em (vii) — iii
Finger 0 2 3 0 0 0
Scale 1 5 1 ♭3 5 1
Note E B E G B E

E (VII) — iii
Finger 0 2 3 1 0 0
Scale 1 5 1 3 5 1
Note E B E G# B E

Fm (i)
Finger 1 3 4 1 1 1
Scale 1 5 1 ♭3 5 1
Note F C F A♭ C F

Additional Diatonic Extensions

F6 (I)
Finger 1 X 0 4 2 3
Scale 1 X 6 3 5 1
Note F X D A C F

FMaj9 (I)
Finger 1 0 3 0 2 0
Scale 1 3 7 2 5 7
Note F A E G C E

F6/9 (I)
Finger X 2 3 1 4 4
Scale X 5 1 3 6 2
Note X C F A D G

Gm6 (ii)
Finger 2 X 1 3 3 3
Scale 1 X 6 ♭3 5 1
Note G X E B♭ D G

Gm9 (ii) — 3rd
Finger 1 3 1 1 1 4
Scale 1 5 ♭7 ♭3 5 2
Note G D F B♭ D A

Gm7add11 (ii)
Finger 3 X 0 4 1 1
Scale 1 X 5 ♭3 4 ♭7
Note G X D B♭ C F

Am7/11 (iii)
Finger X 0 0 0 1 0
Scale X 1 4 ♭7 ♭3 5
Note X A D G C E

Amadd11 (iii)
Finger X 0 0 2 1 0
Scale X 1 4 1 ♭3 5
Note X A D A C E

B♭6 (IV)
Finger X 1 3 0 4 X
Scale X 1 5 6 3 X
Note X B♭ F G D X

B♭Maj9 (IV)
Finger X 1 0 4 2 3
Scale X 1 3 7 2 5
Note X B♭ D A C F

B♭Maj13 (IV)
Finger X 1 1 2 4 4
Scale X 1 4 7 3 6
Note X B♭ E♭ A D G

C9 (V7)
Finger X 2 1 3 3 3
Scale X 1 3 ♭7 2 5
Note X C E B♭ D G

C13 (V7)
Finger X 2 1 3 3 4
Scale X 1 3 ♭7 2 6
Note X C E B♭ D A

C7add11 (V7)
Finger X 3 2 4 1 1
Scale X 1 3 ♭7 1 4
Note X C E B♭ C F

Dm9 (vi) — 3rd
Finger X 3 1 4 4 4
Scale X 1 ♭3 ♭7 2 5
Note X D F C E A

Dm7add11 (vi) — 3rd
Finger X 2 1 3 1 1
Scale X 1 ♭3 ♭7 1 4
Note X D F C D G

Dm11 (vi) — 5th
Finger X 1 3 0 2 0
Scale X 1 5 4 ♭3 2
Note X D A G F E

Em7♭5 (viiø7)
Finger X X 1 3 3 3
Scale X X 1 ♭5 ♭7 ♭3
Note X X E B♭ D G

Em7♭5 (viiø7)
Finger 0 1 3 0 4 0
Scale 1 ♭5 1 ♭3 ♭7 1
Note E B♭ E G D E

E° (vii°)
Finger 0 1 3 0 X X
Scale 1 ♭5 1 ♭3 X X
Note E B♭ E G X X

*The m7♭5 is also referred to as a half diminished chord and can be written as a degree symbol with a slash through it.

Chord Formula Worksheet Up The Neck - Key of F and Dm

F (I) — 3rd
Finger X X 1 4 3
Scale 3 5 1 5 1 3
Note A C F C F A

F (I) — 5th
Finger X 4 3 1 2 1
Scale 5 1 3 5 1 3
Note C F A C F A

F (I) — 8th
Finger X 1 2 3 4 1
Scale 5 1 5 1 3 5
Note C F C F A C

F (I) — 10th
Finger 3 2 1 1 1 4
Scale 1 3 5 1 3 1
Note F A C F A F

I - (1, 3, 5) Extensions - (2), (4), (6), (7)

Bb (IV) — 3rd
Finger 3 2 1 1 1 4
Scale 1 3 5 1 3 1
Note Bb D F Bb D Bb

Bb (IV) — 6th
Finger 1 3 4 2 1 1
Scale 1 5 1 3 5 1
Note Bb F Bb D F Bb

Bb (IV) — 8th
Finger X X 1 2 4 3
Scale 3 5 1 5 1 3
Note D F Bb F Bb D

Bb (IV) — 10th
Finger X 4 3 1 2 1
Scale 5 1 3 5 1 3
Note F Bb D F Bb D

IV - (1, 3, 5) Extensions - (2), (b5), (6), (7)

C (V) — 3rd
Finger X 1 2 3 4 1
Scale 5 1 5 1 3 5
Note G C G C E G

C (V) — 5th
Finger 3 2 1 1 1 4
Scale 1 3 5 1 3 1
Note C E G C E C

C (V) — 8th
Finger 1 3 4 2 1 1
Scale 1 5 1 3 5 1
Note C G C E G C

C (V) — 10th
Finger X X 1 2 4 3
Scale 3 5 1 5 1 3
Note E G C G C E

V - (1, 3, 5) Extensions - (2), (4), (6), (b7)

Dm (vi) —
Finger X 4 2 1 3 X
Scale 5 1 b3 5 1 b3
Note A D F A D F

Dm (vi) — 5th
Finger X 1 3 4 2 1
Scale 5 1 5 1 b3 5
Note A D A D F A

Dm (vi) — 6th
Finger 4 2 1 1 X X
Scale 1 b3 5 1 b3 1
Note D F A D F D

Dm (vi) — 10th
Finger 1 3 4 1 1 1
Scale 1 5 1 b3 5 1
Note D A D F A D

vi - (1, b3, 5) Extensions - (2), (4), (#5), (b7)

Gm (ii) — 5th
Finger X X 1 3 4 2
Scale b3 5 1 5 1 b3
Note Bb A G A G Bb

Gm (ii) — 6th
Finger X 4 2 1 3 X
Scale 5 1 b3 5 1 b3
Note D G Bb D G Bb

Gm (ii) — 10th
Finger X 1 3 4 2 1
Scale 5 1 5 1 b3 5
Note D G D G Bb D

Gm (ii) — 11th
Finger 4 2 1 1 X X
Scale 1 b3 5 1 b3 1
Note G Bb D G Bb G

ii - (1, b3, 5) Extensions - (2), (4), (6), (b7)

Am (iii) —
Finger 4 2 1 1 X X
Scale 1 b3 5 1 b3 1
Note A C E A C A

Am (iii) — 5th
Finger 1 3 4 1 1 1
Scale 1 5 1 b3 5 1
Note A E A C E A

Am (iii) — 7th
Finger X X 1 3 4 2
Scale b3 5 1 5 1 b3
Note C E A E A C

Am (iii) — 8th
Finger X 4 2 1 3 X
Scale 5 1 b3 5 1 b3
Note E A C E A C

iii - (1, b3, 5) Extensions - (b2), (4), (#5), (b7)

* Order of notes as you move up and down a string.

1
b2 (b9)
2 (sus2, 9)
#2 (#9) / (b3 minor)
3
4 (sus, 11)
b5 (b5, #11)
5
#5 (#5, b13) / (+, aug)
6 (6, 13)
b7 (7) Dominant 7th
7 (Maj7)
1

E	A	D	G		E
F	Bb			C	F
		E	A		
G	C	F	Bb	D	G	3rd

| A | D | G | C | E | A | 5th
| Bb | | | | F | Bb |
| | E | | A | D | | 7th
| C | F | Bb | | G | C |
| | | E | | | | 9th
| D | G | C | F | A | D |
| | | | | Bb | |
| E | A | D | G | | E | 12th
| F | Bb | | | C | F |

CHORD SUBSTITUTIONS - KEY OF F AND Dm

1. CHORD EMBELLISHMENTS - EXTENSIONS AND ALTERATIONS

2. MAJOR, MINOR AND DOMINANT SUBSTITUTIONS

Major   **F (I)** Relative minor - **Dm (vi)** or Common Tones - **Am (iii)**

              Bb (IV) Relative minor - **Gm (ii)** or Common Tones - **Dm (vi)**

              C (V) Relative minor - **Am (iii)** or Common Tones - **Em (vii)**

minor   **Dm (vi)** Relative Major - **F (I)** or Common Tones - **Bb (IV)**

              Gm (ii) Relative Major - **Bb (IV)** or Common Tones - **Eb (bVII)**

              Am (iii) Relative Major - **C (V)** or Common Tones - **F (I)**

7th   **C7(V7)** Common Tones - **E°7 (VII°7)** or **Am (iii)** or Tritone - **Gb7**

3. BACKCYCLING (CIRCLE OF 5THS)

(Am7-Dm7-Gm7-C7) - F	**(Dm7-Gm7-Cm7-F7) - Bb**	**(Em7-Am7-Dm7-G7) - C**
(Ebm7-Abm7-Dbm7-Gb7) - Bm	**(Bm7-Em7-Am7-D7) - Gm**	**(Dbm7-Gbm7-Bm7-E7) - Am**

Use the 5th of the chord you're going to to find the letter name of the chord that should proceed it. Here are a couple of variations on backcycling (A7, D7, G7, C7) - F or (Am7, D7, Gm7, C7) - F. The ii-V7 is a very common substitute for a V7 chord. Also don't forget you can just add the secondary dominants before a chord.

4. HALF STEP PROGRESSIONS

This is usually some type of dominant 7th chord.

Major	**E7-F**	**F#7-F**	**A7-Bb**	**B7-Bb**	**B7-C**	**C#7-C**
minor	**Db7-Dm**	**D#7-Dm**	**Gb7-Gm**	**G#7-Gm**	**Ab7-Am**	**A#7-Am**

5. PASSING CHORDS

°7   Diminished 7th chords can be used between diatonic chords to create a *chromatic* chord progression.

          FMaj7(I)-F#°7-Gm7(ii)-G#°7-Am7(iii)-BbMaj7(IV)-B°7-C7(V7)-C#°7-Dm7(vi)

Diatonic   You can also use diatonic chords to fill-in the gaps between chords.

          Here is an example of a *diatonic* type passing chord progression:

          original F(I)-F(I)-F(I)-Bb(IV) becomes F(I)-Gm(ii)-Am(iii)-Bb(IV).

6. TRITONE SUBSTITUTION

You can substitute a dominant 7th chord with another dominant 7th chord based on the flat five of the original dominant 7th chord. Below are the original 7th chords followed by their tritone substitution. You can also use these substitutions in your backcycling to create chromatic bass lines.

A7 to Eb7	Bb7 to E7	B7 to F7	C7 to Gb7	Db7 to G7	Db7 to G7	D7 to Ab7
Eb7 to A7	E7 to Bb7	F7 to B7	Gb7 to C7	Gb7 to C7	G7 to Db7	Ab7 to D7

7. QUALITY CHANGE CHORDS

Majors - (minors, Dominant 7ths), Minors - (Majors, Dominant 7ths), Dominant 7ths - (Majors, minors)

Four Note Extensions Up The Neck - Key of F and Dm

* Use the sections on *Bass Notes* and *Optional Notes* to find other notes you can add to these chords. Also don't forget you don't have to play every note in the chord, only the essential notes that convey the chords family and quality of sound.

FMaj7 (I)
Finger 1 0 3 4 2 0
Scale 1 3 7 3 5 7
Note F A E A C E

FMaj7 (I) — 3rd
Finger X X 1 4 4 4
Scale X X 1 5 7 3
Note X X F C E A

FMaj7 (I) — 5th
Finger X 4 3 1 1 1
Scale X 1 3 5 7 3
Note X F A C E A

FMaj7 (I) — 8th
Finger X 1 3 2 4 1
Scale X 1 5 7 3 5
Note X F C E A C

FMaj7 (I) — 10th
Finger X X 1 1 1 4
Scale X X 5 1 3 7
Note X X C F A E

B♭Maj7 (IV) — 3rd
Finger X X 1 1 1 4
Scale X X 5 1 3 7
Note X X F B♭ D A

B♭Maj7 (IV) — 6th
Finger 1 X 3 4 2 X
Scale 1 5 7 3 5 1
Note B♭ F A D F B♭

B♭Maj7 (IV) — 5th
Finger T X 4 3 2 1
Scale 1 X 1 3 5 7
Note B♭ X B♭ D F A

B♭Maj7 (IV) — 8th
Finger X X 1 4 4 4
Scale X X 1 5 7 3
Note X X B♭ F A D

B♭Maj7 (IV) — 10th
Finger X 4 3 1 1 1
Scale X 1 3 5 7 3
Note X B♭ D F A D

C7 (V7) — 3rd
Finger X 1 3 1 4 1
Scale X 1 5 ♭7 3 5
Note X C G B♭ E G

C7 (V7) — 5th
Finger X X 1 1 1 2
Scale X X 5 1 3 ♭7
Note X X G C E B♭

C7 (V7) — 8th
Finger 1 3 1 2 1 1
Scale 1 5 ♭7 3 5 1
Note C G B♭ E G C

C7 (V7) — 9th
Finger X 2 3 1 4 X
Scale X 5 1 3 ♭7 X
Note X G C E B♭ X

C7 (V7) — 10th
Finger X X 1 3 2 4
Scale X X 1 5 ♭7 3
Note X X C G B♭ E

Dm7 (vi)
Finger X 3 X 2 4 1
Scale X ♭7 X 5 1 ♭3
Note X C X A D F

Dm7 (vi) — 3rd
Finger X 2 1 3 1 4
Scale X 1 ♭3 ♭7 1 5
Note X D F C D A

Dm7 (vi) — 5th
Finger X 1 3 1 2 1
Scale X 1 5 ♭7 ♭3 5
Note X D A C F A

Dm7 (vi) — 6th
Finger X X 2 3 1 4
Scale X X 5 1 ♭3 ♭7
Note X X A D F C

Dm7 (vi) — 10th
Finger 1 3 1 1 1 1
Scale 1 5 ♭7 ♭3 5 1
Note D A C F A D

Gm7 (ii)
Finger 2 1 3 0 4 X
Scale 1 ♭3 ♭7 1 5 X
Note G B♭ F G D X

Gm7 (ii) — 5th
Finger X X 1 3 2 2
Scale X X 1 5 ♭7 ♭3
Note X X G D F B♭

Gm7 (ii) — 8th
Finger X 2 1 3 1 4
Scale X 1 ♭3 ♭7 1 5
Note X G B♭ F G D

Gm7 (ii) — 10th
Finger X 1 3 1 2 1
Scale X 1 5 ♭7 ♭3 5
Note X G D F B♭ D

Gm7 (ii) — 11th
Finger X X 2 3 1 4
Scale X X 5 1 ♭3 ♭7
Note X X D G B♭ F

Am7 (iii)
Finger X 0 2 3 1 4
Scale X 1 5 1 ♭3 ♭7
Note X A E A C G

Am7 (iii) — 5th
Finger 1 3 1 1 1 1
Scale 1 5 ♭7 3 5 1
Note A E G C E A

Am7 (iii) — 7th
Finger X X 1 3 2 2
Scale X X 1 5 ♭7 ♭3
Note X X A E G C

Am7 (iii) — 8th
Finger X 0 3 2 1 0
Scale X 1 ♭3 5 ♭7 5
Note X A C E G E

Am7 (iii) — 10th
Finger X 2 1 3 1 4
Scale X 1 ♭3 ♭7 1 5
Note X A C G A E

Classic Rock Power Chord & Rock-n-Roll Worksheet - Key of F and Dm

I, IV & V Power Chords (1 and 5)

F (I)
Finger 1 3 4 2 1 1
Scale 1 5 1 3 5 1
Note F C F A C F

F5 (I) X X X
Scale 1 5 1 X X X
Note F C F X X X

F5 (I) X X — 8th
Scale 5 1 5 1 X X
Note C F C F X X

Bb (IV) X
Finger X 1 2 3 4 1
Scale X 1 5 1 3 5
Note X Bb F Bb D F

Bb5 (IV) X X
Scale 5 1 5 1 X X
Note F Bb F Bb X X

Bb5 (IV) X X X — 6th
Scale 1 5 1 X X X
Note Bb F Bb X X X

C5 (V) X X O
Finger X 3 X 0 1 4
Scale X 1 X 5 1 5
Note X C X G C G

C5 (V) X X — 3rd
Scale 5 1 5 1 X X
Note G C G C X X

C5 (V) X X X — 8th
Scale 1 5 1 X X X
Note C G C X X X

Flat Major Power Chords

Ab5 (bIII) X X X — 4th
Scale 1 5 1 X X X
Note Ab Eb Ab X X

Ab5 (bIII) X X — 11th
Scale 5 1 5 1 X X
Note Eb Ab Eb Ab X X

Db5 (bVI) X X — 4th
Scale 5 1 5 1 X X
Note Ab Db Ab Db X X

Db5 (bVI) X X X — 9th
Scale 1 5 1 X X X
Note Db Ab Db X X X

Eb5 (bVII) X X X — 6th
Scale 5 1 5 1 X X
Note Bb Eb Bb Eb X X

Eb5 (bVII) X X X — 11th
Scale 1 5 1 X X X
Note Eb Bb Eb X X X

Combinations of notes that can be used to make Power Chords - 1, 5 or 1, 5, 1 called 1st Inversion Power Chords
5, 1 or 5, 1, 5 called 2nd Inversion Power Chords

ii, iii, vi Power Chords

G5 (ii) X X X — 3rd
Scale 1 5 1 X X X
Note G D G X X X

G5 (ii) X X — 10th
Scale 5 1 5 1 X X
Note D G D G X X

A5 (iii) O O X X
Scale 5 1 5 1 X X
Note E A E A X X

A5 (iii) X X X — 5th
Scale 1 5 1 X X X
Note A E A X X X

D5 (vi) X X — 5th
Scale 5 1 5 1 X X
Note A D A D X X

D5 (vi) X X X — 10th
Scale 1 5 1 X X X
Note D A D X X X

Other Power Chord Shapes

(shape) X X
Scale X X 5 1 5 1

(shape) X X
Scale X 5 1 5 1 X

Csus2 (IV) X X O X
Finger X 2 X 0 3 X
Scale X 1 X 5 2 X
Note X C X G D X

X5add9 X X X
Scale 1 5 2 X X X

X5add9 X X X
Scale X 1 5 2 X X

Rock-n-Roll Chord Shapes for I, IV and V Chords

X5 / X6 / X7 X X X X
Scale 1 5 X X X X

X5 / X6 / X7 X X X X
Scale X 1 5 X X X

X5 / X6 / X7 X X X X
Scale X X 1 5 X X

Key of F and Dm Triad Worksheet (1st, 2nd and 3rd strings)

Am (iii) — Scale 1 ♭3 5
F (I) — Scale 3 5 1
C (V) — Scale 5 1 3
D♭ (♭VI) — Scale 5 1 3
F (I) — Scale 3 5 1
F (I) 5th — Scale 5 1 3
F (I) 8th — Scale 1 3 5

B♭ (IV) — Scale 1 3 5
Gm (ii) 3rd — Scale ♭3 5 1
Dm (vi) — Scale 5 1 ♭3
E♭ (♭VII) 3rd — Scale 5 1 3
B♭ (IV) — Scale 1 3 5
B♭ (IV) 6th — Scale 3 5 1
B♭ (IV) 10th — Scale 5 1 3

C (V) 3rd — Scale 1 3 5
Am (iii) 5th — Scale ♭3 5 1
E° (vii°) 3rd — Scale ♭5 1 ♭3
A♭ (♭III) 4th — Scale 3 5 1
C (V) — Scale 5 1 3
C (V) 3rd — Scale 1 3 5
C (V) 8th — Scale 3 5 1

Dm (vi) 5th — Scale 1 ♭3 5
B♭ (IV) 6th — Scale 3 5 1
F (I) 5th — Scale 5 1 3
D♭ (♭VI) 4th — Scale 1 3 5

E° (vii°) 6th — Scale 1 ♭3 ♭5
C (V) 8th — Scale 3 5 1
Gm (ii) 6th — Scale 5 1 ♭3
E♭ (♭VII) 6th — Scale 1 3 5
Dm (vi) — Scale 5 1 ♭3
Dm (vi) 5th — Scale 1 ♭3 5
Dm (vi) 10th — Scale ♭3 5 1

F (I) 8th — Scale 1 3 5
Dm (vi) 10th — Scale ♭3 5 1
Am (iii) 8th — Scale 5 1 ♭3
A♭ (♭III) 8th — Scale 5 1 3
Gm (ii) 3rd — Scale ♭3 5 1
Gm (ii) 6th — Scale 5 1 ♭3
Gm (ii) 10th — Scale 1 ♭3 5

Gm (ii) 10th — Scale 1 ♭3 5
E° (vii°) 11th — Scale ♭3 ♭5 1
B♭ (IV) 10th — Scale 5 1 3
D♭ (♭VI) 9th — Scale 3 5 1
Am (iii) — Scale 1 ♭3 5
Am (iii) 5th — Scale ♭3 5 1
Am (iii) 8th — Scale 5 1 ♭3

Am (iii) 12th — Scale 1 ♭3 5
F (I) 13th — Scale 3 5 1
C (V) 12th — Scale 5 1 3
E♭ (♭VII) 11th — Scale 3 5 1

B♭ (IV) 13th — Scale 1 3 5
Gm (ii) 15th — Scale ♭3 5 1
Dm (vi) 13th — Scale 5 1 ♭3
A♭ (♭III) 11th — Scale 1 3 5
E° (vii°) 3rd — Scale ♭5 1 ♭3
E° (vii°) 6th — Scale 1 ♭3 ♭5
E° (vii°) 11th — Scale ♭3 5 1

Key of F and Dm Triad Worksheet (2nd, 3rd and 4th strings)

F (I)
Scale 1 3 5

C (V)
Scale 3 5 1

Am (iii)
Scale 5 1 ♭3

A♭ (♭III)
Scale 5 1 3

F (I)
Scale 1 3 5

F (I) 5th
Scale 3 5 1

F (I) 10th
Scale 5 1 3

Gm (ii) 3rd
Scale 1 ♭3 5

Dm (vi)
Scale ♭3 5 1

B♭ (IV)
Scale 5 1 3

D♭ (♭VI)
Scale 3 5 1

B♭ (IV)
Scale 5 1 3

B♭ (IV) 6th
Scale 1 3 5

B♭ (IV) 10th
Scale 3 5 1

Am (iii) 5th
Scale 1 ♭3 5

E° (vii°) 3rd
Scale ♭3 ♭5 1

C (V) 5th
Scale 5 1 3

E♭ (♭VII) 3rd
Scale 3 5 1

C (V)
Scale 3 5 1

C (V) 5th
Scale 5 1 3

C (V) 8th
Scale 1 3 5

B♭ (IV) 6th
Scale 1 3 5

F (I) 5th
Scale 3 5 1

Dm (vi) 6th
Scale 5 1 ♭3

A♭ (♭III) 4th
Scale 1 3 5

C (V) 8th
Scale 1 3 5

Gm (ii) 7th
Scale ♭3 5 1

E° (vii°) 8th
Scale 5 1 ♭3

D♭ (♭VI) 6th
Scale 5 1 3

Dm (vi)
Scale ♭3 5 1

Dm (vi) 6th
Scale 5 1 ♭3

Dm (vi) 10th
Scale 1 ♭3 5

Dm (vi) 10th
Scale 1 ♭3 5

Am (iii) 9th
Scale ♭3 5 1

F (I) 10th
Scale 5 1 3

E♭ (♭VII) 8th
Scale 5 1 3

Gm (ii) 3rd
Scale 1 ♭3 5

Gm (ii) 7th
Scale ♭3 5 1

Gm (ii) 11th
Scale 5 1 ♭3

E° (vii°) 11th
Scale 1 ♭3 ♭5

B♭ (IV) 10th
Scale 3 5 1

Gm (ii) 11th
Scale 5 1 ♭3

A♭ (♭III) 8th
Scale 3 5 1

Am (iii)
Scale 5 1 ♭3

Am (iii) 5th
Scale 1 ♭3 5

Am (iii) 9th
Scale ♭3 5 1

F (I) 13th
Scale 1 3 5

C (V) 12th
Scale 3 5 1

Am (iii) 13th
Scale 5 1 ♭3

D♭ (♭VI) 9th
Scale 1 3 5

Gm (ii) 15th
Scale 1 ♭3 5

Dm (vi) 14th
Scale ♭3 5 1

B♭ (IV) 15th
Scale 5 1 3

E♭ (♭VII) 11th
Scale 1 3 5

E° (vii°) 3rd
Scale ♭3 ♭5 1

E° (vii°) 8th
Scale 5 1 ♭3

E° (vii°) 11th
Scale 1 ♭3 ♭5

121

Key of F and Dm Triad Worksheet (3rd, 4th and 5th strings)

Slash Chord Worksheet

Key of F and Dm

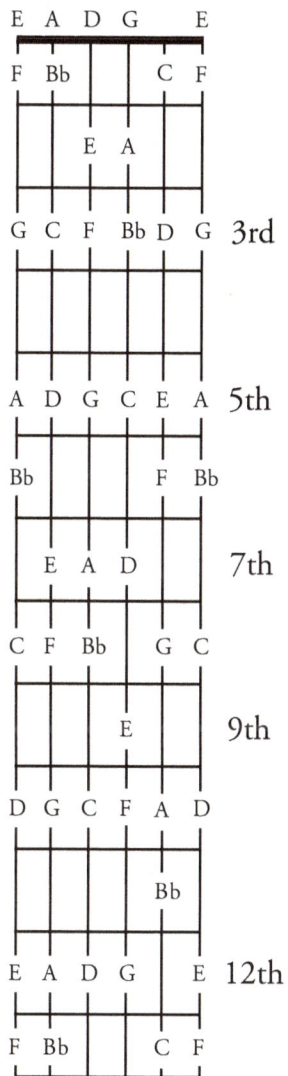

E	A	D	G		E	
F	Bb			C	F	
		E	A			
G	C	F	Bb	D	G	3rd
A	D	G	C	E	A	5th
Bb				F	Bb	
	E	A	D			7th
C	F	Bb		G	C	9th
			E			
D	G	C	F	A	D	
				Bb		
E	A	D	G		E	12th
F	Bb			C	F	

Diatonic and Secondary Dominant Chords

G# minor

B (I)
x
Finger X 1 2 3 4 1
Scale X 1 5 1 3 5
Note X B F# B D# F#

E (IV)
o o
Finger 0 2 3 1 0 0
Scale 1 5 1 3 5 1
Note E B E G# B E

F# (V)
Finger 1 3 4 2 1 1
Scale 1 5 1 3 5 1
Note F# C# F# A# C# F#

F#7 (V7/I)
Finger 1 3 1 2 1 1
Scale 1 5 ♭7 3 5 1
Note F# C# E A C# F#

B7 (V7/IV)
x
Finger X 2 1 3 0 4
Scale X 1 3 ♭7 1 5
Note X B D# A B F#

C#7 (V7/V)
x
Finger X 3 2 4 1 X
Scale X 1 3 ♭7 1 X
Note X C# F B C# X

G#m (vi)
4th
Finger 1 3 4 1 1 1
Scale 1 5 1 ♭3 5 1
Note G# D# G# B D# G#

C#m (ii)
x
4th
Finger X 1 3 4 2 1
Scale X 1 5 1 ♭3 5
Note X C# G# C# E G#

D#m (iii)
x x
Finger X X 3 2 4 1
Scale X X 5 1 ♭3
Note X X F# A# D# F#

D#7 (V7/vi)
x
6th
Finger X 1 2 1 4 1
Scale X 1 5 ♭7 3 5
Note X D A# C# G A#

G#7 (V7/ii)
4th
Finger 1 3 1 2 1 1
Scale 1 5 ♭7 3 5 1
Note G# D# F# C D G#

A#7 (V7/iii)
Finger X 1 2 1 4 1
Scale X 1 5 ♭7 3 5
Note X A# F G# D F

Extensions

BMaj7 (I)
x
Finger X 1 3 2 4 1
Scale X 1 5 7 3 5
Note X B F# A# D# F#

EMaj7 (IV)
x x
Finger X X 1 4 4 4
Scale X X 1 5 7 3
Note X X E B D# G#

F#7 (V7)
x o
Finger X 3 4 2 1 0
Scale X 5 1 3 5 ♭7
Note X C# F# A# C# E

G#m7 (vi)
4th
Finger 1 3 1 1 1 1
Scale 1 5 ♭7 ♭3 5 1
Note G# D# F# B D# G#

C#m7 (ii)
x
4th
Finger X 1 3 1 2 1
Scale X 1 5 ♭7 3 5
Note X C# G# B E G#

D#m7 (iii)
x x
Finger X X 1 3 2 2
Scale X X 1 5 ♭7 ♭3
Note X X D# A# C# F#

Flat Majors

D (♭III)
x x o
Finger X X 0 1 3 2
Scale X X 1 5 1 3
Note X X D A D F#

G (♭VI)
o o o
Finger 3 2 0 0 0 4
Scale 1 3 5 1 3 1
Note G B D G B G

A (♭VII)
x o
Finger X 0 1 2 3 0
Scale X 1 5 1 3 5
Note X A E A C# E

Suspended Chords

Bsus (I)
o o
Finger X 1 3 4 0 0
Scale X 1 5 1 1 4
Note X B F# B B E

Bsus2 (I)
Finger X 1 3 4 1 1
Scale X 1 5 1 2 5
Note X B F# B C# F#

Esus2 (IV)
o o o
Finger 0 1 3 4 0 0
Scale 1 5 2 5 5 1
Note E B F# B B E

F#7sus (V7)
Finger 1 3 1 4 1 1
Scale 1 5 ♭7 4 5 1
Note F# C# E B C# F#

F#sus (V)
Finger 1 2 3 4 1 1
Scale 1 5 1 4 5 1
Note F# C# F# B C# F#

F#sus2 (V)
x x
4th
Finger X X 1 3 4 1
Scale X X 1 5 1 2
Note X X F# C# F# G#

Add 9 Chords

Badd9 (I)
4th
Finger 3 X 1 2 1 4
Scale 1 X 5 2 3 1
Note B X F# C# D# B

Eadd9 (IV)
o o
Finger 0 2 4 1 0 0
Scale 1 5 2 3 5 1
Note E B F# G# B E

Eadd9 (IV)
o o o
Finger 0 2 3 1 0 4
Scale 1 5 1 3 5 2
Note E B E G# B F#

F#add9 (V)
x x
Finger X X 2 3 1 4
Scale X X 1 3 5 2
Note X X F# A# C# G#

Diatonic and Secondary Dominant Chords

B (I)
X

Finger X 1 2 3 4 1
Scale X 1 5 1 3 5
Note X B F# B D# F#

E (IV)
o o o

Finger 0 2 3 1 0 0
Scale 1 5 1 3 5 1
Note E B E G# B E

F# (V)

Finger 1 3 4 2 1 1
Scale 1 5 1 3 5 1
Note F#C#F#A#C#F#

G#m (vi)
4th

Finger 1 3 4 1 1 1
Scale 1 5 1 b3 5 1
Note G#D#G#BD#G#

C#m (ii)
X
4th

Finger X 1 3 4 2 1
Scale X 1 5 1 b3 5
Note XC#G#C#E G#

D#m (iii)
X X

Finger X X 3 2 4 1
Scale X X b3 5 1 b3
Note X XF#A#D#F#

Capo Second Fret

B (I)
X o o

Finger X 0 1 2 3 0
Scale X 1 5 1 3 5
Note X BF# B D#F#

E (IV)
X X o

Finger X X 0 1 3 2
Scale X X 1 5 1 3
Note X X E B E G#

F# (V)
o o o

Finger 0 2 3 1 0 0
Scale 1 5 1 3 5 1
Note F#C#F#A#C#F#

G#m (vi)
2nd

Finger 1 3 4 1 1 1
Scale 1 5 1 b3 5 1
Note G#D#G#BD#G#

C#m (ii)
X
2nd

Finger X 1 3 4 2 1
Scale X 1 5 1 b3 5
Note XC#G#C#E G#

D#m (iii)
X
6th

Finger X 1 3 4 2 1
Scale X 1 5 1 b3 5
Note XD#A#D#F#A#

Capo fourth Fret

B (I)
o o o
4th

Finger 3 2 0 0 0 4
Scale 1 3 5 1 3 1
Note B D#F#BD# B

E (IV)
X o o
4th

Finger X 3 2 0 1 0
Scale X 1 3 5 1 3
Note X EG#B E G#

F# (V)
X X o
4th

Finger X X 0 1 3 2
Scale X X 1 5 1 3
Note X XF#C#F#A#

G#m (vi)
o o o o
4th

Finger 0 2 3 0 0 0
Scale 1 5 1 b3 5 1
Note G#D#G#BD#G#

C#m (ii)
X o o
4th

Finger X 0 2 3 1 0
Scale X 1 5 1 b3 5
Note XC#G#C#E G#

D#m (iii)
X
4th

Finger X 1 3 4 2 1
Scale X 1 5 1 b3 5
Note XD#A#D#F#A#

CAPO PLACEMENT CONSIDERATIONS

As you can see where you place the capo can make a big difference in which chords you'll need to play. In this instance if the song had a lot of minor (vi) and/or (iii) chords you would probably want to put the capo on the 4th fret. However if there were a lot of suspended (IV) chords you might think about putting the capo on the 2nd fret. If you had add9 (IV) chords then the 4th fret would be better.

You should really try several different placements of the capo to decide which gives you the sound and ease of playing you want and need for each song.

Diatonic and Secondary Dominants Chords

Bb Major
Key of (Bb, Eb)
(Capo 1st Fret Use A Major Chords)
G minor

Bb (I) A
Finger X 0 1 2 3 0
Scale X 1 5 1 3 5
Note X Bb F Bb D F

Eb (IV) D
Finger X X 0 1 3 2
Scale X X 1 5 1 3
Note X X Eb Bb Eb G

F (V) E
Finger 0 2 3 1 0 0
Scale 1 5 1 3 5 1
Note F C F A C F

F7 (V7/I) E7
Finger 0 2 0 1 0 0
Scale 1 5 b7 3 5 1
Note F C Eb A C F

Bb7 (V7/IV) A7
Finger X 0 1 0 2 0
Scale X 1 5 b7 3 5
Note X Bb F Ab D F

C7 (V7/V) B7
Finger X 2 1 3 0 4
Scale X 1 3 b7 1 5
Note X C E Bb C G

Gm (vi) F#m
Finger 1 3 4 1 1 1
Scale 1 5 1 b3 5 1
Note G D G Bb D G

Cm (ii) Bm
Finger X 1 3 4 2 1
Scale X 1 5 1 b3 5
Note X C G C Eb G

Dm (iii) C#m
C 4th — 5th
Finger X 1 3 4 2 1
Scale X 1 5 1 b3 5
Note X D A D F A

D7 (V7/vi) C#7
C 4th — 5th
Finger X 1 3 1 4 1
Scale X 1 5 b7 3 5
Note X D A C F# A

G7 (V7/ii) F#7
Finger 1 3 1 2 1 1
Scale 1 5 b7 3 5 1
Note G D F B D G

A7 (V7/iii) G#7
C 4th — 5th
Finger 1 3 1 2 1 1
Scale 1 5 b7 3 5 1
Note A E G C# E A

Extensions

BbMaj7 (I) AMaj7
Finger X 0 2 1 3 0
Scale X 1 5 7 3 5
Note X Bb F A D F

EbMaj7 (IV) DMaj7
Finger X X 0 1 1 1
Scale X X 1 5 7 3
Note X X Eb Bb D G

F7 (V) E7
Finger 0 3 1 2 0 0
Scale 1 5 b7 3 5 1
Note F C Eb A C F

Gm7 (vi) F#m7
Finger 1 3 1 1 1 1
Scale 1 5 b7 b3 5 1
Note G D F Bb D G

Cm7 (ii) Bm7
Finger X 1 3 1 2 1
Scale X 1 5 b7 b3 5
Note X C G Bb Eb G

Dm7 (iii) C#m7
C 4th — 5th
Finger X 1 3 1 2 1
Scale X 1 5 b7 b3 5
Note X D A C F A

Flat Majors

Db (bIII) C
Finger X 3 2 0 1 0
Scale X 1 3 5 1 3
Note X Db F Ab Db F

Gb (bVI) F
Finger 1 3 4 2 1 1
Scale 1 5 1 3 5 1
Note Gb Db Gb Bb Db Gb

Ab (bVII) G
Finger 3 2 0 0 0 4
Scale 1 3 5 1 3 1
Note Ab C Eb Ab C Ab

Suspended Chords

Bbsus (I) Asus
Finger X 0 1 2 3 0
Scale X 1 5 1 4 5

Bbsus2 (I) Asus2
Finger X 0 1 2 0 0
Scale X 1 5 1 2 5

Ebsus2 (IV) Dsus2
Finger X X 0 1 3 0
Scale X X 1 5 1 2

F7sus (V7) E7sus
Finger 0 2 0 3 0 0
Scale 1 5 b7 4 5 1

Fsus (V) Esus
Finger 0 1 2 3 0 0
Scale 1 5 1 4 5 1

Fsus2 (V) Esus2
Finger 0 1 3 4 0 0
Scale 1 5 2 5 5 1

Key of Eb Major

(Bb, Eb, Ab)

(Capo 1st Fret Use D Major Chords)

C minor

Suspended Chords

Ebsus (I) Dsus
X X O
| Finger | X X 0 1 3 4 |
| Scale | X X 1 5 1 4 |

Ebsus2 (I) Dsus2
X X O
| Finger | X X 0 1 3 0 |
| Scale | X X 1 5 1 2 |

Absus2 (IV) Gsus2
X O
| Finger | 2 X 0 1 3 3 |
| Scale | 1 X 5 2 5 1 |

Bb7sus (V7) A7sus
X O O O
| Finger | X 0 1 0 3 0 |
| Scale | X 1 5 b7 4 5 |

Bbsus (V) Asus
X O
| Finger | X 0 1 2 3 0 |
| Scale | X 1 5 1 4 5 |

Bbsus2 (V) Asus2
X O O O
| Finger | X 0 1 2 0 0 |
| Scale | X 1 5 1 2 5 |

Add9 Chords

Abadd9 (IV) Gadd9
X O O
| Finger | 2 X 0 1 0 3 |
| Scale | 1 X 5 2 3 1 |

Diatonic and Secondary Dominants Chords

Eb (I) D
X X
Finger	X X 0 1 3 2
Scale	X X 1 5 1 3
Note	X X Eb Bb Eb G

Ab (IV) G
O O O
Finger	3 2 0 0 0 4
Scale	1 3 5 1 3 1
Note	Ab C Eb Ab C Ab

Bb (V) A
X O
Finger	X 0 1 2 3 0
Scale	X 1 5 1 3 5
Note	X Bb F Bb D F

Bb7 (V7/I) A7
X O O
Finger	X 0 1 0 2 0
Scale	X 1 5 b7 3 5
Note	X Bb F Ab D F

Eb7 (V7/IV) D7
X X O
Finger	X X 0 2 1 3
Scale	X X 1 5 b7 3
Note	X X Eb Bb Db G

F7 (V7/V) E7
O
Finger	0 2 0 1 0 0
Scale	1 5 b7 3 5 1
Note	F C Eb A C F

Cm (vi) Bm
X
Finger	X 1 3 4 2 1
Scale	X 1 5 1 b3 5
Note	X C G C Eb G

Fm (ii) Em
O O O
Finger	0 2 3 0 0 0
Scale	1 5 1 b3 5 1
Note	F C F Ab C F

Gm (iii) F#m
Finger	1 3 4 1 1 1
Scale	1 5 1 b3 5 1
Note	G D G Bb D G

G7 (V7/vi) F#7
Finger	1 3 1 2 1 1
Scale	1 5 b7 3 5 1
Note	G D F B D G

C7 (V7/ii) B7
X O
Finger	X 2 1 3 0 4
Scale	X 1 3 b7 1 5
Note	X C E Bb C F

D7 (V7/iii) C#7
C 4th   5th
Finger	X 1 3 1 4 1
Scale	X 1 5 b7 3 5
Note	X D A C F# A

Extensions

EbMaj7 (I) DMaj7
X X O
Finger	X X 0 1 1 1
Scale	X X 1 5 7 3
Note	X X Eb Bb D G

AbMaj7 (IV) GMaj7
O O O
Finger	3 2 0 0 0 1
Scale	1 3 5 1 3 7
Note	Ab C Eb Ab C G

Bb7 (V) A7
X O O
Finger	X 0 1 0 3 0
Scale	X 1 5 b7 3 5
Note	X Bb F Ab D F

Cm7 (vi) Bm7
X
Finger	X 1 3 1 2 1
Scale	X 1 5 b7 b3 5
Note	X C G Bb Eb G

Fm7 (ii) Em7
O O O O O
Finger	0 2 0 0 0 0
Scale	1 5 b7 b3 5 1
Note	F C Eb Ab C F

Gm7 (iii) F#m7
Finger	1 3 1 1 1 1
Scale	1 5 b7 b3 5 1
Note	G D F Bb D G

Flat Majors

Gb (bIII) F
Finger	1 3 4 2 1 1
Scale	1 5 1 3 5 1
Note	Gb Db Gb Bb Db Gb

Cb (bVI) Bb
X
Finger	X 1 3 3 3 1
Scale	X 1 5 1 3 5
Note	X Cb Gb Cb Eb Gb

Db (bVII) C
X O O
Finger	X 3 2 0 1 0
Scale	X 1 3 5 1 3
Note	X Db F Ab Db F

Diatonic and Secondary Dominant Chords

A♭ (I) G
Finger 3 2 0 0 0 4
Scale 1 3 5 1 3 1
Note A♭ C E♭ A♭ C A♭

D♭ (IV) C
X
Finger X 3 2 0 1 0
Scale X 1 3 5 1 3
Note X D♭ F A♭ D♭ F

E♭ (V) D
X X O
Finger X X 0 1 3 2
Scale X X 1 5 1 3
Note X X E♭ B♭ E♭ G

E♭7 (V7/I) D7
X X O
Finger X X 0 2 1 3
Scale X X 1 5 ♭3 ♭7
Note X X E♭ B♭ D♭ G

A♭7 (V7/IV) G7
O O O
Finger 3 2 0 0 0 1
Scale 1 3 5 1 3 ♭7
Note A♭ C E♭ A♭ C G♭

B♭7 (V7/V) A7
X O
Finger X 0 1 0 2 0
Scale X 1 5 ♭7 3 5
Note X B♭ F A♭ D F

Fm (vi) Em
O O O O
Finger 0 2 3 0 0 0
Scale 1 5 1 ♭3 5 1
Note F C F A♭ C F

B♭m (ii) Am
X O
Finger X 0 2 3 1 0
Scale X 1 5 1 ♭3 5
Note X B♭ F B♭ D♭ F

Cm (iii) Bm
X
Finger X 1 3 4 2 1
Scale X 1 5 1 ♭3 5
Note X C G C E♭ G

C7 (V7/vi) B7
X O
Finger X 2 1 3 0 4
Scale X 1 3 ♭7 1 5
Note X C E B♭ C F

F7 (V7/ii) E7
O O O
Finger 0 2 0 1 0 0
Scale 1 5 ♭7 3 5 1
Note F C E♭ A C F

G7 (V7/iii) F#7
Finger 1 3 1 2 1 1
Scale 1 5 ♭7 3 5 1
Note G D F B D G

Extensions

A♭Maj7 (I) GMaj7
X O O O
Finger 3 X 0 0 0 2
Scale 1 X 5 1 3 7
Note A♭ X E♭ A♭ C G

D♭Maj7 (IV) CMaj7
X O O O
Finger X 3 2 0 0 0
Scale X 1 3 5 7 3
Note X D♭ F A♭ C F

E♭7 (V7) D7
X X O
Finger X X 0 2 1 3
Scale X X 1 5 ♭7 3
Note X X E♭ B♭ D♭ G

Fm7 (vi) Em7
O O O O O
Finger 0 2 0 0 0 0
Scale 1 5 ♭7 ♭3 5 1
Note F C E♭ A♭ C F

B♭m7 (ii) Am7
X O O
Finger X 0 2 0 1 0
Scale X 1 5 ♭7 ♭3 5
Note X B♭ F A♭ D♭ F

Cm7 (iii) Bm7
X
Finger X 1 3 1 2 1
Scale X 1 5 ♭7 ♭3 5
Note X C G B♭ E♭ G

Flat Majors

C♭ (♭III) B♭
X
Finger X 1 3 3 3 1
Scale X 1 5 1 3 5
Note X C♭ G♭ C♭ E♭ G♭

F♭ (♭VI) E♭
X
C 3rd ... 4th
Finger X 4 3 1 2 1
Scale X 1 3 5 1 3
Note X F♭ A♭ C♭ F♭ A♭

G♭ (♭VII) F
Finger 1 3 4 2 1 1
Scale 1 5 1 3 5 1
Note G♭ D♭ G♭ B♭ D♭ G♭

Suspended Chords

A♭sus (I) Gsus
X O O
Finger 3 X 0 0 1 4
Scale 1 X 5 1 4 1

A♭sus2 (I) Gsus2
X O
Finger 2 X 0 1 3 3
Scale 1 X 5 2 5 1

D♭sus2 (IV) Csus2
X O O
Finger X 2 0 0 4 4
Scale X 1 2 5 2 5

E♭7sus (V7) D7sus
X X O
Finger X X 0 2 1 4
Scale X X 1 5 ♭7 4

E♭sus (V) Dsus
X X O
Finger X X 0 1 3 4
Scale X X 1 5 1 4

E♭sus2 (V) Dsus2
X X O
Finger X X 0 1 3 0
Scale X X 1 5 1 2

Add9 Chords

A♭add9 (I) Gadd9
X O O
Finger 3 X 0 2 0 4
Scale 1 X 5 2 3 1

D♭add9 (IV) Cadd9
X O O
Finger X 3 2 0 4 0
Scale X 1 3 5 2 3

Key of Gb Major (Bb, Eb, Ab, Db, Gb, Cb)

(Capo 4th Fret Use D Major Chords)

Eb minor

Suspended Chords

Gbsus (I) Dsus
X X O
Finger X X 0 1 3 4
Scale X X 1 5 1 4

Gbsus2 (I) Dsus2
X X O   O
Finger X X 0 1 3 0
Scale X X 1 5 1 2

Cbsus2 (IV) Gsus2
X O
Finger 2 X 0 1 3 3
Scale 1 X 5 2 5 1

Db7sus (V7) A7sus
X O   O   O
Finger X 0 1 0 3 0
Scale X 1 5 b7 4 5

Dbsus (V) Asus
X O   O
Finger X 0 1 2 3 0
Scale X 1 5 1 4 5

Dbsus2 (V) Asus2
X O   O O
Finger X 0 1 2 0 0
Scale X 1 5 1 2 5

Add9 Chords

Cbadd9 (IV) Gadd9
X O   O
Finger 2 X 0 1 0 3
Scale 1 X 5 2 3 1

Diatonic and Secondary Dominant Chords

Gb (I) D
X X O
4th
Finger X X 0 1 3 2
Scale X X 1 5 1 3
Note X XGbDbGbBb

Cb (IV) G
O O O
4th
Finger 3 2 0 0 0 4
Scale 1 3 5 1 3 1
Note CbEbGbCbEbCb

Db (V) A
X O   O
4th
Finger X 0 1 2 3 0
Scale X 1 5 1 3 5
Note XDbAbDb F Ab

Db7 (V7/I) A7
X O   O
4th
Finger X 0 1 0 2 0
Scale X 1 5 b7 3 5
Note XDbAb B Fb Ab

Gb7 (V7/IV) D7
X X
4th
Finger X X 0 2 1 3
Scale X X 1 5 b7 3
Note X XGbDbE Bb

Ab7 (V7/V) E7
O   O O
4th
Finger 0 2 0 1 0 0
Scale 1 5 b7 3 5 1
Note AbEbGbC EbAb

Ebm (vi) Bm
X
4th
Finger X 1 3 4 2 1
Scale X 1 5 1 b3 5
Note XEbBbEbGbBb

Abm (ii) Em
O   O
4th
Finger 0 2 3 0 0 0
Scale 1 5 1 b3 5 1
Note AbEbAbCbEbAb

Bbm (iii) F#m
4th
Finger 1 3 4 1 1 1
Scale 1 5 1 b3 5 1
Note Bb F BbDb F Bb

Bb7 (V7/vi) F#7
4th
Finger 1 3 1 2 1 1
Scale 1 5 b7 3 5 1
Note Bb F Ab D F Bb

Eb7 (V7/ii) B7
X
4th
Finger X 2 1 3 0 4
Scale X 1 3 b7 1 5
Note XEbGbDbEbBb

F7 (V7/iii) C#7
X
C 4th   8th
Finger X 1 3 1 4 1
Scale X 1 5 b7 3 5
Note X F CEbA C

Extensions

GbMaj7 (I) DMaj7
X X O
4th
Finger X X 0 1 1 1
Scale X X 1 5 7 3
Note X XGbDbF Bb

CbMaj7 (IV) GMaj7
X O O O
4th
Finger 3 X 0 0 0 2
Scale 1 X 5 1 3 1
Note Cb X GbCbEbBb

Db7 (V) A7
X O   O
4th
Finger X 0 1 0 3 0
Scale X 1 5 b7 3 5
Note XDbAbCb F Ab

Ebm7 (vi) Bm7
X
4th
Finger X 1 3 1 2 1
Scale X 1 5 b7 b3 5
Note XEbBbDbGbBb

Abm7 (ii) Em7
O   O
4th
Finger 0 2 0 0 0 0
Scale 1 5 b7 b3 5 1
Note AbEbGbCbEbAb

Bbm7 (iii) F#m7
4th
Finger 1 3 1 1 1 1
Scale 1 5 b7 b3 5 1
Note Bb F AbDb F Bb

Flat Majors

A (bIII) F
4th
Finger 1 3 4 2 1 1
Scale 1 5 1 3 5 1
Note A E A D E A

D (bVI) Bb
X
4th
Finger X 1 3 3 3 1
Scale X 1 5 1 3 5
Note X D A D Gb A

E (bVII) C
X O   O
4th
Finger X 3 2 0 1 0
Scale X 1 3 5 1 3
Note X E Ab Cb E A

129

Contemporary Worship Chords in the Key of E and F (Capo 1st Fret)

E5 (I) — 7th
Finger 0 1 3 4 0 0

E (I)
Finger 0 2 3 1 0 0
Scale 1 5 1 3 5 1
Note E B E G# B E

F5 (I) — 8th
Finger X 1 3 4 0 0

F (I)
Finger 0 2 3 1 0 0
Scale 1 5 1 3 5 1
Note F C F A C F

F#m7add11 (ii)
Finger 2 X 3 4 0 0

F#m7add11 (ii)
Finger 0 3 4 1 0 0
Scale ♭7 5 1 ♭3 4 ♭7
Note E C# F# A B E

Gm7add11 (ii)
Finger 2 X 3 4 0 0

Gm7add11 (ii) — 3rd
Finger 0 3 4 1 0 0
Scale ♭7 5 1 ♭3 4 ♭7
Note F D G B♭ C F

G#m7#5 (iii) — 4th
Finger 2 X 3 4 0 0

G#m5 (iii) — 4th
Finger 0 3 4 1 0 0
Scale #5 5 1 ♭3 ♭3 #5
Note E D# G# B B E

Am7#5 (iii) — 5th
Finger 2 X 3 4 0 0

Am#5 (iii) — 5th
Finger 0 3 4 1 0 0
Scale #5 5 1 ♭3 ♭3 #5
Note F E A C C F

Asus2 (IV)
Finger X 0 3 4 0 0

Asus2 (IV) — 6th
Finger 0 3 4 2 0 0
Scale 5 5 1 3 2 5
Note E E A C# B E

B♭sus2 (IV)
Finger X 0 3 4 0 0

B♭sus2 (IV) — 6th
Finger 0 3 4 2 0 0
Scale 5 5 1 3 2 5
Note F F B♭ D C F

Bsus (V)
Finger X 1 3 4 0 0

Bsus (V) — 8th
Finger 0 3 4 2 0 0
Scale 4 5 1 3 1 4
Note E F# B D# B E

Csus (V)
Finger X 1 3 4 0 0

Csus (V) — 9th
Finger 0 3 4 2 0 0
Scale 4 5 1 3 1 4
Note F G C E C F

C#m7 (vi) — 4th
Finger X 1 3 4 0 0

C#m7 (vi) — 9th
Finger 0 3 4 1 0 0
Scale ♭3 5 1 ♭3 ♭7 ♭3
Note E G# C# E B E

Dm7 (vi) — 5th
Finger X 1 3 4 0 0

Dm7 (vi) — 10th
Finger 0 3 4 1 0 0
Scale ♭3 5 1 ♭3 ♭7 ♭3
Note F A D F C F

(vii) — 6th
Finger X 1 3 4 0 0

(vii) — 11th
Finger 0 2 3 1 0 0
Scale ♭2 ♭5 1 ♭3 #5 ♭2
Note E A D# F# B E

(vii) — 7th
Finger X 1 3 4 0 0

(vii) — 12th
Finger 0 2 3 1 0 0
Scale ♭2 ♭5 1 ♭3 #5 ♭2
Note F B♭ E G C F

The first column in each key is a technique used by Paul Baloche. Notice how the third and fourth fingers never leave the 3rd and 4th strings.

Contemporary Worship Chords in the Key of G with Walking Bass Lines

Em (vi)
Finger 0 2 3 0 0 0
Scale 1 5 1 ♭3 5 1
Note E B E G B E

Em7 (vi)
Finger 0 1 2 0 3 4
Scale 1 5 1 ♭3 ♭7 ♭3
Note E B E G D G

D (V)
Finger X X 0 1 3 2
Scale X X 1 5 1 3
Note X X D A D F♯

Dsus (V)
Finger X X 0 2 3 4
Scale X X 1 5 1 4
Note X X D A D G

D/F♯ (V)
Finger T X 0 1 3 2
Scale 3 X 1 5 1 3
Note F♯ X D A D F♯

Dsus/F♯ (V)
Finger 1 X 0 2 3 4
Scale 3 X 1 5 1 4
Note F♯ X D A D G

C (IV)
Finger X 3 2 0 1 0
Scale X 1 3 5 1 3
Note X C E G C E

C2 (IV)
Finger X 2 0 0 3 4
Scale X 1 2 5 2 5
Note X C D G D G

G (I)
Finger 3 X 0 0 0 4
Scale 1 X 5 1 3 1
Note G X D G B G

G5 (I)
Finger 2 X 0 0 3 4
Scale 1 X 5 1 5 1
Note G X D G D G

G/B (I)
Finger X 1 0 0 0 4
Scale X 3 5 1 3 1
Note X B D G B G

G/B (I)
Finger X 1 0 0 3 4
Scale X 3 5 1 5 1
Note X B D G D G

Am7 (ii)
Finger X 0 2 3 1 0
Scale X 1 5 1 ♭3 5
Note X A E A C E

Am7 (ii)
Finger X 0 2 0 1 4
Scale X 1 5 ♭7 ♭3 ♭7
Note X A E G C G

Am7 (ii)
Finger X 0 2 3 1 0
Scale X 1 5 1 ♭3 5
Note X A E A C E

Am7 (ii)
Finger X 0 2 0 1 4
Scale X 1 5 ♭7 ♭3 ♭7
Note X A E G C G

G/B (I)
Finger X 1 0 0 0 4
Scale X 3 5 1 3 1
Note X B D G B G

G/B (I)
Finger X 1 0 0 3 4
Scale X 3 5 1 5 1
Note X B D G D G

G (I)
Finger 3 X 0 0 0 4
Scale 1 X 5 1 3 1
Note G X D G B G

G5 (I)
Finger 2 X 0 0 3 4
Scale 1 X 5 1 5 1
Note G X D G D G

C (IV)
Finger X 3 2 0 1 0
Scale X 1 3 5 1 3
Note X C E G C E

C2 (IV)
Finger X 2 0 0 3 4
Scale X 1 2 5 2 5
Note X C D G D G

D/F♯ (V)
Finger T X 0 1 3 2
Scale 3 X 1 5 1 3
Note F♯ X D A D F♯

Dsus/F♯ (V)
Finger 1 X 0 2 3 4
Scale 3 X 1 5 1 4
Note F♯ X D A D G

D (V)
Finger X X 0 1 3 2
Scale X X 1 5 1 3
Note X X D A D F♯

Dsus (V)
Finger X X 0 2 3 4
Scale X X 1 5 1 4
Note X X D A D G

Em (vi)
Finger 0 2 3 0 0 0
Scale 1 5 1 ♭3 5 1
Note E B E G B E

Em7 (vi)
Finger 0 1 2 0 3 4
Scale 1 5 1 ♭3 ♭7 ♭3
Note E B E G D G

131

A minor Key of
(Aeolian/Natural)

Am (i)
Finger X 0 2 3 1 0
Scale X 1 5 1 ♭3 5
Note X A E A C E

B° (ii°)
Finger X 1 2 4 3 X
Scale X 1 ♭5 1 ♭3 X
Note X B F B D X

C (III)
Finger X 3 2 0 1 0
Scale X 1 3 5 1 3
Note X C E G C E

E7 (V7/i)
Finger 0 2 0 1 0 0
Scale 1 5 ♭7 3 5 1
Note E B D G# B E

G7 (V7/III)
Finger 3 X 0 0 0 1
Scale 1 X 5 1 3 ♭7
Note G X D G B F

Dm (iv)
Finger X X 0 2 3 1
Scale X X 1 5 1 ♭3
Note X X D A D F

Em (v)
Finger 0 2 3 0 0 0
Scale 1 5 1 ♭3 5 1
Note E B E G B E

F (VI)
Finger 1 3 4 2 1 1
Scale 1 5 1 3 5 1
Note F C F A C F

G (VII)
Finger 3 2 0 0 0 4
Scale 1 3 5 1 3 1
Note G B D G B G

A7 (V7/IV)
Finger X 0 1 0 2 0
Scale X 1 5 ♭7 3 5
Note X A E G# E

B7 (V7/v)
Finger X 2 1 3 0 4
Scale X 1 3 ♭7 1 5
Note X B D# A B F#

C7 (V7/VI)
Finger X 3 2 4 1 0
Scale X 1 3 ♭7 1 3
Note X C E B♭ C E

D7 (V7/VII)
Finger X X 0 2 1 3
Scale X X 1 5 ♭7 3
Note X X D A C F#

Am7 (i)
Finger X 0 2 0 1 0
Scale X 1 5 ♭7 ♭3 5
Note X A E G C E

Bm7♭5 (iiø7)
Finger X 1 2 1 3 X
Scale X 1 ♭5 ♭7 ♭3 X
Note X B F A D X

CMaj7 (III)
Finger X 3 2 0 0 0
Scale X 1 3 5 7 3
Note X C E G B E

Dm7 (iv)
Finger X X 0 2 1 1
Scale X X 1 5 ♭7 ♭3
Note X X D A C F

Em7 (v)
Finger 0 2 0 0 0 0
Scale 1 5 ♭7 ♭3 5 1
Note E B D G B E

FMaj7 (VI)
Finger X X 3 2 1 0
Scale X X 1 3 5 7
Note X X F A C E

GMaj7 (VII)
Finger 3 X 0 0 0 2
Scale 1 X 5 1 3 ♭7
Note G X D G B F#

Key of Am (Harmonic) (G#)

E (V)
Finger 0 2 3 1 0 0
Scale 1 5 1 3 5 1
Note E B E G# B E

E7 (V7)
Finger 0 2 0 1 0 0
Scale 1 5 ♭7 3 5 1
Note E B D G# B E

G#°7 (vii°7)
Finger 2 X 1 3 1 X
Scale 1 X ♭♭7 ♭3 ♭5 X
Note G# X F B D X

132

Key of A minor (Dorian)

(F#)

Am (i)
X O   O

Finger	X	0	2	3	1	0
Scale	X	1	5	1	♭3	5
Note	X	A	E	A	C	E

Bm (ii)
X

Finger	X	1	3	4	2	1
Scale	X	1	5	1	♭3	5
Note	X	B	F#	B	D	F#

C (III)
X   O   O

Finger	X	3	2	0	1	0
Scale	X	1	3	5	1	3
Note	X	C	E	G	C	E

E7 (V7/i)
O   O   O

Finger	0	2	0	1	0	0
Scale	1	5	♭7	3	5	1
Note	E	B	D	G#	B	E

F#7 (V7/vi)

Finger	1	3	1	2	1	1
Scale	1	5	♭7	3	5	1
Note	F#	C#	E	A#	C#	F#

G7 (V7/III)
X O O O

Finger	3	X	0	0	0	1
Scale	1	X	5	1	3	♭7
Note	G	X	D	G	B	F

D (IV)
X X O

Finger	X	X	0	1	3	2
Scale	X	X	1	5	1	3
Note	X	X	D	A	D	F#

Em (v)
O   O O O

Finger	0	2	3	0	0	0
Scale	1	5	1	♭3	5	1
Note	E	B	E	G	B	E

F#° (vii°)
X X

Finger	2	X	X	3	1	4
Scale	1	X	X	♭3	♭5	1
Note	F#	X	X	A	C	F#

G (VII)
O O O

Finger	3	2	0	0	0	4
Scale	1	3	5	1	3	1
Note	G	B	D	G	B	G

A7 (V7/IV)
X O   O

Finger	X	0	1	0	2	0
Scale	X	1	5	♭7	3	5
Note	X	A	E	G	C#	E

B7 (V7/v)
X

Finger	X	2	1	3	0	4
Scale	X	1	3	♭7	1	5
Note	X	B	D#	A	B	F#

D7 (V7/VII)
X X O

Finger	X	X	0	2	1	3
Scale	X	X	1	5	♭7	3
Note	X	X	D	A	C	F#

Am7 (i)
X O   O   O

Finger	X	0	2	0	1	0
Scale	X	1	5	♭7	♭3	5
Note	X	A	E	G	C	E

Bm7 (ii)
X

Finger	X	1	3	1	2	1
Scale	X	1	5	♭7	♭3	5
Note	X	B	F#	A	D	F#

CMaj7 (III)
X   O O O

Finger	X	3	2	0	0	0
Scale	X	1	3	5	7	3
Note	X	C	E	G	B	E

D7 (IV7)
X X O

Finger	X	X	0	1	3	2
Scale	X	X	1	5	♭7	3
Note	X	X	D	A	C	F#

Em7 (v)
O   O O O O

Finger	0	2	0	0	0	0
Scale	1	5	♭7	♭3	5	1
Note	E	B	D	G	B	E

GMaj7 (VII)
X O O O

Finger	3	X	0	0	0	2
Scale	1	X	5	1	3	♭7
Note	G	X	D	G	B	F#

Em (i)

Finger 0 2 3 0 0 0
Scale 1 5 1 ♭3 5 1
Note E B E G B E

F#° (vi°)

Finger 1 2 3 1 X X
Scale 1 ♭5 1 ♭3 X X
Note F# C F# A X X

G (III)

Finger 3 2 0 0 0 4
Scale 1 3 5 1 3 1
Note G B D G B G

E minor
Key of 𝄞 #
(Aeolian/Natural) (F#)

B7 (V7/i)

Finger X 2 1 3 0 4
Scale X 1 3 ♭7 1 5
Note X B D# A B F#

D7 (V7/III)

Finger X X 0 2 1 3
Scale X X 1 5 ♭7 3
Note X X D A C F#

Am (iv)

Finger X 0 2 3 1 0
Scale X 1 5 1 ♭3 5
Note X A E A C E

Bm (v)

Finger X 1 3 4 2 1
Scale X 1 5 1 ♭3 5
Note X B F# B D F#

C (VI)

Finger X 3 2 0 1 0
Scale X 1 3 5 1 3
Note X C E G C E

D (VII)

Finger X X 0 1 3 2
Scale X X 1 5 1 3
Note X X D A D F#

E7 (V7/IV)

Finger 0 2 0 1 0 0
Scale 1 5 ♭7 3 5 1
Note E B D G# B E

F#7 (V7/v)

Finger 1 3 1 2 1 1
Scale 1 5 ♭7 3 5 1
Note F# C# E A# C# F#

G7 (V7/VI)

Finger 3 2 0 0 0 1
Scale 1 3 5 1 3 ♭7
Note G B D G B F

A7 (V7/VII)

Finger X 0 1 0 2 0
Scale X 1 5 ♭7 3 5
Note X A E G C# E

Em7 (i)

Finger 0 2 3 0 0 0
Scale 1 5 ♭7 3 5 1
Note E B D G B E

F#m7♭5 (iiø7)

Finger 2 X 3 4 1 X
Scale 1 X ♭7 ♭3 ♭5 X
Note F# X E A C X

GMaj7 (III)

3rd

Finger 1 X 3 4 2 X
Scale 1 X 7 3 5 X
Note G X F# B D X

Am7 (iv)

Finger X 0 2 0 1 0
Scale X 1 5 ♭7 3 5
Note X A E G C E

Bm7 (v)

Finger X 1 3 1 2 1
Scale X 1 5 ♭7 ♭3 5
Note X B F# A D F#

CMaj7 (VI)

Finger X 3 2 0 0 0
Scale X 1 3 5 7 3
Note X C E G B E

D7 (VII7)

Finger X X 0 2 1 3
Scale X X 1 5 ♭7 3
Note X X D A C F#

Key of Em (Harmonic) (D#)

B (V)

Finger X 1 3 4 2 1
Scale X 1 5 1 3 5
Note X B F# B D# F#

B7 (V7)

Finger X 2 1 3 0 4
Scale X 1 3 ♭7 1 5
Note X B D# A B F#

D#°7 (vii°7)

Finger X X 1 3 2 4
Scale X X 1 ♭5 ♭♭7 ♭3
Note X X D# A C F#

Key of E minor (Dorian)

♯♯ (F#,C#)

Em (i)
Finger 0 2 3 0 0 0
Scale 1 5 1 ♭3 5 1
Note E B E G B E

F#m (ii)
Finger 1 3 4 1 1 1
Scale 1 5 1 ♭3 5 1
Note F#C#F#A C#F#

G (III)
Finger 3 2 0 0 0 4
Scale 1 3 5 1 3 1
Note G B D G B G

B7 (V7/i)
Finger X 2 1 3 0 4
Scale X 1 3 ♭7 1 5
Note X B D#A B F#

C#7 (V7/ii)
4th
Finger X 1 3 1 4 1
Scale X 1 5 ♭7 3 5
Note X C#G#B F G#

D7 (V7/III)
Finger X X 0 2 1 3
Scale X X 1 5 ♭7 3
Note X X D A C F#

A (IV)
Finger X 0 1 2 3 0
Scale X 1 5 1 3 5
Note X A E A C#E

Bm (v)
Finger X 1 3 4 2 1
Scale X 1 5 1 ♭3 5
Note X B F#B D F#

C#o (vio)
Finger X 3 X 0 1 0
Scale X 1 X ♭5 1 ♭3
Note X C#X G C#E

D (VII)
Finger X X 0 1 3 2
Scale X X 1 5 1 3
Note X X D A D F#

E7 (V7/IV)
Finger 0 2 0 1 0 0
Scale 1 5 ♭7 3 5 1
Note E B D G#B E

F#7 (V7/v)
Finger 1 3 1 2 1 1
Scale 1 5 ♭7 3 5 1
Note F#C#E A#C#F#

A7 (V7/VII)
Finger X 0 1 0 2 0
Scale X 1 5 ♭7 3 5
Note X A E G C#E

Em7 (i)
Finger 0 2 3 0 0 0
Scale 1 5 ♭7 ♭3 5 1
Note E B D G B E

F#m7 (ii)
Finger 1 3 1 1 1 1
Scale 1 5 ♭7 ♭3 5 1
Note F#C#E A C#F#

GMaj7 (III)
3rd
Finger 1 X 3 4 2 X
Scale 1 X 7 3 5 X
Note G X F#B D X

A7 (IV7)
Finger X 0 1 0 2 0
Scale X 1 5 ♭7 3 5
Note X A E G C#E

Bm7 (v)
Finger X 1 3 1 2 1
Scale X 1 5 ♭7 ♭3 5
Note X B F#A D F#

DMaj7 (VII)
Finger X X 0 1 1 1
Scale X X 1 5 7 3
Note X X D A C#F#

Bm (i)

Finger	X	1	3	4	2	1
Scale	X	1	5	1	♭3	5
Note	X	B	F#	B	D	F#

C#° (ii°)

Finger	X	3	X	0	1	0
Scale	X	1	X	♭5	1	♭3
Note	X	C#	X	G	C#	E

D (III)

Finger	X	X	0	1	3	2
Scale	X	X	1	5	1	3
Note	X	X	D	A	D	F#

F#7 (V7/i)

Finger	1	3	1	2	1	1
Scale	1	5	♭7	3	5	1
Note	F#	C#	E	A#	C#	F#

A7 (V7/III)

Finger	X	0	1	0	2	0
Scale	X	1	5	♭7	3	5
Note	X	A	E	G	C#	E

Em (iv)

Finger	0	2	3	0	0	0
Scale	1	5	1	♭3	5	1
Note	E	B	E	G	B	E

F#m (v)

Finger	1	3	4	1	1	1
Scale	1	5	1	♭3	5	1
Note	F#	C#	F#	A	C#	F#

G (VI)

Finger	3	2	0	0	0	4
Scale	1	3	5	1	3	1
Note	G	B	D	G	B	G

A (VII)

Finger	X	0	1	2	3	0
Scale	X	1	5	1	3	5
Note	X	A	E	A	C#	E

B7 (V7/IV)

Finger	X	2	1	3	0	4
Scale	X	1	3	♭7	1	5
Note	X	B	D#	A	B	F#

C#7 (V7/v)

Finger	X	3	2	4	1	X
Scale	X	1	3	♭7	1	X
Note	X	C#	F	B	C#	X

D7 (V7/VI)

Finger	X	X	0	2	1	3
Scale	X	X	1	5	♭7	3
Note	X	X	D	A	C	F#

E7 (V7/VII)

Finger	0	2	0	1	0	0
Scale	1	5	♭7	3	5	1
Note	E	B	D	G#	B	E

Bm7 (i)

Finger	X	1	3	1	2	1
Scale	X	1	5	♭7	♭3	5
Note	X	B	F#	A	D	F#

C#m7♭5 (iiø7) 4th

Finger	X	1	2	1	3	X
Scale	X	1	♭5	♭7	♭3	X
Note	X	C#	G	B	E	X

DMaj7 (III)

Finger	X	X	0	1	1	1
Scale	X	X	1	5	7	3
Note	X	X	D	A	C#	F#

Em7 (iv)

Finger	0	2	0	0	0	0
Scale	1	5	♭7	♭3	5	1
Note	E	B	D	G	B	E

F#m7 (v)

Finger	1	3	1	1	1	1
Scale	1	5	♭7	♭3	5	1
Note	F#	C#	E	A	C#	F#

GMaj7 (VI) 3rd

Finger	1	X	3	4	2	X
Scale	1	X	7	3	5	X
Note	G	X	F#	B	D	X

A7 (VII7)

Finger	X	0	1	0	2	0
Scale	X	1	5	♭7	3	5
Note	X	A	E	G	C#	E

Key of Bm (Harmonic) (A#)

F# (V)

Finger	1	3	4	2	1	1
Scale	1	5	1	3	5	1
Note	F#	C#	F#	A#	C#	F#

F#7 (V7)

Finger	1	3	1	2	1	1
Scale	1	5	♭7	3	5	1
Note	F#	C#	E	A#	C#	F#

A#°7 (VII°7)

Finger	X	1	2	0	3	0
Scale	X	1	♭5	♭♭7	♭3	♭5
Note	X	A#	E	G	C#	E

Key of B minor (Dorian)

♯♯ (F#, C#, G#)

Bm (i)
X
Finger X 1 3 4 2 1
Scale X 1 5 1 ♭3 5
Note X B F# B D F#

C#m (ii) — 4th
X
Finger X 1 3 4 2 1
Scale X 1 5 1 ♭3 5
Note X C# G# C# E G#

D (III)
X X O
Finger X X 0 1 3 2
Scale X X 1 5 1 3
Note X X D A D F#

F#7 (V7/i)
Finger 1 3 1 2 1 1
Scale 1 5 ♭7 3 5 1
Note F# C# E A# C# F#

G#7 (V7/ii) — 4th
Finger 1 3 1 2 1 1
Scale 1 5 ♭7 3 5 1
Note G# D# F# C D# G#

A7 (V7/III)
X O O
Finger X 0 1 0 2 0
Scale X 1 5 ♭7 3 5
Note X A E G C# E

E (IV)
O O
Finger 0 2 3 1 0 0
Scale 1 5 1 3 5 1
Note E B E G# B E

F#m (v)
Finger 1 3 4 1 1 1
Scale 1 5 1 ♭3 5 1
Note F# C# F# A C# F#

G#° (vi°)
X O O X
Finger 4 X 0 1 0 X
Scale 1 X ♭5 1 ♭3 X
Note G# X D G# B X

A (VII)
X O O
Finger X 0 1 2 3 0
Scale X 1 5 1 3 5
Note X A E A C# E

B7 (V7/IV)
X O
Finger X 2 1 3 0 4
Scale X 1 3 ♭7 1 5
Note X B D# A B F#

C#7 (V7/v)
X X
Finger X 3 2 4 1 X
Scale X 1 3 ♭7 1 X
Note X C# F B C# X

E7 (V7/VII)
O O O O
Finger 0 2 0 1 0 0
Scale 1 5 ♭7 3 5 1
Note E B D G# B E

Bm7 (i)
X
Finger X 1 3 1 2 1
Scale X 1 5 ♭7 3 5
Note X B F# A D F#

C#m7 (ii) — 4th
X
Finger X 1 3 1 2 1
Scale X 1 5 ♭7 ♭3 5
Note X C# G# B E G#

DMaj7 (III)
X X O
Finger X X 0 1 1 1
Scale X X 1 5 7 3
Note X X D A C# F#

E7 (IV7)
O O O O
Finger 0 2 0 1 0 0
Scale 1 5 ♭7 3 5 1
Note E B D G# B E

F#m7 (v)
Finger 1 3 1 1 1 1
Scale 1 5 ♭7 ♭3 5 1
Note F# C# E A C# F#

AMaj7 (VII)
X O O
Finger X 0 2 1 3 0
Scale X 1 5 7 3 5
Note X A E G# C# E

Key of F# minor (Aeolian/Natural)

F# minor (F#, C#, G#)

F#m (i)
Finger 1 3 4 1 1 1
Scale 1 5 1 ♭3 5 1
Note F#C#F#AC#F#

G#º (iiº)
X 0 0 X
Finger 4 X 0 1 0 X
Scale 1 X ♭5 1 ♭3 X
Note G#X DG#B X

A (III)
X 0 0
Finger X 0 1 2 3 0
Scale X 1 5 1 3 5
Note X A E A C# E

C#7 (V7/i)
X X
Finger X 3 2 4 1 X
Scale X 1 3 ♭7 1 X
Note XC#F B C#X

E7 (V7/III)
0 0 0 0
Finger 0 2 0 1 0 0
Scale 1 5 ♭7 3 5 1
Note E B D G# B E

Bm (iv)
X
Finger X 1 3 4 2 1
Scale X 1 5 1 ♭3 5
Note X B F#B D F#

C#m (v) 4th
X
Finger X 1 3 4 2 1
Scale X 1 5 1 ♭3 5
Note XC#G#C#E G#

D (VI)
X X 0
Finger X X 0 1 3 2
Scale X X 1 5 1 3
Note X X D A D F#

E (VII)
0 0
Finger 0 2 3 1 0 0
Scale 1 5 1 3 5 1
Note E B E G# B E

F#7 (V7/IV)
Finger 1 3 1 2 1 1
Scale 1 5 ♭7 3 5 1
Note F#C#E A#C#F#

G#7 (V7/v) 4th
Finger 1 3 1 2 1 1
Scale 1 5 ♭7 3 5 1
Note G#D#F#C#D#G#

A7 (V7/VI)
X 0 0 0
Finger X 0 1 0 2 0
Scale X 1 5 ♭7 3 5
Note X A E G C# E

B7 (V7/VII)
X 0
Finger X 2 1 3 0 4
Scale X 1 3 ♭7 1 5
Note X B D#A B F#

F#m7 (i)
Finger 1 3 1 1 1 1
Scale 1 5 ♭7 3 5 1
Note F#C#E A C#F#

G#m7♭5 (iiø7)
X X
Finger 2 X 3 4 1 X
Scale 1 X ♭7 ♭3 ♭5 X
Note G#X F# B D X

AMaj7 (III)
X 0 0
Finger X 0 2 1 3 0
Scale X 1 5 7 3 5
Note X A E G#C#E

Bm7 (iv)
X
Finger X 1 3 1 2 1
Scale X 1 5 ♭7 ♭3 5
Note X B F#A D F#

C#m7 (v) 4th
X
Finger X 1 3 1 2 1
Scale X 1 5 ♭7 ♭3 5
Note XC#G#B E G#

DMaj7 (VI)
X X
Finger X X 0 1 1 1
Scale X X 1 5 7 3
Note X X D A C#F#

E7 (VII7)
0 0 0
Finger 0 2 0 1 0 0
Scale 1 5 ♭7 3 5 1
Note E B D G# B E

Key of F#m (Harmonic) (F natural)

C# (V) 4th
X
Finger X 1 3 4 2 1
Scale X 1 5 1 3 5
Note XC#G#C#F G#

C#7 (V7)
X X
Finger X 3 2 4 1 X
Scale X 1 3 ♭7 1 X
Note XC#F B C#X

E#º7 (VIIº7)
X 0 0 X
Finger 2 X 1 3 1 X
Scale 1 X ♭♭7 ♭3 ♭5 X
Note E#X D G B X

138

Key of F#minor (Dorian)

♯♯♯ (F#, C#, G#, D#)

F#m (i)
Finger 1 3 4 1 1 1
Scale 1 5 1 ♭3 5 1
Note F#C#F#AC#F#

G#m (ii) 4th
Finger 1 3 4 1 1 1
Scale 1 5 1 ♭3 5 1
Note G#D#G#BD#G#

A (III)
Finger X 0 1 2 3 0
Scale X 1 5 1 3 5
Note X A E A C# E

C#7 (V7/i)
Finger X 3 2 4 1 X
Scale X 1 3 ♭7 1 X
Note X C# F B C# X

D#7 (V7/ii) 6th
Finger X 1 2 1 4 1
Scale X 1 5 ♭7 3 5
Note X D# A# C# G A#

E7 (V7/III)
Finger 0 2 0 1 0 0
Scale 1 5 ♭7 3 5 1
Note E B D G# B E

B (IV)
Finger X 1 2 3 4 1
Scale X 1 5 1 3 5
Note X B F# B D# F#

C#m (v) 4th
Finger X 1 3 4 2 1
Scale X 1 5 1 ♭3 5
Note X C# G# C# E G#

D#º (viº) 2nd
Finger X 4 X 1 2 1
Scale X 1 X ♭5 1 ♭3
Note X D# X A D# F#

E (VII)
Finger 0 2 3 1 0 0
Scale 1 5 1 3 5 1
Note E B E G# B E

F#7 (V7/IV)
Finger 1 3 1 2 1 1
Scale 1 5 ♭7 3 5 1
Note F#C#E A# C# F#

G#7 (V7/v) 4th
Finger 1 3 1 2 1 1
Scale 1 5 ♭7 3 5 1
Note G#D#F#C#D#G#

B7 (V7/VII)
Finger X 2 1 3 0 4
Scale X 1 3 ♭7 1 5
Note X B D# A B F#

F#m7 (i)
Finger 1 3 1 1 1 1
Scale 1 5 ♭7 ♭3 5 1
Note F#C#E A C# F#

G#m7 (ii) 4th
Finger 1 3 1 1 1 1
Scale 1 5 ♭7 ♭3 5 1
Note G#D#F#BD#G#

AMaj7 (III)
Finger X 0 2 1 3 0
Scale X 1 5 7 3 5
Note X A E G# C# E

B7 (IV7)
Finger X 2 1 3 0 4
Scale X 1 3 ♭7 1 5
Note X B D# A B F#

C#m7 (v) 4th
Finger X 1 3 1 2 1
Scale X 1 5 ♭7 ♭3 5
Note X C#G#B E G#

EMaj7 (VII)
Finger 0 3 1 2 0 0
Scale 1 5 7 3 5 1
Note E B D#G#B E

Key of C# minor (Aeolian/Natural)
(F#, C#, G#, D#)

C#m (i)
x · · · · 4th

Finger X 1 3 4 2 1
Scale X 1 5 1 ♭3 5
Note XC#G#C#EG#

D#°(ii°)
x x · 2nd

Finger X 4 X 1 2 1
Scale X 1 X♭5 1 ♭3
Note XD#X AD#F#

E (III)
o o o

Finger 0 2 3 1 0 0
Scale 1 5 1 3 5 1
Note E B EG#B E

G#7 (V7/i)
↑ 4th

Finger 1 3 1 2 1 1
Scale 1 5 ♭7 3 5 1
Note G#D#F#CD#G#

B7 (V7/III)
x o

Finger X 2 1 3 0 4
Scale X 1 3 ♭7 1 5
Note X BD#AB F#

F#m (iv)

Finger 1 3 4 1 1 1
Scale 1 5 1 ♭3 5 1
Note F#C#F#AC#F#

G#m (v)
4th

Finger 1 3 4 1 1 1
Scale 1 5 1 ♭3 5 1
Note G#D#G#BD#G#

A (VI)
x o o

Finger X 0 1 2 3 0
Scale X 1 5 1 3 5
Note X AE AC#E

B (VII)
x

Finger X 1 2 3 4 1
Scale X 1 5 1 3 5
Note X B F#BD#F#

C#7 (V7/IV)
x x
↑

Finger X 3 2 4 1 X
Scale X 1 3 ♭7 1 X
Note XC#F BC#X

D#7 (V7/v)
x x
↑ 4th

Finger X 3 2 4 1 X
Scale X 1 3 ♭7 3 X
Note XD#GC#D#X

E7 (V7/VI)
o o o o

Finger 0 2 0 1 0 0
Scale 1 5 ♭7 3 5 1
Note E BDG#B E

F#7 (V7/VII)

Finger 1 3 1 2 1 1
Scale 1 5 ♭7 3 5 1
Note F#C#EA#C#F#

C#m7 (i)
x 4th

Finger X 1 3 1 2 1
Scale X 1 5 ♭7 ♭3 5
Note XC#G#B EG#

D#m7♭5 (iiø7)
x x

Finger X X 1 3 3 3
Scale X X 1♭5 ♭7 ♭3
Note X XD#AC#F#

EMaj7 (III)
x x

Finger X X 1 4 4 4
Scale X X 1 5 7 3
Note X X E BD#G#

F#m7 (iv)

Finger 1 3 1 1 1 1
Scale 1 5 ♭7 ♭3 5 1
Note F#C#E AC#F#

G#m7 (v)
4th

Finger 1 3 1 1 1 1
Scale 1 5 ♭7 ♭3 5 1
Note G#D#F#BD#G#

AMaj7 (VI)
x o

Finger X 0 2 1 3 0
Scale X 1 5 7 3 5
Note X AE G#C#E

B7 (VII7)
x o

Finger X 2 1 3 0 4
Scale X 1 3 ♭7 1 5
Note X BD#AB F#

Key of C#m (Harmonic) (C natural)

G# (V)
4th

Finger 1 3 4 2 1 1
Scale 1 5 1 3 5 1
Note G#D#G#CD#G#

G#7(V7)
4th

Finger 1 3 4 2 1 1
Scale 1 5 ♭7 3 5 1
Note G#D#F#CD#G#

B#°7 (vii°7)
x x

Finger X 2 3 1 4 X
Scale X 1♭5 ♭♭7 ♭3 X
Note XB#A#AD#X

140

Key of C#minor (Dorian)
(F#, C#, G#, D#, A#)

C#m (i)
4th

Finger	X	1	3	4	2	1
Scale	X	1	5	1	♭3	5
Note	X	C#	G#	C#	E	G#

D#m (ii)
6th

Finger	X	1	3	4	2	1
Scale	X	1	5	1	♭3	5
Note	X	D#	A#	D#	F#	A#

E (III)

Finger	0	2	3	1	0	0
Scale	1	5	1	3	5	1
Note	E	B	E	G#	B	E

G#7 (V7/i)
4th

Finger	1	3	1	2	1	1
Scale	1	5	♭7	3	5	1
Note	G#	D#	F#	C	D#	G#

B♭7 (V7/ii)
6th

Finger	1	3	1	2	1	1
Scale	1	5	♭7	3	5	1
Note	B♭	F	A♭	D	F	B♭

B7 (V7/III)

Finger	X	2	1	3	0	4
Scale	X	1	3	♭7	1	5
Note	X	B	D#	A	B	F#

F# (IV)

Finger	1	3	4	2	1	1
Scale	1	5	1	3	5	1
Note	F#	C#	F#	A#	C#	F#

G#m (v)
4th

Finger	1	3	4	1	1	1
Scale	1	5	1	♭3	5	1
Note	G#	D#	G#	B	D#	G#

A#° (vi°)

Finger	X	1	X	3	2	0
Scale	X	1	X	1	♭3	♭5
Note	X	A#	X	A#	C#	E

B (VII)

Finger	X	1	2	3	4	1
Scale	X	1	5	1	3	5
Note	X	B	F#	B	D#	F#

C#7 (V7/IV)

Finger	X	3	2	4	1	X
Scale	X	1	3	♭7	1	X
Note	X	C#	F	B	C#	X

D#7 (V7/v)
4th

Finger	X	3	2	4	1	X
Scale	X	1	3	♭7	3	X
Note	X	D#	G	C#	D#	X

F#7 (V7/VII)

Finger	1	3	1	2	1	1
Scale	1	5	♭7	3	5	1
Note	F#	C#	E	A#	C#	F#

C#m7 (i)
4th

Finger	X	1	3	1	2	1
Scale	X	1	5	♭7	♭3	5
Note	X	C#	G#	B	E	G#

D#m7 (ii)
6th

Finger	X	1	3	1	2	1
Scale	X	1	5	♭7	♭3	5
Note	X	D#	A#	C#	F#	A#

EMaj7 (III)

Finger	X	X	1	4	4	4
Scale	X	X	1	5	7	3
Note	X	X	E	B	D#	G#

F#7 (IV)

Finger	1	3	1	2	1	1
Scale	1	5	♭7	3	5	1
Note	F#	C#	E	A#	C#	F#

G#m7 (v)
4th

Finger	1	3	1	1	1	1
Scale	1	5	♭7	♭3	5	1
Note	G#	D#	F#	B	D#	G#

BMaj7 (VII)

Finger	X	1	3	2	4	1
Scale	X	1	5	7	3	5
Note	X	B	F#	A#	D#	F#

141

D minor Key of (Aeolian/Natural) ♭ (Bb)

Dm (i)
X X O
Finger X X 0 2 3 1
Scale X X 1 5 1 ♭3
Note X X D A D F

E° (ii°)
O X X   3rd
Finger 0 X X 1 4 1
Scale 1 X X ♭5 1 ♭3
Note E X X B♭ E G

F (III)
Finger 1 3 4 2 1 1
Scale 1 5 1 3 5 1
Note F C F A C F

A7 (V7/i)
X O O O
Finger X 0 1 0 2 0
Scale X 1 5 ♭7 3 5
Note X A E G C♯ E

C7 (V7/III)
X
Finger X 3 2 4 1 0
Scale X 1 3 ♭7 1 3
Note X C E B♭ C E

Gm (iv)
3rd
Finger 1 3 4 1 1 1
Scale 1 5 1 ♭3 5 1
Note G D G B♭ D G

Am (v)
X O
Finger X 0 2 3 1 0
Scale X 1 5 1 ♭3 5
Note X A E A C E

B♭ (VI)
X
Finger X 1 2 3 4 1
Scale X 1 5 1 3 5
Note X B♭ F B♭ D F

C (VII)
X O O
Finger X 3 2 0 1 0
Scale X 1 3 5 1 3
Note X C E G C E

D7 (V7/IV)
X X O
Finger X X 0 2 1 3
Scale X X 1 5 ♭7 3
Note X X D A C F♯

E7 (V7/v)
O O O O
Finger 0 2 0 1 0 0
Scale 1 5 ♭7 3 5 1
Note E B D G♯ B E

F7 (V7/VI)
Finger 1 3 1 2 1 1
Scale 1 5 ♭7 3 5 1
Note F C E♭ A C F

G7 (V7/VII)
O O O
Finger 3 2 0 0 0 1
Scale 1 3 5 1 3 ♭7
Note G B D G B F

Dm7 (i)
X X O
Finger X X 0 2 1 1
Scale X X 1 5 ♭7 ♭3
Note X X D A C F

Em7♭5 (ii∅7)
X X
Finger X X 1 3 3 3
Scale X X 1 ♭5 ♭7 ♭3
Note X X E B♭ D G

FMaj7 (III)
X X O
Finger X X 3 2 1 0
Scale X X 1 3 5 7
Note X X F A C E

Gm7 (iv)
3rd
Finger 1 3 1 1 1 1
Scale 1 5 ♭7 ♭3 5 1
Note G D F B♭ D G

Am7 (v)
X O O O
Finger X 0 2 0 1 0
Scale X 1 5 ♭7 ♭3 5
Note X A E G C E

B♭Maj7 (IV)
X
Finger X 1 3 2 4 1
Scale X 1 5 7 3 5
Note X B♭ F A D F

C7 (VII7)
X O
Finger X 3 2 4 1 0
Scale X 1 3 ♭7 1 3
Note X C E B♭ C E

Key of Dm (Harmonic) (C♯)

A (V)
X O O
Finger X 0 1 2 3 0
Scale X 1 5 1 3 5
Note X A E A C♯ E

A7 (V7)
X O O O
Finger X 0 1 0 2 0
Scale X 1 5 ♭7 3 5
Note X A E G C♯ E

C♯°7 (vii°7)
X X
Finger X 2 3 1 4 X
Scale X 1 ♭5 ♭♭7 ♭3 X
Note X C♯ G B♭ E X

142

Key of D minor (Dorian)

Dm (i)
X X O

Finger	X	X	0	2	3	1
Scale	X	X	1	5	1	♭3
Note	X	X	D	A	D	F

Em (ii)
O   O O O

Finger	0	2	3	0	0	0
Scale	1	5	1	♭3	5	1
Note	E	B	E	G	B	E

F (III)

Finger	1	3	4	2	1	1
Scale	1	5	1	3	5	1
Note	F	C	F	A	C	F

A7 (V7/i)
X O   O

Finger	X	0	1	0	2	0
Scale	X	1	5	♭7	3	5
Note	X	A	E	G	C#	E

B7 (V7/ii)
X   O

Finger	X	2	1	3	0	4
Scale	X	1	3	♭7	1	5
Note	X	B	D#	A	B	F#

C7 (V7/III)
X   O

Finger	X	3	2	4	1	0
Scale	X	1	3	♭7	1	3
Note	X	C	E	B♭	C	E

G (IV)
O O O

Finger	3	2	0	0	0	4
Scale	1	3	5	1	3	1
Note	G	B	D	G	B	G

Am (v)
X O   O

Finger	X	0	2	3	1	0
Scale	X	1	5	1	♭3	5
Note	X	A	E	A	C	E

B º (viº)
X   X

Finger	X	1	2	4	3	X
Scale	X	1	♭5	1	♭3	X
Note	X	B	F	B	D	X

C (VII)
X   O O

Finger	X	3	2	0	1	0
Scale	X	1	3	5	1	3
Note	X	C	E	G	C	E

D7 (V7/IV)
X X O

Finger	X	X	0	2	1	3
Scale	X	X	1	5	♭7	3
Note	X	X	D	A	C	F#

E7 (V7/v)
O   O   O O

Finger	0	2	0	1	0	0
Scale	1	5	♭7	3	5	1
Note	E	B	D	G#	B	E

G7 (V7/VII)
O O O

Finger	3	2	0	0	0	1
Scale	1	3	5	1	3	♭7
Note	G	B	D	G	B	F

Dm7 (i)
X X O

Finger	X	X	0	2	1	1
Scale	X	X	1	5	♭7	♭3
Note	X	X	D	A	C	F

Em7 (ii)
O   O O O O

Finger	0	2	0	0	0	0
Scale	1	5	♭7	♭3	5	1
Note	E	B	D	G	B	E

FMaj7 (III)
X X   O

Finger	X	X	3	2	1	0
Scale	X	X	1	3	5	7
Note	X	X	F	A	C	E

G7 (IV7)
O O O

Finger	3	2	0	0	0	1
Scale	1	3	5	1	3	♭7
Note	G	B	D	G	B	F

Am7 (v)
X O   O   O

Finger	X	0	2	0	1	0
Scale	X	1	5	♭7	♭3	5
Note	X	A	E	G	C	E

CMaj7 (VII)
X   O O O

Finger	X	3	2	0	0	0
Scale	X	1	3	5	7	3
Note	X	C	E	G	B	E

143

Guide

Quick Reference

Key of C Major

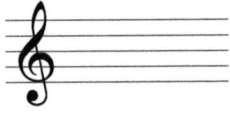

Key of A minor

I	ii	iii	IV	V(7)	vi	vii°
C	Dm	Em	F	G	Am	B°
CMaj7	Dm7	Em7	FMaj7	G7	Am7	B°7
(V7/I)	(V7/ii)	(V7/iii)	(V7/IV)	(V7/V)	(V7/vi)	
G7	A7	B7	C7	D7	E7	
♭III	♭VI	♭VII	II	III	iv	v
E♭	A♭	B♭	D	E	Fm	Gm

Key of G Major

Key of E minor

I	ii	iii	IV	V(7)	vi	vii°
G	Am	Bm	C	D	Em	F♯°
GMaj7	Am7	Bm7	CMaj7	D7	Em7	F♯°7
(V7/I)	(V7/ii)	(V7/iii)	(V7/IV)	(V7/V)	(V7/vi)	
D7	E7	F♯7	G7	A7	B7	
♭III	♭VI	♭VII	II	III	iv	v
B♭	E♭	F	A	B	Cm	Dm

Key of D Major

Key of B minor

I	ii	iii	IV	V(7)	vi	vii°
D	Em	F♯m	G	A	Bm	C♯°
DMaj7	Em7	F♯m7	GMaj7	A7	Bm7	C♯°7
(V7/I)	(V7/ii)	(V7/iii)	(V7/IV)	(V7/V)	(V7/vi)	
A7	B7	C♯7	D7	E7	F♯7	
♭III	♭VI	♭VII	II	III	iv	v
F	B♭	C	E	F♯	Gm	Am

144

Key of A Major

Key of F# minor

I	ii	iii	IV	V(7)	vi	vii°
A	Bm	C#m	D	E	F#m	G#°
AMaj7	Bm7	C#m7	DMaj7	E7	F#m7	G#°7

(V7/I)	(V7/ii)	(V7/iii)	(V7/IV)	(V7/V)	(V7/vi)	
E7	F#7	G#7	A7	B7	C#7	

bIII	bVI	bVII	II	III	iv	v
C	F	G	B	C#	Dm	Em

Key of E Major

Key of C# minor

I	ii	iii	IV	V(7)	vi	vii°
E	F#m	G#m	A	B	C#m	D#°
EMaj7	F#m7	G#m7	AMaj7	B7	C#m7	D#°7

(V7/I)	(V7/ii)	(V7/iii)	(V7/IV)	(V7/V)	(V7/vi)	
B7	C#7	D#7	E7	F#7	G#7	

bIII	bVI	bVII	II	III	iv	v
G	C	D	F#	G#	Am	Bm

Key of B Major

Key of G# minor

I	ii	iii	IV	V(7)	vi	vii°
B	C#m	D#m	E	F#	G#m	A#°
BMaj7	C#m7	D#m7	EMaj7	F#7	G#m7	A#°7

(V7/I)	(V7/ii)	(V7/iii)	(V7/IV)	(V7/V)	(V7/vi)	
F#7	G#7	A#7	B7	C#7	D#7	

bIII	bVI	bVII	II	III	iv	v
D	G	A	C#	D#	Em	F#m

Key of F# Major

Key of D# minor

I	ii	iii	IV	V(7)	vi	vii°
F#	G#m	A#m	B	C#	D#m	E#°
F#Maj7	G#m7	A#m7	BMaj7	C#7	D#m7	E#°7

(V7/I)	(V7/ii)	(V7/iii)	(V7/IV)	(V7/V)	(V7/vi)	
C#7	D#7	E7	F#7	G#7	A#7	

♭III	♭VI	♭VII	II	III	iv	v
A	D	E	G#	A#	Bm	C#m

Key of C# Major

Key of A# minor

I	ii	iii	IV	V(7)	vi	vii°
C#	D#m	E#m	F#	G#	A#m	B#°
C#Maj7	D#m7	E#m7	F#Maj7	G#7	A#m7	B#°7

(V7/I)	(V7/ii)	(V7/iii)	(V7/IV)	(V7/V)	(V7/vi)	
G#7	A#7	C7	C#7	D#7	F7	

♭III	♭VI	♭VII	II	III	iv	v
E	A	B	D#	E#	F#m	G#m

Key of Music	Capo 1st fret	Capo 2nd fret	Capo 3rd fret	Capo 4th fret
Key of C Major			Key of A chords	
Key of G Major		Key of F chords	Key of E chords	
Key of D Major		Key of C chords		
Key of A Major		Key of G chords		Key of F chords
Key of E Major		Key of D chords		Key of C chords
Key of B Major		Key of A chords		Key of G chords
Key of F# Major	Key of F chords	Key of E chords		Key of D chords
Key of C# Major	Key of C chords			Key of A chords

To play in these keys place the capo at the indicated fret and use the chords from the new keys.

Key of C Major

Key of A minor

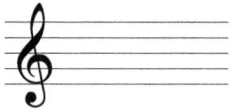

I	ii	iii	IV	V(7)	vi	vii°
C	Dm	Em	F	G	Am	B°
CMaj7	Dm7	Em7	FMaj7	G7	Am7	B°7
(V7/I)	(V7/ii)	(V7/iii)	(V7/IV)	(V7/V)	(V7/vi)	
G7	A7	B7	C7	D7	E7	
♭III	♭VI	♭VII	II	III	iv	v
E♭	A♭	B♭	D	E	Fm	Gm

Key of F Major

Key of D minor

I	ii	iii	IV	V(7)	vi	vii°
F	Gm	Am	B♭	C	Dm	E°
FMaj7	Gm7	Am7	B♭Maj7	C7	Dm7	E°7
(V7/I)	(V7/ii)	(V7/iii)	(V7/IV)	(V7/V)	(V7/vi)	
C7	D7	E7	F7	G7	A7	
♭III	♭VI	♭VII	II	III	iv	v
A♭	D♭	E♭	G	A	B♭m	Cm

Key of B♭ Major

Key of G minor

I	ii	iii	IV	V(7)	vi	vii°
B♭	Cm	Dm	E♭	F	Gm	A°
B♭Maj7	Cm7	Dm7	E♭Maj7	F7	Gm7	A°7
(V7/I)	(V7/ii)	(V7/iii)	(V7/IV)	(V7/V)	(V7/vi)	
F7	G7	A7	B♭7	C7	D7	
♭III	♭VI	♭VII	II	III	iv	v
D♭	G♭	A♭	C	D	E♭m	Fm

Key of Eb Major

Key of C minor

I	ii	iii	IV	V(7)	vi	vii°
Eb	Fm	Gm	Ab	Bb	Cm	D°
EbMaj7	Fm7	Gm7	AbMaj7	Bb7	Cm7	D°7
(V7/I)	(V7/ii)	(V7/iii)	(V7/IV)	(V7/V)	(V7/vi)	
Bb7	C7	D7	Eb7	F7	G7	
bIII	bVI	bVII	II	III	iv	v
Gb	Cb	Db	F	G	Abm	Bbm

Key of Ab Major

Key of F minor

I	ii	iii	IV	V(7)	vi	vii°
Ab	Bbm	Cm	Db	Eb	Fm	G°
AbMaj7	Bbm7	Cm7	DbMaj7	Eb7	Fm7	G°7
(V7/I)	(V7/ii)	(V7/iii)	(V7/IV)	(V7/V)	(V7/vi)	
Eb7	F7	G7	Ab7	Bb7	C7	
bIII	bVI	bVII	II	III	iv	v
Cb	Fb	Gb	Bb	C	Dbm	Ebm

Key of Db Major

Key of Bb minor

I	ii	iii	IV	V(7)	vi	vii°
Db	Ebm	Fm	Gb	Ab	Bbm	C°
DbMaj7	Ebm7	Fm7	GbMaj7	Ab7	Bbm7	C°7
(V7/I)	(V7/ii)	(V7/iii)	(V7/IV)	(V7/V)	(V7/vi)	
Ab7	Bb7	C7	Db7	Eb7	F7	
bIII	bVI	bVII	II	III	iv	v
Fb	A	Cb	Eb	F	Gbm	Abm

Key of Gb Major

Key of Eb minor

I	ii	iii	IV	V(7)	vi	vii°
Gb	Abm	Bbm	Cb	Db	Ebm	F°
GbMaj7	Abm7	Bbm7	CbMaj7	Db7	Ebm7	F°7

(V7/I)	(V7/ii)	(V7/iii)	(V7/IV)	(V7/V)	(V7/vi)	
Db7	Eb7	F7	Gb7	Ab7	Bb7	

bIII	bVI	bVII	II	III	iv	v
A	D	E	Ab	Bb	Cbm	Dbm

Key of Cb Major

Key of Ab minor

I	ii	iii	IV	V(7)	vi	vii°
Cb	Dbm	Ebm	Fb	Gb	Abm	Bb°
CbMaj7	Dbm7	Ebm7	FbMaj7	Gb7	Abm7	Bb°7

(V7/I)	(V7/ii)	(V7/iii)	(V7/IV)	(V7/V)	(V7/vi)	
Gb7	Ab7	Bb7	B7	Db7	Eb7	

bIII	bVI	bVII	II	III	iv	v
D	G	A	Db	Eb	Fbm	Gbm

Key of Music	Capo 1st fret	Capo 2nd fret	Capo 3rd fret	Capo 4th fret
Key of F Major	Key of E chords		Key of D chords	
Key of Bb Major	Key of A chords		Key of G chords	
Key of Eb Major	Key of D chords		Key of C chords	
Key of Ab Major	Key of G chords		Key of F chords	Key of E chords
Key of Db Major	Key of C chords			Key of A chords
Key of Gb Major	Key of F chords	Key of E chords		Key of D chords
Key of Cb Major		Key of A chords		Key of G chords

To play in these keys place the capo at the indicated fret and use the chords from the new keys.

CAPO Chart

Major Keys

Capo Location	C	G	D	A	E	F
0	C	G	D	A	E	F
1	C#/Db	Ab	Eb	Bb	F	F#/Gb
2	D	A	E	B	F#/Gb	G
3	Eb	Bb	F	C	G	Ab
4	E	B	F#/Gb	C#/Db	Ab	A
5	F	C	G	D	A	Bb
6	F#/Gb	C#/Db	Ab	Eb	Bb	B
7	G	D	A	E	B	C

minor Keys (Aeolian/Natural) / Using chords from this Major scale

Capo Location	Am/C	Em/G	Bm/D	F#m/A	C#m/E	Dm/F
0	Am	Em	Bm	F#m	C#m	Dm
1	A#m Bbm	Fm	Cm	Gm	Dm	D#m Ebm
2	Bm	F#m	C#m	G#m	D#m Ebm	Em
3	Cm	Gm	Dm	Am	Em	Fm
4	C#m	G#m	D#m Ebm	A#m Bbm	Fm	F#m
5	Dm	Am	Em	Bm	F#m	Gm
6	D#m Ebm	A#m Bbm	Fm	Cm	Gm	G#m
7	Em	Bm	F#m	C#m	G#m	Am

TIPS ON PLAYING-BY-EAR

The underlying premise of this book is to teach you to play-by-ear, so how do you get started?

To make things a little easier try printing out the lyrics of the song you want to learn. (There are lots of websites that have just the lyrics of a song you can use for this step.) This will give you something to write your chords on and a way of referencing were the chord changes occur in the song. As you get better you'll be able to skip this step.

The next step is to determine the key of the song. This can be the hardest part of playing by ear. If you're planning on playing the song in its original performance key try humming the first note in the melody along with the song and then try to find that note on your guitar. Use the first and second strings, moving up and down until you find the right note. You may need to go up an octave to get it on one of these strings. Just knoodle around until you find the right note. If you're not interested in playing along with the song on a CD or YouTube you can just hum what sounds right and again find the note on the guitar. This may take some practice, but it's definitely do able, even for those of us not so gifted with perfect pitch.

Once you have the first note of the melody try playing the three Major chords listed at the end of this section with the highest note of the chord playing that melody note. If the song is in a Major key one of the chords should sound right. If the song is in a minor key you will need to switch to the minor chords. Usually the first chord in a song will be the key of the song as well. Use the "1" in the chords listed to determine the letter name of the key. The idea is that the melody note will be a part of the chord, but you won't know if it's the root note, the 1, or the 3rd or 5th of the chord. Let your ear tell you which sounds right. You can use this same method if you get stuck later in the song and are not sure what chord to play. Just play the melody note on top of the chord and try the three different inversions until one sounds right.

Another method is to hum a note along with the first part of a song that sounds right through several chord changes. This note will often be the root note of the "I" chord of the key. The reason for this is the root note of the I chord is also in the IV and vi chord, popular chords in many songs. If the song is in a natural minor key the root note of the vi chord is also in the ii and IV chords. Once you find the note that sounds good

through the chord changes all you need to do is determine if the song is Major or minor. If this doesn't work you may have found the 3rd or 5th of the chord instead of the root. Try the different inversions with the note you've found on top to see if you can find the right key.

Once you know what key the song is in make sure you're familiar with the chords in that key. You don't have to know all the chords from the chord charts, but you should at least be familiar with the basic diatonic chords and their extensions on the first page.

Once you know the key of the song, and which chord starts the song, just keep playing that chord until you need to change. One thing you may notice when you start playing by ear is you may want to change chords when you don't need to change. But don't change unless the chord clashes with the melody. Keep playing until it's obviously wrong. (It can be really frustrating looking for another chord when the one you were playing is the one you want.) When the chord clashes with the melody use the chords from the chord chart to find the next chord in the song. At first this will be a trial and error process, but with practice it will become much easier.

This is when things can get tricky. You may be able to play the wrong chord with the melody without it clashing. But that's okay. Just stick with it for now. In the beginning you're just building the foundation. Once you have things fairly nailed down, use the chord substitution section to see if you can make it sound better. Remember chord substitutions work because many times the chords have two or more notes in common. So you may have a chord that works over a melody, but you can tell it's just not quite right. That's when you go back and try some other chords from the chord chart.

I talked about this a little in the *How to Use this Book* and *Progression* section, but you really need to keep in mind the style of music you're playing as well. If it's a classic rock song you're no doubt going to use the Flatted Major chords. If it's a folk song or older country song the diatonic chords are probably all you'll need. If it's a modern country song then you're probably going to run into some Flatted Major chords as well. If the song has a blues feel to it you're going to need to think about dominant 7th chords. By thinking about the style of music you should be able to predict the type of chords used. With practice you'll be able to connect progressions with styles of music as well. All this can help you narrow things down when you're looking for that next chord that fits over the melody line.

The most important thing is to practice. It's so easy to just look up a song on the internet and never learn the skill of playing-by-ear. But all the great musicians have shown the value of this skill and you can learn it too if you put some time into it. It can be great fun and give you a real sense of accomplishment when you can sit down and figure out a song on your own.

melody is a D located on the second string 3rd fret. You then use the "2nd string melody note" chords to determine the key by playing each chord with the D as the highest note in that chord. That means you would play the first Major chord on the 2nd fret with the D on tope, the second chord 3rd fret with the D on top and the third chord 3rd fret with the D on top. When you find one of these chords that sounds right, you've probably located the (I) chord. You can determine the letter name of the chord, and therefore the key by looking at the 1 in the chord that works.

If none of them sound right drop down to the minor chords and find one that works. If one of the minor chords work then the song is probably in a minor key and this will be the (vi) chord. These are just general rules and will not work all the time, sometimes songs start on other chords besides the (I) or (vi), but this process will at least get you the first chord in the song. You can use this method to determine the chords that fit with other melody notes as well.

One other problem you may encounter is when two chords sound very similar and you're not sure which is right. For instance it can be hard to tell if a C chord is being played or an Am7. Both chords have the same notes. So how do you tell which is right? There are a couple of ways to approach this problem. First try and determine what note is being played in the bass. If the bass player is playing a C then go with the C chord, if they're playing an A then go with the Am7. Another way is to just play the Am chord, instead of the Am7. By playing just the Am instead of it's extension you get a truer since of the chord's quality and if it fits or not. If it sound good then you probably need to play the Am7, instead of a C.

Fretboard diagram

```
  E A D G B E
  F       C F
    B E A
  G C F   D G   3rd
        B
  A D G C E A   5th
          F
  B E A D   B   7th
  C F     G C
      B E       9th
  D G C F A D
  E A D G B E   12th
  F       C F
```

1st string melody note

Major 1st String	Major 1st String	Major 1st String
Scale X X 5 1 3 5	Scale X X 1 3 5 1	Scale X X 3 5 1 3

minor 1st String	minor 1st String	minor 1st String
Scale X X 5 1 b3 5	Scale X X 1 b3 5 1	Scale X X b3 5 1 b3

2nd string melody note

Major 2nd String	Major 2nd String	Major 2nd String
Scale X 1 3 5 1 X	Scale X 3 5 1 3 X	Scale X 5 1 3 5 X

minor 2nd String	minor 2nd String	minor 2nd String
Scale X 1 b3 5 1 X	Scale X b3 5 1 b3 X	Scale X 5 1 b3 5 X

Here's an example of how to use the chords and fretboard above. Lets say you want to play a song by ear and you determine through humming along with the song and knoodling around on the guitar that the first note in the

THE CIRCLE OF FIFTHS

The Circle of Fifths gives you the order of Sharps when moving clockwise and flats when moving counter clockwise. The fifth referred to in this Circle of Fifths is an interval of a perfect fifth or seven frets apart. Just think of it as the fifth note in a Major scale. For instance the G is the fifth note in a C Major scale, the D is the fifth note in a G Major scale, the A is the fifth note in a D Major scale etc..

You can also use this circle to create chord progressions by moving counter clockwise around the circle. Let's say you're playing an Am in the key of C Major and you want to move from the Am to a C Major chord. You could stick a Dm then a G7 chord between the Am and C. This is a technique called backcycling. You can use as many chords as you have room for to get to your ultimate destination chord. These extra chords can be played as dominant 7th chords or minors. A lot of times minors are used until the last chord before your destination chord and then a dominant 7th chord is used. Here are a couple of examples for how you might approach a G Major chord; Em - Am - D7 - G or E7 - A7 - D7 - G.

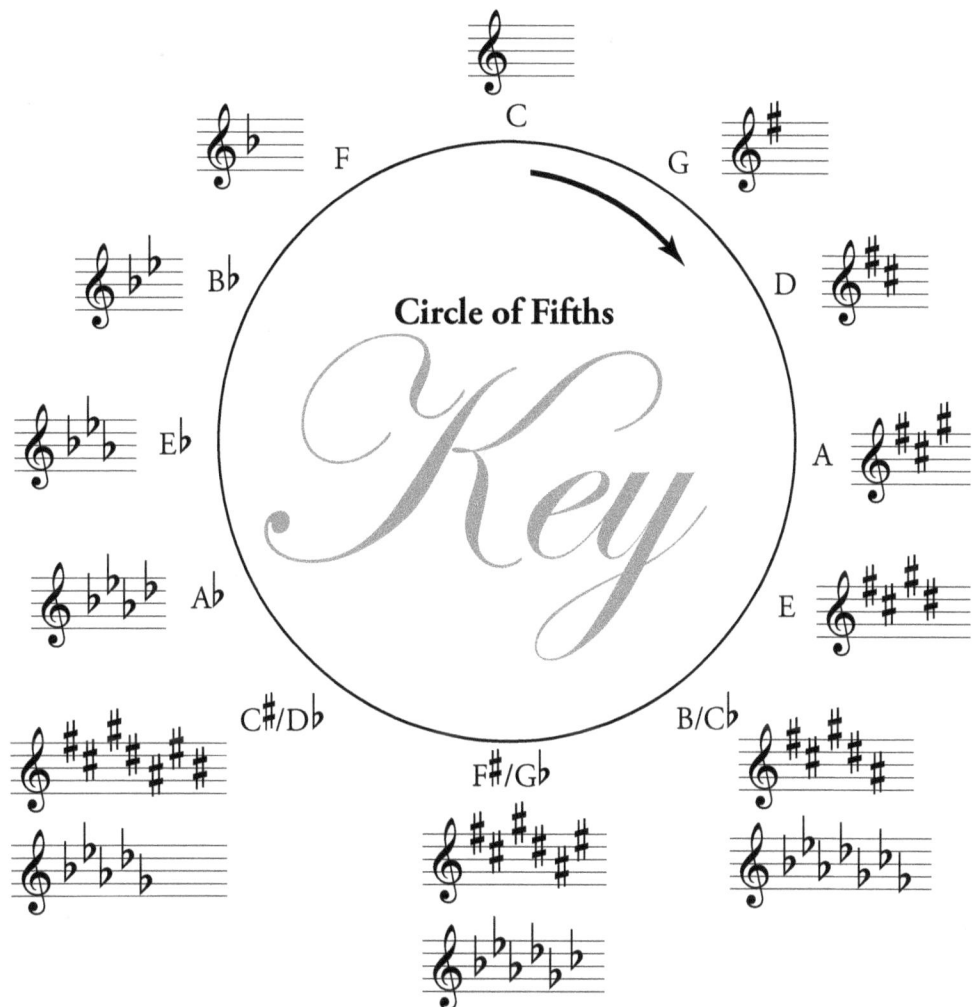

Circle of Fifths Key

Memory helps for the Sharp Keys:

If you raise the last sharp in the key signature one half step you will have the name of the Major key. The sharps are added in intervals of fifths F-C-G-D-A-E-B. If you need help memorizing the notes on the staff you can use these two memory helps. The spaces on the musical staff starting from the bottom spell out the word FACE and the lines, starting from the bottom are, E, G, B, D, F or Every Good Boy Does Fine

Memory helps for the Flat Keys:

If you look at the second to the last flat in the key signature you will have the name of the Major key. (You'll just have to memorize the first one which is F) The flats are added in the reverse order of the sharps B-E-A-D-G-C-F.

I do sincerely appreciate your support. I hope through this book you've gained a much greater understanding of music and can use that to make your playing even that much more enjoyable and fun.

If you would like a condensed version of this book you can carry around with you on your iPhone, iPad or Kindle check out my book *CHORDS by KEY FOR GUITAR . . . THE BASICS*.

Thanks again,

Tim Wemple

Thank you !

On the next several pages you'll find worksheets you can copy and use with the worksheet sections in each key. Look at the examples in the front of the book for ideas on how to use these worksheets.

Chord Extensions Worksheet -Moving Lines in a Chord

Finger _ _ _ _ _
Scale _ _ _ _ _
Note _ _ _ _ _

Finger _ _ _ _ _
Scale _ _ _ _ _
Note _ _ _ _ _

Finger _ _ _ _ _
Scale _ _ _ _ _
Note _ _ _ _ _

Finger _ _ _ _ _
Scale _ _ _ _ _
Note _ _ _ _ _

Finger _ _ _ _ _
Scale _ _ _ _ _
Note _ _ _ _ _

Finger _ _ _ _ _
Scale _ _ _ _ _
Note _ _ _ _ _

Finger _ _ _ _ _
Scale _ _ _ _ _
Note _ _ _ _ _

Finger _ _ _ _ _
Scale _ _ _ _ _
Note _ _ _ _ _

Finger _ _ _ _ _
Scale _ _ _ _ _
Note _ _ _ _ _

Finger _ _ _ _ _
Scale _ _ _ _ _
Note _ _ _ _ _

Finger _ _ _ _ _
Scale _ _ _ _ _
Note _ _ _ _ _

Finger _ _ _ _ _
Scale _ _ _ _ _
Note _ _ _ _ _

Finger _ _ _ _ _
Scale _ _ _ _ _
Note _ _ _ _ _

Finger _ _ _ _ _
Scale _ _ _ _ _
Note _ _ _ _ _

Finger _ _ _ _ _
Scale _ _ _ _ _
Note _ _ _ _ _

Finger _ _ _ _ _
Scale _ _ _ _ _
Note _ _ _ _ _

Finger _ _ _ _ _
Scale _ _ _ _ _
Note _ _ _ _ _

Finger _ _ _ _ _
Scale _ _ _ _ _
Note _ _ _ _ _

Finger _ _ _ _ _
Scale _ _ _ _ _
Note _ _ _ _ _

Finger _ _ _ _ _
Scale _ _ _ _ _
Note _ _ _ _ _

Chord Progression Worksheet - Ascending and Descending Bass lines, and Pedal notes

Finger _ _ _ _ _
Scale _ _ _ _ _
Note _ _ _ _ _

Finger _ _ _ _ _
Scale _ _ _ _ _
Note _ _ _ _ _

Finger _ _ _ _ _
Scale _ _ _ _ _
Note _ _ _ _ _

Finger _ _ _ _ _
Scale _ _ _ _ _
Note _ _ _ _ _

Finger _ _ _ _ _
Scale _ _ _ _ _
Note _ _ _ _ _

Finger _ _ _ _ _
Scale _ _ _ _ _
Note _ _ _ _ _

Finger _ _ _ _ _
Scale _ _ _ _ _
Note _ _ _ _ _

Finger _ _ _ _ _
Scale _ _ _ _ _
Note _ _ _ _ _

Finger _ _ _ _ _
Scale _ _ _ _ _
Note _ _ _ _ _

Finger _ _ _ _ _
Scale _ _ _ _ _
Note _ _ _ _ _

Finger _ _ _ _ _
Scale _ _ _ _ _
Note _ _ _ _ _

Finger _ _ _ _ _
Scale _ _ _ _ _
Note _ _ _ _ _

Finger _ _ _ _ _
Scale _ _ _ _ _
Note _ _ _ _ _

Finger _ _ _ _ _
Scale _ _ _ _ _
Note _ _ _ _ _

Finger _ _ _ _ _
Scale _ _ _ _ _
Note _ _ _ _ _

Finger _ _ _ _ _
Scale _ _ _ _ _
Note _ _ _ _ _

Finger _ _ _ _ _
Scale _ _ _ _ _
Note _ _ _ _ _

Finger _ _ _ _ _
Scale _ _ _ _ _
Note _ _ _ _ _

Finger _ _ _ _ _
Scale _ _ _ _ _
Note _ _ _ _ _

Finger _ _ _ _ _
Scale _ _ _ _ _
Note _ _ _ _ _

Chord Substitution Worksheet

Finger _ _ _ _ _
Scale _ _ _ _ _
Note _ _ _ _ _

Finger _ _ _ _ _
Scale _ _ _ _ _
Note _ _ _ _ _

Finger _ _ _ _ _
Scale _ _ _ _ _
Note _ _ _ _ _

Finger _ _ _ _ _
Scale _ _ _ _ _
Note _ _ _ _ _

Finger _ _ _ _ _
Scale _ _ _ _ _
Note _ _ _ _ _

Finger _ _ _ _ _
Scale _ _ _ _ _
Note _ _ _ _ _

Finger _ _ _ _ _
Scale _ _ _ _ _
Note _ _ _ _ _

Finger _ _ _ _ _
Scale _ _ _ _ _
Note _ _ _ _ _

Finger _ _ _ _ _
Scale _ _ _ _ _
Note _ _ _ _ _

Finger _ _ _ _ _
Scale _ _ _ _ _
Note _ _ _ _ _

Finger _ _ _ _ _
Scale _ _ _ _ _
Note _ _ _ _ _

Finger _ _ _ _ _
Scale _ _ _ _ _
Note _ _ _ _ _

Finger _ _ _ _ _
Scale _ _ _ _ _
Note _ _ _ _ _

Finger _ _ _ _ _
Scale _ _ _ _ _
Note _ _ _ _ _

Finger _ _ _ _ _
Scale _ _ _ _ _
Note _ _ _ _ _

Finger _ _ _ _ _
Scale _ _ _ _ _
Note _ _ _ _ _

Finger _ _ _ _ _
Scale _ _ _ _ _
Note _ _ _ _ _

Finger _ _ _ _ _
Scale _ _ _ _ _
Note _ _ _ _ _

Finger _ _ _ _ _
Scale _ _ _ _ _
Note _ _ _ _ _

Finger _ _ _ _ _
Scale _ _ _ _ _
Note _ _ _ _ _

Chord Substitution Worksheet

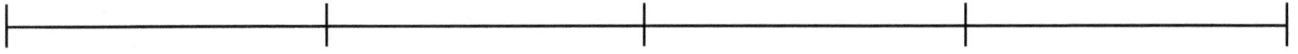

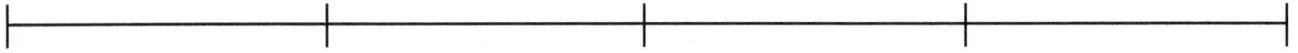

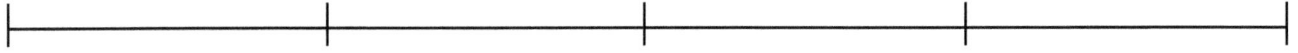

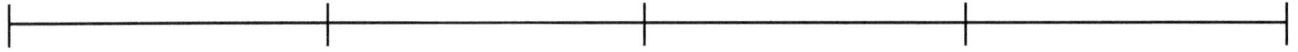

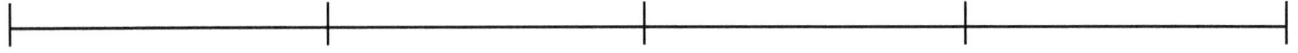

Power Chord Worksheet

Finger _ _ _ _ _
Scale _ _ _ _ _
Note _ _ _ _ _

Finger _ _ _ _ _
Scale _ _ _ _ _
Note _ _ _ _ _

Finger _ _ _ _ _
Scale _ _ _ _ _
Note _ _ _ _ _

Finger _ _ _ _ _
Scale _ _ _ _ _
Note _ _ _ _ _

Finger _ _ _ _ _
Scale _ _ _ _ _
Note _ _ _ _ _

Finger _ _ _ _ _
Scale _ _ _ _ _
Note _ _ _ _ _

Finger _ _ _ _ _
Scale _ _ _ _ _
Note _ _ _ _ _

Finger _ _ _ _ _
Scale _ _ _ _ _
Note _ _ _ _ _

Finger _ _ _ _ _
Scale _ _ _ _ _
Note _ _ _ _ _

Finger _ _ _ _ _
Scale _ _ _ _ _
Note _ _ _ _ _

Finger _ _ _ _ _
Scale _ _ _ _ _
Note _ _ _ _ _

Finger _ _ _ _ _
Scale _ _ _ _ _
Note _ _ _ _ _

Finger _ _ _ _ _
Scale _ _ _ _ _
Note _ _ _ _ _

Finger _ _ _ _ _
Scale _ _ _ _ _
Note _ _ _ _ _

Finger _ _ _ _ _
Scale _ _ _ _ _
Note _ _ _ _ _

Finger _ _ _ _ _
Scale _ _ _ _ _
Note _ _ _ _ _

Finger _ _ _ _ _
Scale _ _ _ _ _
Note _ _ _ _ _

Finger _ _ _ _ _
Scale _ _ _ _ _
Note _ _ _ _ _

Finger _ _ _ _ _
Scale _ _ _ _ _
Note _ _ _ _ _

Finger _ _ _ _ _
Scale _ _ _ _ _
Note _ _ _ _ _

Triad Worksheet

Finger _ _ _ _ _
Scale _ _ _ _ _
Note _ _ _ _ _

Finger _ _ _ _ _
Scale _ _ _ _ _
Note _ _ _ _ _

Finger _ _ _ _ _
Scale _ _ _ _ _
Note _ _ _ _ _

Finger _ _ _ _ _
Scale _ _ _ _ _
Note _ _ _ _ _

Finger _ _ _ _ _
Scale _ _ _ _ _
Note _ _ _ _ _

Finger _ _ _ _ _
Scale _ _ _ _ _
Note _ _ _ _ _

Finger _ _ _ _ _
Scale _ _ _ _ _
Note _ _ _ _ _

Finger _ _ _ _ _
Scale _ _ _ _ _
Note _ _ _ _ _

Finger _ _ _ _ _
Scale _ _ _ _ _
Note _ _ _ _ _

Finger _ _ _ _ _
Scale _ _ _ _ _
Note _ _ _ _ _

Finger _ _ _ _ _
Scale _ _ _ _ _
Note _ _ _ _ _

Finger _ _ _ _ _
Scale _ _ _ _ _
Note _ _ _ _ _

Finger _ _ _ _ _
Scale _ _ _ _ _
Note _ _ _ _ _

Finger _ _ _ _ _
Scale _ _ _ _ _
Note _ _ _ _ _

Finger _ _ _ _ _
Scale _ _ _ _ _
Note _ _ _ _ _

Finger _ _ _ _ _
Scale _ _ _ _ _
Note _ _ _ _ _

Finger _ _ _ _ _
Scale _ _ _ _ _
Note _ _ _ _ _

Finger _ _ _ _ _
Scale _ _ _ _ _
Note _ _ _ _ _

Finger _ _ _ _ _
Scale _ _ _ _ _
Note _ _ _ _ _

Finger _ _ _ _ _
Scale _ _ _ _ _
Note _ _ _ _ _

www.ingramcontent.com/pod-product-compliance
Lightning Source LLC
Chambersburg PA
CBHW062102090426
42741CB00015B/3303